GRAYWOLF FORUM 4

The Private I

GRAYWOLF FORUM ONE
  Tolstoy's Dictaphone: Technology and the Muse
  Edited by SVEN BIRKERTS

GRAYWOLF FORUM TWO
  Body Language: Writers on Sport
  Edited by GERALD EARLY

GRAYWOLF FORUM THREE
  *The Business of Memory: The Art of Remembering
  in an Age of Forgetting*
  Edited by CHARLES BAXTER

GRAYWOLF FORUM 4

The Private I
Privacy in a Public World

Edited by
MOLLY PEACOCK

GRAYWOLF PRESS : SAINT PAUL

Publication of this volume is made possible in part by a grant provided by the Minnesota State Arts Board through an appropriation by the Minnesota State Legislature, and by a grant from the National Endowment for the Arts. Significant support has also been provided by the Bush Foundation; Dayton's Project Imagine with support from Target Foundation; the McKnight Foundation; a Grant made on behalf of the Stargazer Foundation; and other generous contributions from foundations, corporations, and individuals. To these organizations and individuals we offer our heartfelt thanks.

Special funding for this volume was provided by the College of Saint Benedict and the Star Tribune Foundation.

Published by Graywolf Press
2402 University Avenue, Suite 203
Saint Paul, Minnesota 55114
All rights reserved.

www.graywolfpress.org

Published in the United States of America

ISBN 1-55597-313-2

2   4   6   8   9   7   5   3   1
First Graywolf Printing, 2001

Library of Congress Card Number: 00-107648

Cover photograph: Patricia McDonough
Series and cover design: A N D

Contents

. . . .

Introduction

.   .   .   .

Close that door! This is a very personal book about privacy—from the quirky points of view of people living their private lives in this public world. How we get privacy and how we lose it grips these writers' imaginations, and their essays flush out a panoply of essential desires—from sex to solitude, from intimacy to the simple need to be left alone. While *The Private I* explores the secrets of privacy from childhood to death, in contexts rural and urban, aesthetic and legal, flamboyant and reserved, it has no pretensions to be comprehensive. The eccentric and passionate points of view of its authors give their essays the lushness and depth that only personally chosen secret places have.

Privacy, seemingly one of our hottest issues, in fact has taken over a century to ignite. Beginning in 1890 with the famous Brandeis and Warren opinion on the "right to be let alone," and fed by judicial, domestic, social, and scientific debates throughout the twentieth century, privacy issues really began to sizzle during the Cold War, when government spying was advanced by surveillance technology, according to a conversation with University of Pennsylvania Professor of Law, Anita L. Allen. International spy technology turned domestic with the investigation of participants in the Civil Rights movement and the Vietnam War protests. Then the courts weighed in with rulings on abortion, birth control, and the right to read pornography in the privacy of our houses. In the sciences, neonatal-care innovations, gene mapping, and the right-to-die movement raised bioethical concerns. In the 1970s federal legislation about computer privacy began, attempting to insure financial records from prying eyes. And, after Watergate, the media began to assume an unprecedented degree of intrusion on the lives of public figures. The frenzy flash point, Professor Allen concludes, now is the Internet.

Into all this comes our *Private I*. We begin with Janna Malamud Smith's definitions of solitude, anonymity, reserve, and intimacy, then enter the realm of personal life with Josip Novakovich's ode to childhood's secret places in the former Yugoslavia. Next sassy Bronwyn Garrity explores Internet privacy through the lenses of teen web sites. While Dorothy Allison insists that fiction creates both truth and privacy, Vivian Gornick reacts to her mother's response to her memoir, and then lays out her tough-minded views on personal writing. Michael Groden, having made a scholar's bargain to hide behind his subject, describes his astonishment at suddenly finding himself exposed. I admit that, as his wife, I'm the one who did the exposing in my memoir *Paradise, Piece by Piece*. My own essay explores privacy and creativity, my mother and her near-contemporary Anne Sexton, and how the revealing of secrets actually preserves privacy.

Physical boundaries define solitude, and Cathleen Medwick, a self-acknowledged intruder on private interiors for shelter magazines, delicately unfolds the character of privacy as it is built in rooms. But Yusef Komunyakaa's East Village rooms are invaded by multiple burglaries. He reconfigures his zone of privacy in a literary meditation—ending in a walk on a nude beach. Dr. F. Gonzalez-Crussi introduces us to an antique chamber pot, talisman of a Chinese empress (who was never left unattended), while he muses about the polarity of warm Latin community versus cold North American isolation.

We can't always take our private lives this seriously, so Victoria Roberts places two cartoons on intimacy's altar. Actor Barbara Feldon, best known as Agent 99 on the 1960s *Get Smart* TV comedy series, exhorts us to reweave the veil of glamour for celebrities, and Wayne Koestenbaum meditates on stardom as he peeks into the scandal of Lana Turner. Inverting the public-private telescope, Jonathan Franzen claims both that the Clinton-Lewinsky scandal invaded his private citizen's life—and that the public isn't all that pumped up about privacy after all. Legal philosopher Anita L. Allen compares Clinton to Oscar Wilde as she makes an argument for lying by public figures about sexual affairs. Evans D. Hopkins takes sex to the jail cell, and Wendy Lesser examines the issue of public attendance at executions. Penultimately, attorney Robin West argues against legislating for privacy altogether in favor of a bias toward community. How can an individual live privately in community? Kathleen Norris provides the last word as she tracks the trails of gossip in a tiny South Dakota town.

How did I, a tell-all poet, come to edit a book on private life? I've been writing over and under the line between personal and public for decades. Then, when I wrote a memoir about how I made my most important deci-

.   .   .   .

sions, particularly deciding to become a poet and deciding not to have children . . . well, *The Private I* has turned out to be so personal that even the editor, usually hiding behind her choices, has had to submit to scrutiny. My husband's essay outs some of my motives. Personal life in a public age? The searchlight is everywhere, especially at home.

Each essayist in this book sails a special zone between the undiscovered and the revealed. Each discovers that, very much like a river, the issue of privacy will not stay still. It keeps on flowing. Trying to capture it, finding the vocabulary for its ideas, is like painting light on water. It can only be almost done. Yet we all feel we know absolutely when our privacy is sovereign and when it is trespassed. And these writers establish those certain uncertainties of personal life.

MOLLY PEACOCK
New York City and London, Ontario

GRAYWOLF FORUM 4

The Private I

Privacy and Private States

.   .   .   .

by
JANNA MALAMUD SMITH

One way of beginning to understand privacy is by looking at what happens to people in extreme situations where it is absent. Recalling his time in Auschwitz, Primo Levi observed that "solitude in a Camp is more precious and rare than bread."[1] Solitude is one state of privacy, and even amidst the overwhelming death, starvation, and horror of the camps, Levi knew he missed it.

Uprooted by the Second World War from his life as a chemistry student and beginning chemist, Levi, a twenty-four-year-old Italian Jew from Turin, was arrested and deported to the Nazi labor camp at Auschwitz in February 1944. Six hundred and fifty other men, women, and children traveled with him. When he returned home a year and a half later, he was one of twenty who had survived. Levi spent much of his life finding words for his camp experience. How, he wonders aloud in *Survival in Auschwitz*, do you describe "the demolition of a man," an offense for which "our language lacks words."[2]

Many people carry a mental image of a Jew in a concentration camp. We see the striped jacket, the starved face with shaved head and unseeing eyes. To Levi, the picture of an emaciated man "with head dropped and shoulders curved, on whose face and in whose eyes not a trace of thought is to be seen" encloses "all the evil of our time."[3]

During the past century we have learned much about how to create an individual and how to destroy one—not that such knowledge hasn't always existed. But we have had particular opportunity to observe and explore ideas about both individual worth and mass human destruction, including the ways to destroy an individual short of outright murder. Destroying his privacy and his safety in private is one way.

A basic ingredient in such destruction is terror. I am walking with a friend in the Dordogne region of France. It is a warm midsummer day, and the blackberry bushes are flowering. During the war, my friend recounts, pointing up at an old stone house set on a small hill, a family lived there who joined the Resistance. The SS arrested the husband, tortured him, and then delivered him back to their door. The captors waited until the family, overjoyed that he was alive, ran out to hug him. Then they shot him in front of his wife and children.

Hitler's accomplices understood—as many have before and since—that if you kill an enemy, his loved ones will grieve, but if you kill him in a way that also terrorizes them, you will accomplish more effective harm. Psychologically fractured by fear, these "enemies" will find it harder to oppose you. Yet they remain alive and able to till fields that feed your troops. The English who fought Indians in seventeenth-century Virginia summed up this approach neatly, observing that "terrour . . . made short warres."[4]

When you set out to destroy someone psychologically, destroying his privacy turns out to be one effective and common tactic. When Primo Levi talks about solitude in the camp being more precious and rare than bread, he helps us understand its place in life. One function of privacy is to provide a safe space away from terror or other assaultive experiences. When you remove a person's ability to sequester herself, or intimate information about herself, you make her extremely vulnerable.

Consider Vera Wollenberger, a woman who spent much of her young adulthood protesting East German communism. For her dissent she was harassed, fired from her job, and imprisoned. After communism collapsed, Wollenberger, elected to Parliament, helped enact a law allowing people to read the secret files kept on them by the East German government. Reading her own, she realized with horror that the intimate and damaging information that filled it could only have been offered by her husband. No one else knew the particular details.[5] Violating the privacy she expected to hold in common with him, her husband took advantage of her trust in their intimacy (a private state) to betray and exploit her, probably in the hope of increasing his own power. What must it have been like to recognize that her spouse was responsible for her imprisonment? After such a betrayal, what would happen to her ability to love?

The totalitarian state watches everyone, but keeps its own plans secret. Privacy is seen as dangerous because it enhances resistance. Constantly

spying and then confronting people with what are often petty trans-
gressions is a way of maintaining social control and unnerving and dis-
empowering opposition. While spying efforts sometimes backfire and
increase the loyalty of friends and intimates, too often they succeed. And
even when one shakes real pursuers, it is often hard to rid oneself of the
feeling of being watched—which is why surveillance is an extremely powerful way to control people. The mind's tendency to still feel observed
when alone (a phenomenon related to Freud's idea of the superego) is
probably biologically and culturally indispensable, but it can also be in-
hibiting. Used malevolently, surveillance badly harms individuals in part
by really endangering them, in part by overstimulating their vigilance.
Feeling watched, but not knowing for sure, nor knowing if, when, or how
the hostile surveyor may strike, people often become fearful, constricted,
and distracted.

Nadezhda Mandelstam was married to the Russian poet Osip Mandelstam who was arrested and imprisoned by Stalin and eventually died in a
labor camp. In her memoir, *Hope Against Hope*, Mandelstam relates the
terrible havoc wreaked by Stalinism, and she details the insidious psychological harm of surveillance. She describes how the dictatorship destroyed
trust—often by destroying the sanctuary within privacy—and "atomized"
the society. Anything a person said in private could be reported to government spies, and used against him to demonstrate his disloyalty, for which
he was then imprisoned and often killed. Spies were everywhere, and
when unable to find damaging material, they made it up. Since the conversations they reported had theoretically occurred in private, no one
could disprove the accusations. Mandelstam observes how, when such
practices destroy people's safety, everyone becomes a little mad:

> An existence like this leaves its mark. We all became slightly unbalanced men-
> tally—not exactly ill, but not normal either: suspicious, mendacious, confused
> and inhibited in our speech, at the same time putting on a show of adolescent
> optimism. What value can such people have as witnesses? The elimination of
> witnesses was, indeed, part of the whole program.[6]

Constrained and frightened, harassed people often lose their efficacy.
Their privacy has been destroyed by surveillance and fear. (It is the same
phenomenon as it sometimes occurs in family life that serious discussions
on talk shows attempt to witness and describe and that psychotherapists
treat.)

It is of course not just communist or fascist governments that use such tactics. The United States has often spied on and persecuted dissidents: Emma Goldman, the Wobblies, and Malcolm X are a few who come to mind. Surveillance and harassment have grown in America along with the rest of government. Curt Gentry's eight-hundred-page biography of J. Edgar Hoover offers an endless catalogue of the FBI chief's appalling misuse of spying sometimes for political, sometimes for more self-serving, purposes. Here is a small example:

> On learning that one magazine publisher was considering an expose of the FBI and its long-tenured director, Hoover struck first, viciously. Favored newspaper contacts all over the country received a plain brown envelope with no return address. Inside was a packet of photographs showing the publisher's wife engaged in fellatio with her black chauffeur.[7]

Such surveillance betrays intimacy—and all privacy—by observing people while they are enjoying the freedom of being unobserved. The FBI's attempt to make Martin Luther King commit suicide by sending him and his wife tapes of his sexual infidelities is another example of this approach. Along with the videos, King received an anonymous letter. Knowing that he had attempted suicide as a twelve-year-old child, the writer, an FBI agent, encouraged King to end his life.[8] As we learn more about J. Edgar Hoover, his morbid shame about his own sexuality, his secrecy, and decadence, the way he persecuted others in the name of patriotism seems not only awful, but obviously self-defensive. But such insight is cold comfort to the people whose lives he destroyed or harmed.

Safe privacy is an important component of autonomy, freedom, and love, and thus psychological well-being, in any society that values individuals. In fact, by reversing to the smallest detail all that was perpetrated against Levi, Mandelstam, Wollenberger, and King, we can extract a standard. Summed up briefly, a statement of "how not to dehumanize people" might read: Don't replace names with numbers. Don't beat or torture. Don't terrorize or humiliate. Don't starve, freeze, exhaust. Don't demean or impose degrading submission. Don't force separation from loved ones. Don't make demands in an incomprehensible language. Don't refuse to listen closely. Don't destroy privacy. Terrorists of all sorts destroy privacy both by corrupting it into secrecy and by using hostile surveillance to undo its useful sanctuary.

But if we describe a standard for treating people humanely, why does stripping privacy violate it? And what is privacy? In his landmark book,

Privacy and Freedom, Alan Westin names four states of privacy: solitude, anonymity, reserve, and intimacy.[9] The reasons for valuing privacy become more apparent as we explore these states.

Solitude is the most complete state of privacy. A person seeking solitude separates from others so that she cannot be seen or heard, and so that she is not easily intruded upon. In solitude, as opposed to the other states of privacy, she is most free to relax her body.

What is considered physically private varies in different cultures and different families. Anthropologists suggest that most people, no matter where or when they live, seek privacy for sex and defecation.[10] But other habits are more local and temporary. In private today, a person might remove undergarments, use the toilet, sleep, pick his nose, masturbate, examine and cleanse parts of his body, or sniff his own odors. The heroine in Marie Cardinal's memoir/novel *The Words to Say It* describes her adeptness at discreetly reaching her hand down under her clothing to check her menstrual flow. And when alone, she privately examines her blood. "I remember taking out the tampon that stopped the blood, which I began to watch gently flowing, drop by drop. . . . It was an activity to watch the blood work its way out of me; it had a life of its own now, it could discover the physics of earth-bound things, weight, density, speed, duration. It kept me company and at the same time was delivered over to the indifferent and incomprehensible laws of life."[11]

Similarly, in his memoir *Self-Consciousness,* John Updike describes the close attention he paid to his body because of his psoriasis. Years later he remembers the smell of the medicine, the "insinuating odor deeply involved with my embarrassment. Yet, as with our own private odors, those of sweat and earwax and even of excrement, there was something satisfying about this scent, an intimate rankness that told me who I was."[12]

Alone with our bodies, we allow ourselves to know them thoroughly—the shape of an arm, the bend of a toenail, the pattern of freckles or scars. In private we learn and continually update our knowledge of the small details that make up our physical being. It is a vast and fundamental entry in the lexicon of our identity. Freud believed that the primary ego is a body ego—that the first and most basic knowledge we have of ourselves is through the feelings in our body, our physical gratification, pain, hungers, and needs. The body is the plowed field in which the self grows. As the body changes, it alters and recreates the self. Souls and private scents are inextricably commingled.

It is not only when we are alone that we come to know our bodies. The touch of others is critical for comfort because it allows us to learn where we begin and end. It can offer pleasure or pain. A baby deprived of human touch is a baby unlikely to survive infancy. But in the presence of others, once out of earliest childhood, the intimate and thorough explorations of the body are limited and inhibited by demands for propriety and conformity.

In some Catholic orders, a nun was forbidden to examine her own body. Even when she bathed, she was covered with sheets. While the repression of sexuality is obvious (though it's easy to imagine such an effort backfiring by creating a tabooed eroticism), more subtle is the impact such strictures must have had on the woman's sense of self and individuality. Did she collect knowledge with her fingertips instead of her eyes? Or was her mind so completely on God that she just didn't care? Diminishing individual identity heightens receptivity to authority—something military leaders have understood for centuries. Discouraging people from private knowledge of their bodies probably eases that process. An opposite approach is that of feminist doctors who hand women mirrors and encourage them to examine their own vulvas.

Solitude frequently gets represented by a man alone in nature—something that television commercials play upon endlessly. Often the image replaces the experience: Urban highways are crowded with Land Rovers and Jeeps theoretically designed to allow people to go alone into the wilderness—to drive beyond the roads or to ford streams. Gas guzzlers, short on comfort, awkward on crowded streets, these cars have little practical purpose in city life except, I suspect, the profound one of maintaining the fantasy of solitude in nature against the besieging reality.

Americans have long loved the idea of the man alone in nature. Whether of Thoreau, Natty Bumppo, a Native American, or a cowboy, the image is deeply held. Entering nature we identify with him, like children with superheroes. The solitude he inhabits is a child's fantasy of life without dependency, of sublime confidence, of conflict without ambiguity or compromise. The nature that frames him is a stage set, a passive backdrop for human assertion constructed to flatter him as separate, free, and strong.

Real accounts of nature describe the difficulty of physical toil and the constant danger of dying—men in their fishing boats lost at sea, women frozen in storms, children eaten by wolves. The perception of beauty and freedom is set against the deep fear, even terror, of harm and death. The natural world that the Pilgrims encountered was, according to William Bradford, "a hideous and desolate wilderness, full of wild beasts and wild men." New England fishermen understand this feeling. Only when summer people started visiting the coast did houses get fitted with decks and picture windows. People who daily worked and died at sea had no urgency to contemplate the water from their kitchen tables.

In the suburban world, wilderness dangers are overshadowed by civilization's; we fear stalkers more than bears. People generally possess a more distant and split image of nature. On the one hand, it is a weakened and perhaps dying leviathan harpooned by overpopulation, technology, toxic waste, and the pollution of contemporary life—not a place to seek solitude. On the other hand, the contemporary sense of nature is still the wide-open spaces, pristine—or at least pastoral—beauty, a spiritual haven, the site of personal liberty, freedom, and autonomy. The nature in which one seeks solitude has often already been subdued. Nineteenth-century transcendentalists and romantic poets, facing the encroachments of industrial society, wrote about solitude in this nature and tried to define why it mattered.

"I went to the woods," Thoreau asserts in a famous passage from *Walden*, "because I wished to live deliberately." Or, as he states earlier, because he wished to be awakened by the "undulations of celestial music instead of factory bells."[13] Solitude allows people to regulate their rhythms and behaviors away from the influence of others. No one controls what you do or when. No one else's alarm clock wakes you. No one's questions or need interrupt your train of thought or feeling, or your solitary pursuits. Solitude does not have to be in nature, but when set there, frees people most completely from the regulation, control, and constraint of society. Even more than the factory bells, it is the direct influence of other people, particularly in their more oppressive and intrusive dimensions, that one temporarily eludes in solitude.

Why is it that I am drawn to sit alone on a small beach watching the ocean, the circling gulls and ospreys, the piles of smooth stones surrounded by wild indigo, morning glory, and hawkweed? My answer is common. I love the peace of not having to take account of others. I am amazed by the beauty. I am reminded that my concerns are small and that what good or damage I do is small. The large wild domain indifferent to my existence is both soothing and thrilling. Alone in nature, one confronts its grandeur. Sensing its scope, it is the rare person who feels no awe. Solitude in nature places a person directly in contact with a vivid, original force.

One may, like Wordsworth, experience nature as a moral force that reinforces and enhances one's virtues. Nature, he asserts, is "the anchor of my purest thoughts, the nurse, the guide, the guardian of my heart, and soul of all my moral being." By closely watching nature, he believes, one uncovers the divine and feels its resonance within the self. A related use of solitude occurs in some kinds of meditation, when people sit alone in order to examine and reflect more rigorously. When this ancient practice is undertaken as part of a religious pursuit, people seek to become closer to a god or to holiness. Otherwise, it is to calm oneself, or use contemplation as a route to knowledge.

Seeking solitude, but not nature, people wish for time alone to "center" or to "get back in touch" with themselves. But what does this mean? Since I have had children, commuting to work forty minutes in traffic has changed from onerous to almost pleasant. It is privacy I can count on having. As the traffic inches along, my thoughts drift freely to situations at work, exchanges at home or with friends, problems I need to solve, plans, feelings, and fantasies. If a story on the radio is sad and my eyes tear, no child looks at me with worry. If an old song reminds me of a good time and I sing along, no adolescent passenger complains that it's a bad song and I'm off-key. A car in traffic is not completely private, yet it suffices.

We seek solitude because our psyches are permeable membranes. When we come in contact with others, we tend to absorb feelings, thoughts, moods, and opinions. A child says you're unfair for making her start her book report today. Are you? A client asks to change his appointment from Tuesday to Monday. Can you? A spouse gives you a look that suggests it's your turn to fold the laundry. Is it? A friend describes events that have made her sad. Is that why you now feel sad? We separate from others to sort through all we have taken in, to replay pieces of exchanges, to evaluate them, to rework them—and ultimately for the peace in which to listen attentively until we can hear our own notes amidst the jangle.

The essence of solitude, and all privacy, is a sense of choice and control. You control who watches or learns about you. You choose to leave and return. Even Thoreau left his cabin to seek companionship. Often we are all our own worst company, and nothing can relieve us except the comfort of others. Unchosen solitude quickly becomes painful isolation. Frederick the Great, wishing to hear the original language he believed had been spoken before the Tower of Babel, reportedly isolated a group of infants in hopes that when they talked, they would speak the ancient lost language. Though fed and clothed, they died.

. . . .

People in solitary confinement have to fight constantly against madness. In fact, the way they often preserve their sanity is by learning to dissociate, to alter their own mental state, and use fantasy to evoke images, memories, and feelings of loved ones. Yamil Kouri, a doctor jailed in solitary confinement in Cuba for allegedly conspiring to overthrow Castro, recalls that he survived the darkened two-foot-by-two-foot cell for two and a half years by meditating continually.[14] Paradoxically, one can defy isolation by evoking memories of intimacy.

Enforced or protracted solitude is unbearable to most people. But solitude in moderation, held in check by its being a sought and limited departure from the company of others, allows freedom. Alone, we create stories about ourselves as we would wish to be. We can feel our own feelings free from the direct influence of others, think our thoughts uninterrupted, spin out fantasies, and follow the images of the imagination. In his book *Solitude,* the psychoanalyst Anthony Storr argues that its value has been hidden in this century because of psychology's obsession with intimacy. Storr suggests that many highly creative people, like Beethoven and Kipling, were extremely solitary and that solitude is often a prerequisite for creativity. Some people want to be left alone to imagine.[15]

People need privacy from others so that they can rest from the strain of being what others desire—responsive, civil, engaged, conventional. "We pray to be conventional," writes Ralph Waldo Emerson, "but the wary Heaven takes care you shall not be, if there is anything good in you!"[16] To think and create, people often need solitude because its privacy allows not only mental continuity, quiet, and relief from feeling noticed, but latitude to experiment with half-formed ideas and ridiculous solutions.

Still, that image neglects the full cycle. Solitude is half a heartbeat. Artists seek solitude so that they can create what they then must take before the public. Without an eventual audience, no matter how small, solitude can become, in Emerson's words, "the safeguard of mediocrity."[17]

Most images of solitude are male: men alone, men in nature, men making art. Almost the only time women traditionally were allowed solitude was in prayer—as they conversed with a saint or a god. Emerson's mother, who bore eight children of whom five survived, sought solitude to pray. "She led a deeply religious life. Every day after breakfast she retired to her room for reading and contemplation. She was not to be disturbed."[18] At the hearth, surrounded by children and family, in the imagination, we place women in the presence of others. A woman alone is usually perceived not as seeking solitude, but as abandoned, unattractive, isolated, and lonely, or conversely as dangerous, unattached, destabilizing. A woman without a man is a woman after your man—ask any country western singer.

When women venture out alone—whether into wilderness or empty alleys—they often feel apprehensiveness about their own vulnerability. It is not wolves or snakes that raise contemporary fears, but the violence of men. In a chilling *New York Times* "Hers" column, Susan Brison describes setting out alone for a country walk on a beautiful summer day in southern Europe:

> I sang to myself as I set out, stopping to pet a goat and pick some wild straw-berries along the way. An hour later, I was lying near death, pleading for my life with a brutal assailant who had jumped me from behind. I hadn't heard or seen him coming. He dragged me off the road and into a deep ravine, beat me with his fist and with a rock, sexually assaulted me, choked me repeatedly and, after I had passed out four times, left me for dead.[19]

A woman alone is a woman easily overpowered and hurt. And while all the ramifications of such violence are terrible, one of the worst is the way it harms women's freedom to relish solitude. The story includes a cautionary tale about solitude: It can be dangerous. It may be that we associate the glory of solitude with men, and its liabilities with women. Underlying that unfortunate polarization is the recognition that the aloneness people seek can be risky; it can undermine communal life, or make individuals too vulnerable.

A second state of privacy is *anonymity*. To be anonymous is to be unidentified, unnamed, unnoted: a walker in a city, a member of a crowd. With the absence of recognition can come a liberating privacy. People often seek anonymity when the conventions of their surroundings, when the burden of being known, threatens to obliterate vital dimensions of their being. It seems no coincidence, for example, that the nineteenth-century feminist Margaret Fuller fell passionately in love and had a child while living in Italy, not in New England. Being surrounded by people at home with narrow ideas about women hindered her wish to have both passion and a mind. In Rome, she found freedom in not knowing or being known. (To find equal freedom, an Italian woman of her era might have expatriated herself elsewhere.) So, too, in *My Own Country,* Abraham Verghese, a doctor in Tennessee treating people with HIV, describes how frequently gay men left their small hometowns and moved to the city to find a place where they could possess their sexuality and their lives.

Anonymity in an urban setting is in some ways equivalent to solitude in nature. Like solitude, anonymity offers space. But because we are surrounded by other people, our aloneness is less complete and more easily disrupted. In an anonymous state, we are alone because we don't stand out or invite identification. No one interrupts us, we believe that no one notices us—though that is not certain. We may notice others and create their meaning without having to entertain their subjectivity. Anonymity, you might say, is privacy for people who don't want to be really alone.

Ernest Hemingway liked to write in places where he could be in the private world of his work, but still among people. In *A Moveable Feast*, he describes sitting and writing in a café when a pretty girl comes in. He would like to approach her, but he realizes she is waiting for someone—he assumes another man. Nevertheless, she becomes "his" because he can fantasize and write about her. He writes, "I've seen you, beauty, and you belong to me now, whoever you are waiting for and if I never see you again, I thought. You belong to me and all Paris belongs to me and I belong to this notebook and this pencil."[20]

Anonymity allows people to express thoughts or feelings they might suppress in a relationship where they feel ashamed, vulnerable, or frightened. Writing about the way anonymity permitted intimacy in the letters women wrote to the birth control crusader Margaret Sanger, her biographer Ellen Chesler recounts: "They wrote of strict and falsely modest mothers who had told them nothing of sex or birth control, of callous physicians who claimed ignorance of reliable methods, of husbands who abandoned them when they chose continence over the risk of another pregnancy, of illegal abortionists who cost them their fertility. They wrote with a sisterly affection and intimacy made possible by distance and anonymity."[21] When not worried about being identified, people will say what they are otherwise ashamed to say.

Anonymity is a tentative and unsteady state of privacy. In a hurry to get somewhere, a neighbor, stuck behind a car dawdling at a stoplight, honked her horn angrily. A few seconds later she became embarrassed when the driver, an elderly man, turned around and recognized her. She had expressed her dismay rudely because she felt anonymous. She assumed that her behavior would not be identified with her. This response and the embarrassment it sometimes occasions, familiar to all of us, is the stuff of contemporary urban life.

Honk a horn, deface a sign, state an unacceptable wish—anonymity supports the mischievous, the petty vandalisms against each other and authorities that give us room to mock perceived hegemonies and to release "incorrect" but genuine feelings. Unfortunately, crime and serious assaults are also based in anonymity. The terrorist, bank robber, housebreaker, and rapist cover their faces to hide their identities and to avoid social sanctions. They may know their victim, but hope not to be recognized by him.

The proliferation of certain kinds of crime testifies to the overabundance of anonymity in contemporary life. Like solitude, anonymity offers the most when it is temporary—and freely chosen. When undesired, anonymity leads to dehumanization and isolation. Many people, though they have friends, feel alienated and reduced because they participate in fragmented communities too large and impersonal to recognize or value them. Their anonymity becomes burdensome.

Sitting before computers linked by modems, some users of the Internet make up names, identities, true or untrue stories about themselves, and exchange unverifiable messages with other people. Good things come of it: vital exchanges, useful information, psychological adventure, creativity, and recreation. Yet the Internet reflects the culture's dilemma of too much anonymity. No one on it has to answer for himself. People make contact with each other, start to build relationships, exchange information, and cannot verify what is fantasy and what is fact. While this is an age-old problem, usually embodied in a story of a deceiving stranger who arrives in a village—like Wickham in *Pride and Prejudice*—it reaches almost absurd heights in computer relationships where no observing community is present to contradict an individual's deceptions.

Reserve, the third state of privacy is forbearance, tact, restraint. In a state of reserve, unlike solitude, we are together with people, and unlike anonymity, we are usually known to them. We may be intimate. Our state is private simply because we do not choose to reveal the full extent of what we feel, observe, think, or experience. We set aside our immediate perceptions, sometimes our frankest opinions—preserving them (and often us) for the future. Reserve is a house with glass walls, but no one mentions it.

Highly variable among cultures, reserve tends to be a type of privacy available in the absence of most others. The Utku Eskimos, who during the long arctic winters share close quarters with a number of family members, signal their wish for privacy by withdrawing into their own sleeping space, not speaking or responding to people around them. They are awake, but no one approaches them.[22] Kids on subways often use head-

. . . .

phones to the same end, or family members, television. In situations where other privacy is denied or undesirable, reserve offers an opportunity to move away. The state is most easily sustained when surrounding people agree not to intrude.

Levels of reserve vary from person to person, family to family, neighborhood to neighborhood. Standards continually shift. At the end of *The Age of Innocence,* Edith Wharton's novel set in late-nineteenth-century New York society, Dallas Archer talks openly with his father, Newland Archer, about his parents' relationship. Contrasting Dallas to his parents, Wharton observes, "it had never been possible to inculcate in him even the rudiments of reserve."

On this occasion, Dallas brings up the passionate love for another woman that his father once felt and then renounced. He startles his father with the news that his mother knew about her husband's feelings. She told Dallas that Newland had given this love up at her request. Wharton writes:

> Archer received this strange communication in silence. His eyes remained unseeingly fixed on the thronged, sunlit square below the window. At length he said in a low voice: "She never asked me."
>
> "No. I forgot. You never did ask each other anything, did you? And you never told each other anything, you just sat and watched each other, and guessed at what was going on underneath. A deaf-and-dumb asylum, in fact! Well, I back your generation for knowing more about each other's private thoughts than we ever have time to find out about our own."[23]

Wharton suggests that in a state of reserve people do not necessarily know less about each other's private experience; they just learn by watching rather than speaking, and they preserve privacy by not speaking about what they believe they know. While Wharton—through Dallas—gently ridicules the idea, she also romanticizes it, implying that reserve does not obscure understanding, that perhaps it enhances it. In this sense, the privacy of reserve is the privacy of not being forced to openly acknowledge what it is known that you know.

Words can be indelicate, and can tear the fragile gauze of lifelong intimacy. In their inexactness or awkwardness, they may cause unnecessary pain by making something too explicit. Over a long marriage, each partner's love has vicissitudes. Does it do more harm or more good to document them aloud? When people live at close quarters, small irritations are frequent. Some are better unnamed. Some feelings can be universally understood to be present, and thus do not warrant expression.

Various types of reserve dominate most exchanges. Sometimes we lower our eyes or look away. Frequently adults admonish children, "Don't stare." We offer privacy by not letting our interest be noticed, by pretending not to hear something that is said, by deflecting with silence or platitude a remark that threatens to intrude into private space or to reveal "too much." Reserve is a cornerstone of civility. Its premise is that most exchanges are better off partial, most days improved by not telling much to many.

The disadvantages of reserve, and particularly the price to a person's life of being overly reserved, are explored in Kazuo Ishiguro's novel *The Remains of the Day*. The story is narrated by a butler who has devoted his life so entirely to serving a rich Englishman in a large mansion that he has forgotten himself. He has not married or had children. Stevens prides himself on being a superb butler, for whom reserve is an essential professional quality. One evening, in the middle of looking after his lordship's guests, Stevens is called to the attic bedside of his father who has just suffered a stroke and is dying. Though others gathered around the bed are visibly distraught, Stevens shows no emotion, saying dryly, "This is most distressing. Nevertheless, I must now return downstairs."[24]

For Stevens, it is a point of honor neither to show emotion nor to acknowledge feelings or behaviors in others that might reveal their personal state. The lack of acknowledgment preserves privacy. Reserve is the essence of the butler's art because a butler must be extremely intimate with the people he serves without developing the habits or expectations of intimacy. Normally, if you help or watch someone change from nightclothes to street clothes, you share a close relationship. You are good friends or lovers or a parent with a young child. But a butler often must view his employer intimately without taking it as an invitation to closeness. Unfortunately, Ishiguro implies, the demands of the job are ultimately so dehumanizing that anyone expert at it is rendered useless for more intimate human relationships.

Too much reserve leaves people isolated, misunderstood, and guessing. Do you like me or hate me? Are you angry or sad? Am I helping or hurting? People get edgy when they cannot figure out where they stand. Yet almost all exchanges require some holding back of what is thought or felt because our most private thoughts and feelings are too idiosyncratic, vacillating, boring, unsocialized, and bald to be more than occasionally tolerable to other people. The capacity for reserve is as important to sustaining intimacy as disclosure is. It offers a basic form of emotional safety.

"There are people," the psychoanalyst Leston Havens has observed, "to whom we would say nothing. Even when the hot iron comes toward us and the manacles are clamped tight, we will say nothing."[25] Havens is referring to the way in which we instinctively and at times powerfully recognize that revealing something about ourselves—no matter how trivial—to someone we judge as untrustworthy will harm us. Without the capacity and the freedom to stay silent, to guard one's psychic privacy, there is no possibility for authentic relationships. Sometimes reserve is the only way to resist people who have more power. It allows us to choose to whom we speak.

One evening after a large Los Angeles earthquake, I turn on the television news. The story begins innocuously enough with footage of a twisted freeway filmed from a circling helicopter. We see rubble, destroyed buildings, fires, broken water mains, and listen to residents recount ordeals. The scene shifts. We are at the site of an attempted rescue. An apartment has collapsed, and men and bulldozers are digging in the rubble. They have just found the body of a woman's only child, her daughter. The woman is out of sight, and then she comes into the camera frame, screaming.

I expect the camera to offer us one look at her and then cut away. But it does not. She is wearing a gray pantsuit and sunglasses, and she cannot stop running and screaming. Her husband tries to grab her and pull her into his arms, but her grief is so intense, her body cannot allow itself to be held still. A man at the scene stands looking away from her, his reserve intuitively granting her the privacy that the camera refuses to offer. I look away and back, in my mind telling them to stop, and finally when she settles for a moment in her husband's arms, the screen cuts back to the somber faces of our local news anchors.

As I go to bed, I cannot shake the profound trauma of a woman I have never met. Does the television news editor feel I must see her to understand that earthquake? Her grief is vivid and somehow timeless. She looks like a mother would look. Parents digging children out of the ash around Pompeii two thousand years ago would know just how she felt. The horror of the event is vividly transmitted. But there is something wrong with witnessing the intimate traumas of people we don't hold close. Violating her privacy by allowing the camera to defy reserve, we violate a collective standard of honoring life and death by shielding people when their suffering is extreme.

Intimacy is the fourth state of privacy.

I am standing with a friend on a long, crowded beach. It is a hot day, and we have rolled our slacks so that foam from the waves hits our ankles and splatters our legs. My children swim in the glare and green water, and we both watch them, vigilantly tracking their movements among those of other swimmers. People walk by us. We talk, but with eyes fixed on the water, we do not often look at each other. Standing with arms almost touching but eyes rarely meeting is conducive to good talk. This beach reminds my friend of one she used to visit as a child. She describes it, and then speaks of her life growing up. I am content, caught up in her story, and the large umbrella of intimacy with which it shelters us. In "Midrash on Happiness," Grace Paley writes about how much her happiness depends upon such moments. "To walk in the city arm in arm with a woman friend (as her mother had with aunts and cousins so many years ago) was just plain essential. Oh! Those long walks and intimate talks, better than standing alone on the most admirable mountain or in the handsomest forest or hay-blown field."[26]

Intimacy is a private state because in it people relax their public front either physically or emotionally or, occasionally, both. They tell personal stories, exchange looks, or touch privately. They may ignore each other without offending. They may have sex. They may speak frankly using words they would not use in front of others, expressing ideas and feelings—positive or negative—that are unacceptable in public. (I don't think I ever got over his death. She seems unable to stop lying to her mother. He looks flabby in those running shorts. I feel horny. In spite of everything, I still long to see them. I am so angry at you I could scream. That joke is disgusting, but it's really funny.) Shielded from forced exposure, a person often feels more able to expose himself.

At moments, questions of intimacy become euphemistic questions of sex. "Are they intimate?" often means "Have they had sexual intercourse?" An intimate relationship may sometimes be observed in the way couples touch, kiss, or stand close in public, but many expressions of physical intimacy are private. Deep kissing, the touching with hands, mouths, or genitals or breasts, buttocks, and genitals tend to be private expressions of physical intimacy. Not all physical touching, even when it occurs in private, is intimate. One characteristic of violence is that it is contact—often to intimate areas of the body—without consent.

Sometimes out of lust, joy, lack of privacy, or the wish to shock, private touching occurs in public. Sometimes people get a kick (or an orgasm) out of being seen, of having others witness their pleasure. But often, making it public diminishes intimacy.

The heart of intimacy, its essence, is that in it one comes as close as one is capable of, or as close as one feels permitted, to revealing oneself to another person. One attempts to express frankly to another one's inner experiences, desires, feelings, and perceptions—though the expression is inevitably limited and incomplete. Intimacy requires trust and confidentiality. Intimacy may grow simply through experiencing events together, but often it grows through the sharing of private thoughts and feelings. The warp and woof of its development are the alternating cycles of revelation, bearable response, and gradually heightened trust. In the course of falling in love, each lover tells his beloved a story of his life. Othello recounts the effect of telling Desdemona about himself.

> She thank'd me
> And bade me, if I had a friend that lov'd her,
> I should but teach him how to tell my story,
> And that would woo her. Upon this heat I spoke.
> She lov'd me for the dangers I had pass'd,
> And I lov'd her that she did pity them.[27]

Desdemona is wooed by Othello's story. She feels awe and tenderness, feelings that deepen love. He offers her a man she can admire, a person worthy of her affection. So, too, her sympathy wins him. He has revealed himself without feeling shame.

In *War and Peace*, Princess Natasha and Princess Marya, originally enemies, become intimate friends while sitting together at the deathbed of Prince Andrei—Marya's brother and Natasha's onetime fiancé. After Andrei dies, Natasha risks telling Marya of her love:

> "Masha," she said, timidly drawing Princess Marya's hand toward her."
> Masha, you don't think I'm wicked, to you? Masha, darling, how I love you!
> Let us be real, bosom friends!" . . .
> From that day there sprang up between them one of those tender, passionate friendships that exist only between women. They were continually kissing and saying tender things to each other and spent most of their time together. If one went out, the other became restless and hastened to join her. Together they felt more in harmony than when apart. A tie stronger than friendship was established between them: that special feeling of life being possible only in each other's company.[28]

Love and intimacy are often wound together—though not always. We may preserve a habit of intimacy with people we no longer love. Loving someone, we desire increased intimacy. Put in a situation with another person where intimacy grows, we often come to feel love. And ultimately, love is private. Displayed too long before an audience, it becomes performance.

Intimate expressions occur in private because revelation makes people feel vulnerable. Imagine an intimate moment, then imagine it observed, and it changes. The sensibility jumps back, like an animal startled by a loud noise. Privacy not only sanctions intimacy, but appears to be a precondition of its most complete expression.

When people are not held, thrown, or forced together by geography, tradition, enslavement, simple dominance, economics, or kinship, then intimacy, chosen closeness based in love or tenderness, becomes a desirable alternative. Even were it not intrinsic to creativity, autonomy, and dignity, privacy would be invaluable simply for its role in supporting the possibility of rich and pleasurable intimacy.

A compelling image of Franklin Roosevelt is of him on his yacht relaxing by fishing, sleeping, and spending time with close friends. While president, Roosevelt drew enormous sustenance from the laughter, gossip, sexual intrigue, and warm friendships that privacy permitted. In the face of impossible political situations, he appreciated that creative public solutions often first came to mind when one was enjoying privacy. While Eleanor Roosevelt rarely relaxed, she too used private relationships for emotional sustenance. Whenever she wished to muster courage for a task that frightened or overwhelmed her, she would create intense, intimate friendships. The love emboldened her. Doris Kearns Goodwin's biography *No Ordinary Time* describes how much the courage and political force of both Roosevelts rested on their personal relationships.

Why is intimacy so sustaining? This question is key to understanding the importance of privacy. If aloneness is our predicament, then everything rests on finding ways to bear it. Love and friendship fulfill this mission. Love because it suggests we are acceptable and thus deserve to give and get respite. Friendship because it puts a person near us proffering this possibility. When, as Grace Paley suggests, we metaphorically or actually walk "arm in arm" with a lover or a friend, we have company with whom we can comment freely upon the passing scene, and each of us is allowed to be.

NOTES

1. Primo Levi, *Survival in Auschwitz and The Reawakening*, p. 329.
2. Ibid., p.15.

. . . .

3. Ibid., p. 67.

4. Bernard Bailyn, review of *The American Revolution in Indian Country* by Colin B. Calloway, *New York Review of Books*, 42–15, Oct. 5, 1995, p. 16.

5. Stephen Kinzer, "East Germans Face Their Accusers," *New York Times Magazine*, Apr. 12, 1992, p. 24.

6. Nadezhda Mandelstam, *Hope Against Hope*, p. 88.

7. Curt Gentry, *J. Edgar Hoover: The Man and the Secrets*, p. 388.

8. Ibid., p. 572.

9. Alan F. Westin, *Privacy and Freedom*, p. 31.

10. John Bowlby, quoted in Barrington Moore, Jr., *Privacy: Studies in Social and Cultural History*, p. 59.

11. Marie Cardinal, *The Words to Say It*, p. 17.

12. John Updike, *Self-Consciousness*, p. 43.

13. Henry David Thoreau, *Walden*, pp. 65, 66.

14. Julie Hatfield, "For a Cuban, Yoga Was a Lifesaver," *Boston Globe*, Nov. 16, 1992, p. 30.

15. Anthony Storr, *Solitude: A Return to the Self*, p. 140.

16. Ralph Waldo Emerson, "Culture," p. 155.

17. Ralph Waldo Emerson, "Society and Solitude," p. 7.

18. Robert D. Richardson, *Emerson: The Mind on Fire*, p. 21.

19. Susan Brison, "Survival Course," *New York Times Magazine*, Mar. 21, 1993, p. 20.

20. Ernest Hemingway, *A Moveable Feast*, p. 6.

21. Ellen Chesler, *Woman of Valor: Margaret Sanger and the Birth Control Movement in America*, p. 224.

22. Moore, Jr., *op. cit.*, p. 11.

23. Edith Wharton, *The Age of Innocence*, p. 282.

24. Kazuo Ishiguro, *The Remains of the Day*, p. 104.

25. Leston Havens, Cambridge Hospital Forum, Nov. 13, 1991.

26. Grace Paley and Vera B. Williams, "Midrash on Happiness," in *Long Walks and Intimate Talks*, unpaged.

27. William Shakespeare, *Othello*, Act 1, Scene 3, Lines 163–168, p. 29.

28. Leo Tolstoy, *War and Peace*, p. 1292.

SOURCES

Cardinal, Marie. *The Words to Say It*. Cambridge: VanVactor and Goodheart, 1983.

Chesler, Ellen. *Woman of Valor: Margaret Sanger and the Birth Control Movement in America*. New York: Simon & Schuster, 1992.

Emerson, Ralph Waldo. "Culture." *Conduct of Life: The Complete Works of Ralph Waldo Emerson, Vol. 6*. Cambridge: Riverside, 1904: 131–166.

——, "Society and Solitude." *Essays, First Series: The Complete Works of Ralph Waldo Emerson, Vol. 7*. Cambridge: Riverside, 1904: 1–16.

Gentry, Curt. *J. Edgar Hoover: The Man and the Secrets*. New York: Plume, 1992.

Hemingway, Ernest. *A Moveable Feast*. New York: Bantam, 1964.

Ishiguro, Kazuo. *The Remains of the Day*. New York: Vintage, 1990.

Levi, Primo. *Survival in Auschwitz and The Reawakening: Two Memoirs*. Trans. Stuart Woolf. New York: Summit, 1985.

Mandelstam, Nadeszhda. *Hope Against Hope: A Memoir*. Trans. Max Hayward. New York: Atheneum, 1970.

Moore, Barrington, Jr. *Privacy: Studies in Social and Cultural History*. Armonk, NY, and London: M.E. Sharpe, 1984.

Paley, Grace, and Vera B. Williams. *Long Walks and Intimate Talks*. Women and Peace Series. New York: Feminist Press, 1991.

Richardson, Robert D. *Emerson: The Mind on Fire*. Berkeley: University of California Press, 1995.

Shakespeare, William. *The Tragedy of Othello*. The Yale Shakespeare. Ed. Tucker Brooke and Lawrence Mason New Haven and London: Yale University Press 1947, 1965.

Storr, Anthony. *Solitude: A Return to the Self*. New York: Ballantine, 1989.

Thoreau, Henry David. *Walden*. New York: Signet Classic, 1960.

Tolstoy, Leo. *War and Peace*. New York: Signet Classic, 1968.

Updike, John. *Self-Consciousness: Memoirs*. New York: Knopf, 1989.

Westin, Alan F. *Privacy and Freedom*. New York: Atheneum, 1968.

Wharton, Edith. *The Age of Innocence*. New York: Signet Classic, 1962.

Secret Spaces of Childhood

. . . .

by
JOSIP NOVAKOVICH

The setting (Daruvar, Croatia) in which I was growing up was highly in-
imical to the notion of privacy. Yugoslavia in the early 1960s was a
staunchly communist country, Stalinist really, but since Tito couldn't get
along with the Soviet Union, Yugoslavia practiced its own brand of totalitarian socialism. Our ideologues regarded privacy as a bourgeoisie disease; everything was public or was to end up being public. What need was
there of possessing a book when you could go to the library and read one
there? What need was there for hiding anything in our society guided by a
beautiful motto, Brotherhood and Unity? The emphasis on doing everything together was tremendous. You wouldn't go out and run alone; you
would do it in a group, at school. You'd be geared toward playing group
sports—soccer, basketball, European handball, volleyball—and hardly toward individual ones. I think Yugoslavia (and its offspring countries) has
the highest ratio of medals won in group sports versus individual sports in
the world.

And for me, there was an additional agency exerting pressure against
privacy: the Baptist church, in which I was raised as a member of that
scorned minority. I grew up with the notion that God sees everything, and
no matter what you do and where you hide, God will watch you.

So privacy was a disease (for Socialists) and sin and illusion (for Baptists). It was a hopeless case, not worth attempting, apparently.

And yet, precisely because both groups exerted, or attempted to, such
total control over me, I desperately wanted some place to hide. But before
I could worry about space, I worried about time. We went to school six
days a week, and on the seventh I had to be in church most of the day,

listening to zealots who measured the intensity of their inspiration by how long they could carry on their sermons—we'd sit there for four hours, listening to the same lines of reasoning being repeated ten times. As if that weren't enough, we Baptists went to church every Thursday evening for a prayer meeting and every Tuesday for a youth group meeting—and these again could stretch for hours.

Perhaps because I had to spend so much time in public, I created a portable private space within me—I grew to be shy. I never let on in public what I really thought and believed. I didn't like to be scrutinized, and if anyone's gaze rested on me for more than a couple of seconds, I interpreted his action as an attack aiming to expose me. It was one thing to have the inevitable and just eye of God scrutinize me. It was another to have the eyes of neighbors, siblings, and uncles search through me.

To make matters worse, we were a society of gazers. There were many talented spies all around, employed and unemployed. This was not simply a matter of politics, but of some remnant of tribalism, of *zadruga* (an ancient agricultural collective of several extended families living together) that used to be common among the Slavs. It takes a whole village to raise a child is a maxim that worked in the old zadruga system, and which people in small towns still wanted to employ, not necessarily with the benevolent aim of bringing up a healthy child, but more frequently with the aim of discrediting your neighbor's child so you'd feel better about your own—or simply, in those still mostly nontelevision years, the scrutiny was a form of entertainment, a continuous soap opera of the whole village or town that throve on disclosed secrets and shame. On the other hand, the whole town braced itself against the same collective gaze that it exerted upon itself. No Stalin or God could change the desperate need for a bit of private turf.

And indeed, a construction craze swept the town with a modicum of prosperity that occurred when Tito managed to borrow a lot of money from the IMF and we still did not have to return it. Moreover, many people began to work in Germany as Gastarbeiter with the sole aim of building their own homes. And so houses with solid brick walls laid on concrete foundations sprang up around the town. The windows were protected with solid roller-shutters that could sink your house in total darkness in the middle of the day. Of course, this all may have sprung from some kind of sensation of threat, as though another war was about to come—we were constantly expecting a Soviet invasion—and clearly people weren't completely wrong about that. The casualty statistics in the

. . . .

wars to come, in the 1990s, would be much higher if it hadn't been for such solid construction that could indeed withstand a lot of bombing.

One of the first houses to be constructed in this bunker-like mode was my father's. In 1959, when I was three years old, we moved from a little house into a large one that was one-third finished. He kept working on it piecemeal—finishing a room here, a terrace, a garage, and so on, but leaving, still in the middle of the house, a wood-storage room. Nine years later, when my father died, the house was not yet finished. The yard went through similar construction attempts. He built one workshop, where he made wooden shoes, and then a shack, and a sheep stall. As soon as he finished the stall, the new town ordinance forbade keeping livestock. Our garden was large, an acre. The whole place was a construction zone and work chaos. Planks of wood, sand, bricks, granite rocks, iron rods—they all lay in piles here and there. And then, there was a large sawdust pile beneath my favorite walnut tree. The workshop hosted circular and band saws, rotary rasps, and all sorts of adzes and knives. Above the workshop was an attic, with piles of neatly stacked wooden soles. So if I were to hide anything (including myself), there was no shortage of space. Whenever I did something wrong, which could result in flogging—my parents believed in the Don't-Spare-the-Rod style of upbringing—I hid. One particularly effective hiding space was among the bales and stacks of cowhide in the dark attic of the main house. Here, I could insert several wooden soles and create a hidden cave within the cowhides. I would crawl into the cave and stay still. Nobody knew of my technique.

I had many locations where I could hide, even in the public park and nearby forests. Several of us played Robin Hood in the woods south of the town. Here we'd hide swords that I made in my father's workshop, using his variety of wood-carving knives, to make smooth weapons. We also made bows and arrows, with reed, turkey feathers, and large nails. Then, we stole oxhide from my father and made shields stretched on wooden frames. There were several cave-like formations, which we covered with branches and leaves and used as storage spaces. We spent more time carving weapons and storing them than actually playing Robin Hood, although sometimes we did manage to hold archery tournaments, wrestling and boxing and fencing matches.

We all had our secret spaces. A friend of mine, when he moved into a large office building that was too decrepit to hold offices any longer, proudly displayed all sorts of beams and dark corners under the roof in the attic. At one end of the attic, his mother smoked ham, so we cut off very flimsy slices so she wouldn't notice that anything was missing. He hid small bottles of plum brandy he'd stolen from his father, and this, too, we'd sip in minute quantities, just for the fun of experiencing the burning of our throats. In a way, the more intriguing the secret spaces of your home, the higher your social appeal would be; in making a new friend, you'd try to impress him by what strange and unexplored worlds you could offer—at any rate, that was my attitude in both offering friendship and seeking friendship. And for these explorations, we were left alone. I don't think this sort of privacy is possible in the States these days. You wouldn't leave two ten-year-old boys to roam unobserved in attics and basements, and then to slip into the streets, and to play till eleven at night in a forest. Yet our parents didn't panic, didn't call the police, didn't even worry that much. The only reproach we'd get was that dinner was prepared in vain if we weren't there to eat it. Frequently, for a meal, we'd jump a fence and eat fruits and vegetables in someone's garden.

On the other hand, if you stayed at a friend's place, his mother would feed both of you, but as we didn't use the phone there was no way to notify your mother that you wouldn't be home till midnight. And once we did get home, my brother and I didn't like to announce that we were home. We had our own tree, a large and knotty apricot, that we could climb to the second floor and jump directly into our bedroom. We scoffed at using the staircase.

Now, I think that the amount of freedom that we enjoyed was possible precisely because the town was full of official and unofficial spies. The town was tremendously safe. Nearly all the boys and many girls freely roamed in the town of 10,000 (with a busy downtown, such as not even a 100,000 people make in the States). There were people on foot in almost all the streets of the town. I don't know of a single case of a child being stolen or abducted—something that's a constant fear for parents in the States. Even during the war, while visiting Croatia, I saw children walking to school, sometimes two to three miles away, either by themselves or with other children. As a child, you used to live and still perhaps do in a blessed zone of unconscious safety over there. I remember a friend of mine in Zadar complaining that the war changed everything, that now she was so nervous she couldn't let her son leave her sight for more than a minute without her running to check on him. While she talked like that, she completely forgot about her seven-year-old, and only an hour later, when we paid for the pizza bill, it occurred to us (to me first), Well, where is Dinko? We found him on the next block playing in the Roman ruins with a couple of other unsupervised boys, even though it was the middle of a busy summer. I don't even know of cases of sexual abuse—and many of my peers said they couldn't recall anything like that either. Now and then, there would be elderly single men who liked to talk to young boys, and they'd invite us to walk with them in the park, but they only talked, and talked very interestingly without ever touching us. Perhaps because the eyes of the town were everywhere, there was hardly any possibility in public places to cross the forbidden lines. So I'd say the tremendous scrutiny that we were subjected to in the streets—sometimes you'd even discern figures behind the curtains of windows peering out and eavesdropping—created such a safety nexus that we could be left alone. Strangely enough, although my assignment here is to talk about my private spaces, I talk about the spaces of my generation in my town, for our privacy was a commune of sorts.

Best friendships were forged in these hideouts, where we smoked our first cigarettes and had our first sips of brandy—years later, many of us are still in touch.

Of course, I can remember different sorts of private spaces—books. I read them in different corners, in the attic, with shafts of sunlight hitting the page through cracks in the roof. I read Jules Verne, Alexandre Dumas, Mark Twain, and various Westerns. Those were certainly important, but somehow, the impression that I have when I think of privacy is that of a space into which special friends could be invited for long conversations about whether God existed, what the best form of communism would be, whether we would all end up living in a commune, and about many other matters, personal and political. Caught in the cross fire between Baptists and communists, many basic questions were a matter of life and death to me, even eternal life and death. I didn't fit the church requirements, and I didn't fit the party requirements, to qualify as a perfectly acceptable boy, and I had to find a way of surviving psychologically, for standing on my own, because I didn't want to end up like everybody in church or everybody in the party. I craved—and in a way created—an alternative because I couldn't completely give up faith in God nor could I give up the school and society. And so there we were, with our underground alternative society, thousands of children crouching in corners, basements, all over the country as though a bombing were already in progress.

Some Cyberspace of Her Own:
DrRogue's Intelligent Life

.   .   .   .

by
BRONWYN GARRITY

> I am no doubt not the only one who writes in order to have no face. Do not
> ask who I am and do not ask me to remain the same.
>   MICHEL FOUCAULT

Ever since I was assigned to read *A Room of One's Own* in college eight
years ago, I have kept it close for support. Besides the fact that, like Virginia Woolf, I had also read Leo Tolstoy's journals and was similarly enraged by the clarity he exhibited at such a young age, I felt she was onto
something. "A room of one's own" however, wasn't quite it.

I grew up in the 1980s, inside a charming if small, Spanish-style California home with a mom, a sister, a piano, many dogs, and two brothers
who were relentless in their efforts to ply my locks with butter knives. Although I liked to think I had my own room, the space's original and (now
that I'm an adult I can say it) *idiotic* plans called for its doubling as a
shortcut to one of the house's more popular bathrooms. I went to great
and occasionally violent lengths to discourage use of this particular feature. The results? Ha, as DrRogue would say.

Time and time again, my brothers broke triumphantly in, capturing me
on my bed writing in my journal. I smile now, but back then, those intrusions enraged me. You see, unlike those jerks, I was becoming a woman
and it was making me miserable. I liked being a girl. And, it wasn't necessarily that I was surprised to discover that girls became women—in a rational way, I knew it happened all the time. It was just that I found the
obvious sexuality of it offensive. It was clear to me that once breasts made
their appearance against a shirt, a person could not be taken seriously.

I looked around at school and saw happy, pretty girls who went to the beach. They seemed content being female, and I liked boys too, so I did what they did. Then I went home depressed, slammed my doors, locked them, and wrote to my journal about how much I loathed myself, until my brothers broke in after school. Here is a genuine entry from November 4, 1988: *I've gained five lbs. in a week if that's possible. I loathe myself. I'm sick of being regarded as "muscular"—I want to be petite like Kate. Sports have ruined me.*

Yes, you could say I was self-involved, melodramatic, petty. Worse, I was repetitive: November 4, 1988 was no date with an epiphany. Nonetheless, I was in pain. All I knew was that I'd gone from being an outspoken girl interested in everything to someone withdrawn and incapable of participating in class. I was depressed, but more than that I was hating myself for being a woman. I'd slipped onto a path that is as vicious and uncreative as it is a cliché of young womanhood. In a rare moment of teen lightness, I named it the Dark Horrible Sucking Trail of the Lost Voice. The Trail shouldn't be underestimated. Every day, another girl gets stuck in its mud.

1

Virginia Woolf would have liked DrRogue, a bright, confident writer with a lashing wit. As to whether DrRogue is a genius as defined by Woolf, only time will tell. In the meantime, she manages beyond the confines of a tiny school (there are just five girls in her class), her parents' limited financial means, and oh yes, childhood, to find both experience and "a room of her own" for the cultivation of her talents. You see, DrRogue is known to those in her small New England town as thirteen-year-old Arabella.

We meet on July 14, 2000. I'm a part-time producer of commercial web sites for teen girls, and am spending some time perusing the vast number of "homepages" linked to one another on the Internet. There are thousands out there, colorful and animated, with names like Glitter Girl, Fairy Dawn, Overcooked, Pixie Kitten, Foily Tin, Quasi Grrrl, Peppermint, and Intelligent Life. They can be constructed at established homepage-building areas of sites such as gURL, ChickClick, Lycos, and Bolt. Or, they can be created independently, then hooked into freer-floating web rings such as Shut Up You're Only 16! and Music Girl. Some are smart; some are sappy. Most are filled with poetry. If you visit, you may find writings, drawings, photos, interactive games, and the creator's deepest, darkest secret. But, you won't ever find her. Instead, your experience will be that of discovering an anonymous diary on a crowded city street. You can read it, and learn everything about its owner, but look up and she's long gone.

DrRogue however, is right here. I have no idea who she is.

DrRogue: Hello!

She flashes onto my screen, an insistent clump of text in a small, square dialogue box aboard America Online's ubiquitous Instant Messenger (IM).

DrRogue: Hey, Bronwyn!

Aha, exclamation points. Dead giveaway. DrRogue, I now know, is one of the dozen or so teen girls whom I have e-mailed about their home-pages. By now, I've visited enough to identify the prints.

I flip through my list of teen e-mails. DrRogue is Arabella, the one with the web site called "Intelligent Life." Evidently, she has made a note of my AOL e-mail address and posted it to her "buddy list" to see when I'm on-line. She's flashing again.

DrRogue: Hello, it's Arabella.

Slowness, you see, is terminal here.

BGAR2: Yes, Arabella, of Intelligent Life. Hello.

DrRogue: Yeah, yeah, just thought I'd reiterate.

In my web travels, I've discovered that most Internet-savvy, homepage-creating girls provide only first names on their sites and to people they meet online. Discussing this find via e-mail with many different young women, I learn that the "first name only" policy is pretty strictly followed in these parts. Not every teen, of course, approaches her online develop-ment in the same way. Web sites like Goosehead, for example, the work of a fifteen-year-old student, her parents, and a growing staff, serves up a huge number of provocative photos of the pretty tenth-grade founder. For self-run sites however, those who forgo anonymity are just throwing bait to bad people. "Avoid the psychopaths," as DrRogue says.

Anonymity is one of the hallmarks of safety online. And both ano-nymity and online safety, I learn, are crucial to privacy. If you'd asked me in high school what privacy meant in my life, I might have said, locked physical space that cannot be invaded with a butter knife. I mention this to DrRogue. It becomes clear that things have changed.

DrRogue: Privacy is [about] having your personal space in a more intellectu-ally abstract, metaphysical sense. It is making sure that no one can find out

too much about your real life through your online follies, keeping relationships strictly anon and not putting yourself at risk of psychopaths.

Evidently, DrRogue's issues go beyond keeping her brother out of her
room (although this is cited as an ancillary goal). No matter the "horror
stories blown up by newscasters," Arabella asserts that she doesn't "feel
threatened that [her] anonymity is slipping away." On the contrary, she
blames the media for exacerbating the situation with their stupidity:

> DrRogue: Newscasters report the invasion of my privacy very sternly, as
> though they're the ones decoding the human genome. From the way they
> speak, as though every technical word is new and unknown, it's clear that
> they're still asking their kids how to log on to the Internet.

Notwithstanding adult ignorance, DrRogue's understanding of privacy,
"metaphysical" as it may be, is still predominantly about hiding the chord
that could lead "psychopaths" to the "real" her. But, *isn't this paranoia for
good reason?* I ask. Haven't we all heard stories of "psychopaths" locating
teenagers from clues carelessly dropped in chatrooms? DrRogue blisters at
this one.

> DrRogue: And then we have, "Cyber stalkers! Are your kids safe on the
> net?" If they have an IQ higher than a rock. Never give your full, real name,
> specific location, or phone number to a stranger. EVERY kid should know
> that!

"Keeping relationships strictly anon" in fact, is just the beginning of
what a user, child or adult, must learn about the web, according to Dr-
Rogue. Sensing my ignorance, she outlines society's paranoia, the real issues as she sees them, and the solutions—albeit in a somewhat mocking
tone:

> DrRogue: Companies are putting something called COOKIES onto your hard
> drive to TRACK WHAT SITES YOU VISIT! screams the television. Anyone
> with a brain and a mouse should know that you can clear all the cookies off
> your hard drive anytime, or even set your computer to not accept them at all.
> CREDIT CARD FRAUD! is another big one. If you have a grain of sense, you
> won't give your credit card number to sites with names like Bob's Discount
> Warehouse. If you're not sure it's credible, DON'T SHOP THERE.
> "A new virus is spreading like wildfire around the world and through major
> corporations!" Major corporations where the employees are so out of touch,
> apparently, that they'll download anything. My rule of thumb: never down-
> load attachments, unless it's from a close friend and is attached to a message
> obviously composed by them.

Although DrRogue, and most of the teens I encounter online, are very careful about their privacy, the Annenberg Public Policy Center's study of *The Internet and the Family* 2000 reports that 75 percent of teens consider it acceptable to reveal what the study has defined as "private family information" in exchange for gifts, online. These "older kids," aged thirteen to seventeen, are even more likely, according to the study, than younger ones to divulge personal details, including the names of their own and their parents' favorite stores, the type of car their family drives, whether their parents talk about politics, and what their parents do on the weekends.

In the adult world, while a person's concern for her own physical safety goes without saying, the current discourse surrounds public image more than it does personal safety. In a *New York Times Magazine* article on privacy and technology, Jeffrey Rosen states that through the interception of e-mails, the tracking of browsing habits and purchases online, and statements made in chatrooms, one's "public identity may be distorted by fragments of information that have little to do with how you define yourself."

Indeed, we've all heard stories about e-mail fragments being taken out of context by employers and others. The *Washington Post* described the case of James Rutt, the CEO of Network Solutions Inc., who feared his years of candid postings about sex, politics, and his weight problem might be taken out of context, thus damaging his reputation and his ability to run his company effectively. Consequently, the new CEO employed Scribble, a software encryption program, to erase his online past.[1]

Rutt's story is not unusual. This fear of being taken for a "fragment" of information is enough for most of us to employ private e-mail accounts we switch to at work when we have something personal to communicate. Even though we take these precautions, everyone I know goes to great lengths to erase all of her business e-mails when leaving a company. Why? Because the medium is seductive, web travel is about exploration, and e-mails begun as impersonal memos often become more intimate exchanges. Intimacy does not translate well to third parties.

Take the 1997 example Rosen cites of Harvard professor Lawrence Lessig's e-mailed comment to a friend that he had "sold his soul" in downloading Microsoft Internet Explorer. Lessig, who had downloaded Explorer simply to enter a contest for a Powerbook, was not stating a biased opinion about the company, he was flippantly quoting a song. However, Judge Thomas Penfield Jackson, who had chosen him as an advisor in the

. . . .

Microsoft antitrust suit, was forced to take such a bias seriously, removing Lessig as his advisor.

Jeffrey Rosen makes the point that we all wear different social "masks" in different settings and with different people. This may be true even as it is socially taboo. From our estimations of Joan of Arc down to President Clinton, we celebrate and trust those with consistent (and consistently good) characters, and criticize those who "waffle," or behave as if they are "spineless." Because we do not know how to define someone who changes with each new setting, we call her things like: "mercurial," a "chameleon," or "two-faced." Consequently, the web induces fear in an adult not just for the things online crooks might do to social security numbers and other personal information, but what a user herself may do to complicate her own "character."

However, while the adult world may suffer from a preoccupation with consistency, teens have the peculiar advantage of being dismissed as inconsistent before they begin. Adolescence is the societally condoned window in which we may shuffle through identities with abandon. My older sister, for example, horrified my grade-school self by morphing from punk to hippie to hare krishna to surfer girl all in the next room. Yet, by the time I graduated high school, I'd been through a few of those identities myself.

Besides their assumed role as explorers, teens may actually face fewer risks of this kind than their adult counterparts. Statistics relate that around 45 percent of companies monitor their employees' e-mail accounts,[2] while few junior highs and high schools in America offer all their students computers or e-mail accounts. Even if they did, chances are "monitoring" of kids' private mail in public schools would raise countless legal issues. DrRogue's school is just now hooking up six new computers for the whole school of fifty-six students and has no intention of providing students with e-mail accounts. Ironically, it is this deprivation that has made monitoring less of an issue for students than it is for employees at big companies.

2

For girls like DrRogue who create and maintain personal homepages, and explore the web's massive serving of chatrooms and boards, safety is not the only motivation for anonymity. "Bodilessness," it seems, can be the means to a more intellectual objective: credibility. Says Peppermint, a seventeen-year-old writer,

I definitely feel "bodiless" when writing for my page. The Internet has provided me with an audience that will forever be my biggest fan and my worst enemy. Just as I can say what I want on my site without fear of rejection, others can e-mail me their honest thoughts without the face-to-face consequences of criticism. My audience, as well as my privacy, is crucial to my development as a writer.

In a world with, as DrRogue sees it, "a seemingly endless supply of people to talk to and sites to visit, from all around the world," immediate, physical privacy gives some young women confidence they don't have when they're attached to developing physiques, school cliques, or societal and familial expectations.

Anonymity as executed by DrRogue can preserve privacy and enhance creativity and self-expression. Only bodiless, confess some girls, can they relate certain ideas and thoughts at all. Indeed, screen names have become so popular that AOL is currently offering the option of seven aliases to the users of Instant Messenger. DrRogue herself has five that she can "remember." In addition, girls can, if only for the experience, switch genders online. (Studies suggest 40 percent have done it.) "The ONLY reason I go into a chatroom is to pretend to be someone else!" insists DrRogue. Other young women are altogether wary of chatrooms. "I don't believe in chatrooms," explains Peppermint, "they've become a forum for online popularity contests and cyber sex." Does the monitoring of chatrooms add to its problems?

> DrRogue: I've never felt like I was being monitored, because a monitor would do a better job of kicking out the scum.

Bodiless, many girls use their homepages as a "sounding board" before taking ideas out into "the real world." Others put the space and the "audience" to work on facets of themselves or ideas they plan to confine permanently there.

Peppermint, whose "real-life" friends know her as Caitlin, addresses the consequences that she believes her physicality can have upon the reception of her ideas. "I do not post pictures of myself," she states in an e-mail, "simply because I want to be perceived as 'more than just a pretty face.'" Peppermint is so adamant that her physical self be distinct from her online self that she does not give her web-site address to "real-life" friends. She explains:

> I don't allow friends that I have known in person to have my web-site address. The web is a sacred place for me to speak to a receptive and critical

. . . .

audience, while at the same time, I do not need to worry about making a first impression, [about] coming off how I'd like to, or [about] what will happen the next time I see them. Because I don't need to make impressions, I am who I am, and I am being honest.

During adolescence, asserts Carol Gilligan, whose groundbreaking studies of female adolescence have illuminated many of the issues facing young women in our culture, girls are acutely sensitive to hypocrisy in themselves and in others. Young women admit to "pretending, performing, or impersonating the right kind of girl," behavior that puts them, as the girls themselves see it, "in jeopardy" of losing touch with their real selves. That Peppermint must confine her "honest" feelings to a forum outside "real life" seems tragic. Yet, even as she struggles with conformity, she actively nourishes her "honest" feelings in a place where she will not lose touch with them.

Another reason for anonymity on Peppermint's web site is her explorations of bisexuality, albeit in a bodiless forum. "[Online] I feel free to make references to my bisexuality or even openly talk about it. In life, I feel that telling someone . . . could completely change the relationship that we have. . . ."

DrRogue has her own reasons for anonymity. Asking her to discuss them results in a flurry of responses:

> DrRogue: ha! Why is it important? Anonymity [on the web] is important because people can't judge you on how you look
>
> DrRogue: only what you say
>
> DrRogue: you can say anything and there are no personal repercussions, you can also interact with lots of sites and people without putting yourself at risk.

While DrRogue uses the physical privacy of the web to overcome, in a sense, the handicap of youth, Peppermint believes her femininity and "real-life" identity can negatively affect the reception of her ideas. Observes Peppermint: "As a woman, I think we will always be viewed as sexual objects. [I want a person] to be able to look past the outside and realize that there is an opinionated, intelligent, creative young woman behind the pretty face." DrRogue, who, at thirteen, is really just entering adolescence, simply may not have experienced her femininity as a handicap yet. If all goes well, she never will.

To many, appearance is the essential problem of female development. With the world standing by to notice her changing body, a young woman begins to perceive her somewhat limited access to what psychologist Lyn

Mikel Brown calls "the patriarchal framework of [her] culture." From
here, a struggle to retain her childhood identity and value system ensues,
followed typically by a loss of voice, the narrowing of desires and expectations, and the capitulation to conventional notions of womanhood. [3]
Yes, the Dark Horrible Sucking Trail of the Lost Voice is so trodden it
is cliché. We've all seen countless articles on the phenomenon, but that
doesn't make it any less prevalent now than it was 100 years ago.

Believe it or not, the Father of Psychology developed his own unfortunate theories on the self-conscious transition of girls into women within a
patriarchy. Puberty, postulated Freud, "which brings about so great an
accession of libido in boys, is marked in girls by a fresh wave of repression." The repression in question, confirms Freud, is an acknowledgment
of the female's "castration," and a simultaneous stripping of our childhood's "masculine sexuality."[4] If girls weren't traumatized enough by observing what would be their future roles in society, Freud's perspective
should have sufficiently condemned them to life on the Trail.

With Freud's thesis airborne, Virginia Woolf published *A Room of
One's Own* just three years later. It was no wonder to Woolf that with
their hostile introduction to life and the pathetic theories concerning their
development, even women of genius were resentful. Such anger though,
however valid, "jerked" through their work, something which Woolf
could not abide. Famously, of *Jane Eyre*'s Charlotte Brontë, she said: "She
will write in a rage where she should write calmly. She will write foolishly
where she should write wisely. She will write of herself where she should
write of her characters. She is at war with her lot. How could she help but
die young, cramped and thwarted?"[5] Woolf's prescription for peaceful,
brilliant writing: talent, an inheritance, and "a room of one's own."

Woolf instructed us to go back and become boys—that would have
been more easily achieved for most of us. Nonetheless, things are substantially better politically for women today than they were for Charlotte
Brontë and even Virginia Woolf (whose gender notably kept her out of an
established university library, among other inconveniences). Yet, as Peppermint can attest, young women remain under tremendous pressure to
conform to feminine standards they didn't create: a challenge to creativity
that Woolf underestimated. Sociolinguists tell us that girls' voices become
breathy, whispery, and higher-pitched before puberty—that is, before
there is actually any physiological basis for it. Perhaps squeaky voices
wouldn't be a problem if they weren't also heard as "less competent, less
potent, and less truthful" than lower-pitched voices.[6]

Less publicized, though more interesting than the pervasiveness of the Sucking Trail, is Gilligan and Brown's identification of a period before adolescence—when girls' "voices" are at their most powerful. Young women, most of whom I imagine to be variations on DrRogues, actively resist dominant cultural notions of femininity at the edge of puberty.[7] Finding a means to connect, harness, and preserve the loud, defiant voices may empower girls to defy cultural norms, and in the process eclipse the resentment that Virginia Woolf so protested.

A foe like Freud may seem laughable today, but with members of this generation still fearing their own "pretty faces," we may be only laughably closer to instilling a feeling of worth in today's young women. On the one hand, Peppermint's sensitivity to a societal bias we'd like to think has passed is tragic. On the other hand, unlike those of us who were teenagers even ten years ago, Peppermint and DrRogue can literally construct their own worlds, with their own standards, where the only thing that matters is their ideas. They can't live in it forever, but maybe a few hours a day is long enough to change their lives.

3

BGAR2: how many hours do you spend online each day?
DrRogue: 1, usually.
BGAR2: really? That's nothing.
DrRogue: 2, really.
BGAR2: hmmm.
DrRogue: 3, if I'm bored.
BGAR2: still, I imagined more.
DrRogue: well, I'm prolly scaling down a lot.
BGAR2: why's that?
DrRogue: let's just say I've had to LIMIT my online time in the past.
BGAR2: ahh. los padres?
DrRogue: si.
BGAR2: how much time did you spend yesterday?
DrRogue: lemme check my log.
DrRogue: ok, I lied. I spent 4 hours online.

Called Intelligent Life, DrRogue's latest homepage, which makes vague note of a Arabella somewhere in the meat of its smart, sometimes acerbic,

·   ·   ·   ·   ·   ·   ·   ·   ·   ·

steadfastly spelling-error-free content, is exactly what it sounds like: a literal SOS for brain activity in a spectrum overwrought with misspelled emotion. Intelligent Life is just a month old, has already received nearly 400 visitors, and that's during the summer. Whether they're up to Dr-Rogue's standards is another matter. Requests Intelligent Life:

> I'm not being snobbish or narrow-minded, the time has simply come to draw
> the line. I want to meet people (of any age) who are bright and exciting,
> funny, kind, and intelligent. I want to meet people who are clearly individuals,
> not stereotypical, bumbling, senseless teenagers with limited vocabularies
> who take extreme liberties with spelling.

In short, do not visit Intelligent Life if you are, and there's no easy way to say this, a "ditz." Ding.

> DrRogue: Have you been to Narly Carly yet?

Narly Carly's Super Awesome Page, to be specific, is DrRogue's spoof site—she recommended I look at it for research. Pulling the purple page with the rotating star up onto the screen, I see another reactionary move by DrRogue: a parody of the many sunny, earnest, "overwrought" teen sites splattered across the web. In the usual autobiographical style of these things, the fictional Narly Carly describes herself and her life, albeit without any of the eloquence DrRogue saves for, well, DrRogue. "I am a junior at Willingford High!" screams Narly at her visitors, "Go Wolfs!!!"

Although, to the naked eye, Narly Carly's Super Awesome Page looks quite a lot like any other teen site, its status as a farce lies in its suspicious abuse of, ironically, exclamation marks; the word "like" and its overload of personal information, among other things. Narly gives away reels of intimate details—for the visitors who "get it"; this is a reproach of lax security. There is, after all, no one currently policing the Internet to keep people from divulging too much about themselves. In this era, something like Narly Carly serves as a gentle warning—as gossip does in a small town—to keep people in line. The irony is, of course, that a real Narly Carly may not understand irony.

Narly Carly bears the treadmarks of an adolescent critical of hypocrisy in older girls, making Arabella appear to be someone Gilligan might identify as a "resister." Before they give up any measure of voice, and shift into idealized femininity, girls are louder than ever, embodying what Gilligan believes may be the political potential of an active adolescent underground.[8] Whatever Arabella's reasons are for building an older "teenybopper's" site, they are her own. However, the underground political potential, along with Arabella's strength and clarity of character, are palpable on Narly Carly. Indeed, a handful of the guestbook's visitors, whether male or female, passed the first test—they "got it." Said one visitor: "This page is so evil! I know whoever made it did this intentionally. No 'real' person acts this pathetic. And 'like' was WAY back in the '80s. I know this is a joke and the person who made it is laughing their head off reading the guestbook. I would Nya-hahaha *more evil laughter* pauses* again MORE evil laughter."

> DrRogue: hello?
> BGAR2: I'm looking at it now. Pretty funny.
> DrRogue: hehe. I'm actually quite proud of Narly Carly's page.
> BGAR2: Why's that?
> DrRogue: Well, see, a lot of girls have "rants" on their pages. And some of these might deal with the Narly-Carly type person.
> BGAR2: "Rants."

DrRogue picks up on my confusion.

> DrRogue: I'll call it a "why do cliques have to exist and why do they pick on me, everyone should be themselves"–type rant.
> BGAR2: Mmm, earnest criticism? Yes, I've seen this.
> DrRogue: Yes. I wanted mine to be humorous, to trick people, provoke a reaction, and I sure did.

Indeed, the fictionally popular Narly Carly covers such topics as "why losers have to share the same locker room as cool people." I look up the number of visitors who have dropped off notes in Narly's guestbook: 209—many of them earnest, responding to previous posts, as well as to the site itself. Culture, it seems, is not much different online than it is in, say, downtown New York City. Where there is art, there is criticism.

> DrRogue: I've tricked about 3/4 of the visitors.

And, there are people who don't get the art. In other matters, I'm not responding fast enough for DrRogue, and am fearing termination.

> DrRogue: people are not so smart these days.

Truly, if Narly's guestbook is any indication, this may be a fact. Its latest posting, entered today by an anonymous visitor, with idiosyncratic spelling, reads: "Ok, your a junior, right? Well, no offence, but you obviously have the common since of a nat. Why on earth would you tell people where you lived especially on the Internet? And can't you use spell check? Again, no offence, but you sound as if your 12 not 16–17."

Then again, whether one "gets" the art doesn't really matter. There's still the "party," the conversation, and for the hovering artist checking the guestbook, the criticism—just as there is at any hyper-postmodern art opening. The objective for the creators I've spoken to? Hanging out, more or less depending on their needs, in the shadows, listening.

BGAR2: Nice work, Arabella.

DrRogue: Hehe. I get a kick out of it, if no one else.

4

Hamlet, the archetypal teenager, is given to studying himself. Rather than revealing his character to his audience over time, however, Hamlet reveals himself to himself through soliloquies, actions, and utterances, developing as a human being before our eyes.[9] He has seven soliloquies in a play 4,000 lines long: a work so massive only a few directors have ever attempted a complete performance of it. Harold Bloom has attributed the play's length to Hamlet's speaking so much of it. Indeed, the prince's ever-burgeoning consciousness takes up a lot of space.

DrRogue is, more than Ethan Hawke, a modern Hamlet. She has, rather reluctantly, given me a list of six other web sites to view: all of them her own from the past two years or so (when she began inhabiting space on the Internet). Although similar, tightly worded text and harsh user instructions mark each piece, the many pages feel dramatically different in tone and purpose. The first, Billy Sunshine, is chirpy, even childish, but then DrRogue would have been just eleven when she built it. Another called Encoded was inspired by *The Matrix,* and is kind of sci-fi. The vastly popular Shooting Star Light and Shooting Star Light Afterglow sites are parts of what DrRogue deems "the teenybopper kingdom." Regardless, the works offer a preserved fragment of their creator's character at one moment in time. As I expected, preservation is not some literary metaphor lost on DrRogue—rather it is her objective.

Having spotted me online again, she appears in her usual box.

DrRogue: yo

Nary a period after this greeting. DrRogue is in a mood. I can play this game.

BGAR2: o, you're back.

DrRogue: yep

BGAR2: looked at your sites. found the matrix one quite intriguing.

The only similarity among the sites, as far as I am concerned, is that the links, the buttons connecting one page to another—are broken. I feel the failure needs to be addressed. Ding.

BGAR2: I did notice, with some frustration, that a few of the links go nowhere.

DrRogue: hehe. MOST of the links.

BGAR2: ok, yes, most.

DrRogue: that's what happens

BGAR2: eh?

DrRogue: I create sites, then abandon them

BGAR2: why's that?

DrRogue: "someday I'll finish it"

BGAR2: but you don't

DrRogue: no. when I'm done, I abandon it and create a new one.

The web, however brief its life, is already a "wasteland," says DrRogue. Most users she knows have the same processes: create a site, pour in heart and soul and some slick designs, and then dump it. I don't like the idea—it clutters my personal image of the web, and seems unfair to the people these homesteaders call their "audience." DrRogue points out the circular truth that the "audience" is composed of homesteaders, most of whom build and abandon sites, too. The web is beginning to look like a heavily populated ghost town.

With DrRogue contributing to the "wasteland," the similarity between her and Shakespeare's greatest contribution to world literature may not be immediately obvious. However, like the creative forces behind the ghost towns, Hamlet himself takes refuge in a number of incarnations (and perhaps in more dimensions than even DrRogue), abandoning them and moving on as the tortured adolescent essays to reconcile his identity.

Not to mention the more obvious, restless shifts of character the young prince undergoes (from mourning prince to lunatic, for example), *Hamlet* the play has had its own identity struggle. Many years before the *Hamlet* most of us know, existed another, similar, not quite so ingenious script known as *Ur-Hamlet*. So distinct is this ur-lier version, that scholars suggest it wasn't written by Shakespeare at all, but another writer named

Thomas Kyd. Harold Bloom refutes this supposition, asserting that *Ur-Hamlet* was just the immature dabbling of a young genius.

Who knows. What's interesting is how different the incantations of Hamlet are. Like DrRogue's first site Billy Sunshine, *Ur-Hamlet* is not only immature in its verbal execution (its technology), but the Prince of Denmark himself is so substantially different as to be another character entirely from the one we now know. As the eleven-year-old DrRogue does in cyberspace, Ur-Hamlet and the one we all know live on in their separate scripts. The web takes this doppelganger effect to the next level, allowing the many incarnations to live on as if brand-new in the same space. Consequently, the "wasteland," is home to an abundance of characters—all of them alive and dead at the same time.

In yet an earlier manifestation of the prince's character, records show that Shakespeare's only son, Hamnet, died when he was just eleven years old. Although the *Hamlet* of Shakespeare's stage is surely not intended to represent the lost child,[10] perhaps Hamnet was somehow an inspiration. The boy himself was an incarnation of Shakespeare as any son is of his father. And, Hamlet is a living manifestation of the son himself who, like the prince, never grew to maturity. Similarly, DrRogue's early sites and all their broken links leave the visitor with a feeling of incompletion.

I mention this to DrRogue who has only just read *Romeo and Juliet*. I tell her that *Hamlet* is better. She puts it on her list of "to reads." We return to the subject at hand.

> DrRogue: it's not like I'm being charged for using space. And anyway, I like knowing they're there.
> BGAR2: still, it would seem annoying to visitors.
> DrRogue: I'm the only one who knows they're dead.
> BGAR2: hmm. Like Hamlet was the only one who knew who killed his father.
> DrRogue: anyway it's like a virtual progression chart. "oh, look how stupid I was a year ago."
> BGAR2: so you leave these up to show the world and yourself how stupid you were a year ago?
> DrRogue: not the world.
> DrRogue: well, the world can see.
> DrRogue: more for my own benefit. I like being able to see how I've changed.

In the latest movie version of *Hamlet*, Ethan Hawke's character records his own soliloquies: he films them—and then studies them later. Hamlet (and all stage characters) directs his soliloquies at his audience.

· · · · · · · · · ·

DrRogue (and all homesteaders) directs her homepages at what she deems her "audience." The blasé observation "well, the world can see" seems odd when one considers that these things were created for the "world." It all sounds like something Hamlet might have said. One of his own comments is remarkably similar to DrRogue's as he shows his own production *The Mousetrap* to his audience: "You that look pale and tremble at this chance/That are but mutes or audience to this act." That the soliloquy's purpose is lost on both the prince and DrRogue suggests something of its seductive powers, and the all-consuming act of personal transformation.

Perhaps it is the unusual setting of observed privacy that draws both DrRogue and Hamlet to the expressive mediums. FairyGlitter, a site hooked into a web ring called Shut Up You're Only 16! blurs even further the lines between soliloquy and homepage. In a confession that could easily pass for one of Hamlet's own questioning speeches, FairyGlitter cries:

> How do I sleep at night? All these voices, thoughts, images, wants, sorrows, sometimes to the point where I cry & can't stop. So many things that I can't block out when I'm awake, but can, somehow when I drift. I clutch tightly to the pillow, trying to sleep & erase things about the day, my life, me, my mind, my soul. Do you ever scream inside your head so loud that you can't hear anything on the outside?

Had Hamlet lived to web-browse he might have been validated to find another tortured young soul wondering whether to be or not to be. The ostensible purpose for the soliloquy is to allow the audience into the character's mind—to include them in a sense, to burden or enlighten them with knowledge other characters don't have. Hamlet, with his many soliloquies, seems to feel progressively less empathy for the other characters, and never expresses anything, spare mockery, for his audience. Those watching him exist to help him, to witness each word as it falls so that he can hear it, feel lighter, be changed by it, and move on. The character seems to know intrinsically the unburdening power of this action, remaining nonetheless indifferent to his helpers.

When I argue that web diarists like herself must be a bit self-conscious, DrRogue seethes: "People really put themselves out on these things!" Unlike my diaries though, they also get visitors who comment and provide discourse and insight, making the creator feel less alienated, making them actually useful methods of growth. Not to knock the diary—I certainly got somewhere venting in my own. Anaïs Nin, kept a journal to "free" herself of "personae." The web is, in some ways, a more evolved journal, even as

it is so many other things. Studies have shown that students write better
papers and learn foreign languages more fluently when they actually have
something to communicate to another person.[11]

> BGAR2: so these sites are like journals.
>
> DrRogue: exactly.
>
> BGAR2: couldn't you print them out and store them in a closet or something
> and then delete them?
>
> DrRogue: AH no!
>
> DrRogue: that would defeat the purpose of the web!
>
> BGAR2: what's the purpose?
>
> DrRogue: interactivity, for one.
>
> DrRogue: longevity of information, two. I can visit the Arabella of a year ago.
> she's there in the same place, just as alive.
>
> BGAR2: but how do you know when you're done?
>
> DrRogue: I stop visiting it. I'm sick of it.

D.W. Winnicott defined a process of imaginative "saturation" in children's play in which the child plays with a certain toy or enacts an imaginative experience until all of the emotional ambivalence, fear, anxiety,
etc.—are diffused from that action or thing.[12] DrRogue, FairyGlitter, and
Hamlet may be "playing" out their emotions to make offline "reality" less
emotional. As Nietzsche said in *The Twilight of the Idols*: "That for which
we find words is something already dead in our hearts." I ask DrRogue if
this might be the case with her.

> DrRogue: mmmhmm. great quote. who said that?
>
> BGAR2: nietzsche. want the exact quote? I have it here somewhere.
>
> DrRogue: your paraphrasing is fine for me. but the idea is right.

Selfishly, while she contributes to the textual "wasteland," DrRogue hates
to stumble upon a "haunted" site herself.

> DrRogue: It makes me feel really bad, manipulated almost, when I'm brows-
> ing a site, and then there's a date, and that date is like, March 13, 1996.
>
> BGAR2: why, because it's old?
>
> DrRogue: "does this person still exist?"
>
> BGAR2: hmm
>
> DrRogue: because I spent time getting to know the person
>
> BGAR2: is it a waste if it's old?
>
> DrRogue: it depends.

. . . .

DrRogue: I like retail sites because they're constantly busy.

BGAR2: yeah, the idea of an updated site is good.

DrRogue: like someone's alive.

A good character's job is to "manipulate" her audience. Perhaps then, a date is some sort of narrative flaw that pulls DrRogue out of the story. What should a date matter to her anyway, I wonder: she will never meet the site's creators. Why does she care whether she or he is still "alive?" The presence of a date on a site is like an actor's mustache falling off—it brings reality back into focus. The notion that a retail site would suggest someone's being "alive" to DrRogue is puzzling. In describing how an author goes about creating character, E. M. Forster explained:

> the novelist makes up a number of word-masses, gives them names and sex, assigns them plausible gestures, and causes them to speak by the use of inverted commas. These word-masses are his characters.[13]

DrRogue's sense that a "word-mass" such as a retail site might have human qualities, or something resembling a heartbeat, implies her ability to suspend disbelief so that the mechanism—words on the web—dissolves. Further, it suggests a narrative view of the Internet, a desire to read and live through other people's stories. Arabella seeks to learn about the world, about people, and about herself, insight she can glean from any good story, regardless of its medium. I express some weariness of the homepages.

DrRogue: but they're so interesting.

BGAR2: why?

DrRogue: like finding someone's diary. People really put themselves out on these things.

BGAR2: but they do it for publication. There's something bizarre in that.

DrRogue: no! no one knows who they are. They change names. [Their experiences are not] really unique, but [are] nonetheless interesting.

BGAR2: how?

DrRogue: but reading about the everyday doings and dramatics of ANYONE'S life is fascinating.

DrRogue: sort of makes you feel like you're not the only person who does certain things. Or like, "good, their life is boring, too."

BGAR2: ha!

DrRogue: triumphant, almost.

BGAR2: I'd be interested in reading a diary only of a person I knew.

DrRogue: ooh, that's fun. But fun for a different reason.

DrRogue: It's a different story on the web. Sort of like having someone's life for a minute.

Stories, like "playing," can be powerful agents of personal transformation. "The right stories can open our hearts and change who we are," says Janet Murray, a professor of a digital fiction course at MIT. Indeed, ultimately the best stories render their technologies transparent so that we experience only the power of the characters and the story itself.[14]

DrRogue created Intelligent Life to find other people, to hear their stories, to "have someone's life for a minute." In exchange, she shares her own experiences, and in doing so develops a bit more as a human being. Logging on has enabled DrRogue to get beyond her small town, her age, her financial situation, and has allowed her through narrative, to experience the world.

5

Somehow, maybe because she pummels me with IMs whenever I log on, I have come to associate the web with DrRogue. It is her "room," you might say.

DrRogue: yo

BGAR2: yo

BGAR2: shouldn't you be at camp or something

DrRogue: I said ALL my friends were at camp. I'm not so fortunate.

BGAR2: oh. sucks. well, you have the web.

DrRogue: I have the web.

Writing has always allowed people to step outside of their skin, to try on different identities, to see through other perspectives. Lyn Lifshin, who edited a collection of women's journals by both professional writers and others, recalled that contributors' friends were often shocked at the people represented in the diaries. For Foucault, writing was about growth and escaping the confines of identity. No one understands this better than the growth-hungry DrRogue, who, thanks to technology, can go even further in her explorations. She can gain experience of the world from a tiny room in Vermont.

Cyberspace was coined by William Gibson, the prolific sci-fi novelist, to define the virtual landscape of a human being's consciousness. It is voyeurism, entertainment, education, communication, interaction, and self-expression all at once. Above all, it is a human environment, an extension of, rather than an escape from, the "real world." As such, it poses "real-world" risks, as well as opportunities. For young women like Dr-Rogue and Peppermint, it is the real stories, the sense of community and communication, that keep them coming back. Says Peppermint:

> Receiving responsive e-mail to something I've written is the most rewarding part of the experience. I've received in excess of fifty letters, especially from girls a few years younger than myself, saying that I've taught them that there is nothing wrong with being yourself. This is a lesson that I wish I had learned at their age, and to know that I have taught it to someone younger than me is an incredible feeling.

> DrRogue: IGG. (I gotta go.) Time to do something productive today.

> BGAR2: Go write your novel.

I forgot to mention that, since she's not going to camp, DrRogue is writing a novel. It's tentatively entitled: *Teen Girls: Not as Stupid as You Think*.

NOTES

1. Jeffrey Rosen, "The Eroded Self," *The New York Times Magazine*, p. 51.

2. Ibid., p. 50.

3. Lyn Mikel Brown, *Raising Their Voices: The Politics of Girls' Anger*, p. vii.

4. Sigmund Freud, *The Complete Psychological Works of Sigmund Freud*, Vol. VII, p. 253.

5. Virginia Woolf, *A Room of One's Own*, pp. 69–70.

6. Carol Gilligan, *In a Different Voice*, p. 110.

7. Brown, *op. cit.*, p. vii.

8. Gilligan, *op. cit.*, p. xi.

9. Harold Bloom, *Shakespeare: The Invention of the Human*.

10. Ibid., p. 413.

11. Janet H. Murray, *Hamlet on the Holodeck: The Future of Narrative in Cyberspace*, p. 5.

12. Ibid., p. 169.

13. E. M. Forster, *Aspects of the Novel*.

14. Murray, *op. cit.*, p. 26.

SOURCES

Bloom, Harold. *Shakespeare: The Invention of the Human*. New York: Riverhead Books, 1998.

Brown, Lyn Mikel. *Raising Their Voices: The Politics of Girls' Anger*. Cambridge, MA: Harvard University Press, 1998.

Forster, E.M. *Aspects of the Novel*. London: Arnold, 1927.

Gibson, William. *Neuromancer*. New York: Ace Books, 1983.

Gilligan, Carol. *In a Different Voice*. Cambridge, MA: Harvard University Press, 1982.

Lifshin, Lyn. *Ariadne's Thread: A Collection of Contemporary Women's Journals*. New York: Harper and Row, 1982.

Murray, Janet H. *Hamlet on the Holodeck: The Future of Narrative in Cyberspace*. New York: The Free Press, 1997.

Rosen, Jeffrey. "The Eroded Self," *The New York Times Magazine*, April 30, 2000.

Shakespeare, William. *Hamlet*.

The Complete Psychological Works of Sigmund Freud. Edited by J. Strachey. Vol. VII. London: Hogarth Press, 1961.

Woolf, Virginia. *A Room of One's Own*. New York: Harcourt Brace Jovanovich, Inc., 1929.

Privacy Is Not the Issue

.   .   .   .

by
DOROTHY ALLISON

1

As a girl, I was a reader, a bookworm, and secretive—my mother's pride, but no one's prize. There was book-smart and street-smart. I was the first, but not the second. We all agreed on that fact—my sisters and I, my mother and her friends. I remember looking up from one book or another to see how they looked at me, the curiosity in their faces and, now and then, the pity. My sisters would marry, everyone agreed. They would make babies and do what they did. What I would do was unimaginable, or darkly imaginable like the covers of the paperback books on the back racks at the drugstore. I read those books. I searched for myself in them. But somehow the plot turned and nothing came out as I was told it would.

Thirty years past my girlhood, I live in San Francisco with my partner and our child. One thing has not changed. My comfort is still in the bent head and the voice of the text. I read as passionately as I did as a girl, and stockpile books to reassure me that there will always be one to hand no matter how uncertain my everyday life may become. This means that every other week I am in one bookstore or another. In the company of other book lovers, I am at ease, nodding in recognition while shifting a couple of volumes from one arm to the other, running one finger down the stacks of used paperbacks and exclaiming when I find one I had missed.

Max is the guy who handles the cash register at my favorite used bookstore just off Market Street. I have been shopping there since I moved to California more than a dozen years ago. They used to give great trading discounts, so this was where I brought my boxes of review copies. The discounts are no longer as generous, but the turnover on the shelves is steady, and I can usually find half a dozen books I want. It also doesn't hurt that my long-standing account lets me get many of them for less than cover price.

"More of this stuff, huh?" Max says as I pile up my selections. "Damn," he adds. "No one keeps secrets anymore."

I watch him frown balefully at the stack of paperbacks I have put together. They are memoirs mostly, though I have leavened the pile with various poetry chapbooks. He picks up the volume of Mary Karr's poetry, and lets it fall onto *The Kiss* by Kathryn Harrison. We have argued about memoir before. I like them. Max doesn't. He did perversely decide he liked Frank McCourt's *'Tis*, when it got a less than rave review in a local journal, but he says what he is waiting for is for McCourt to try a novel.

"If we don't watch out, people going to quit writing novels," Max complains.

I resist the urge to make excuses for my selections. I don't want to explain that I have assembled this package for a young woman who let me talk to her about what it is like to wake up from a coma. If I tell Max that, he will want to talk about the novel I am writing, and I'm not at a place where that would be easy to do. Worse, Max might get the idea I could be coaxed into teaching a class his girlfriend could attend—something he has been asking about for a long time. I have read two stories by this girlfriend and know I have nothing to teach her. But that, too, is not something I want to explain to Max.

Near the end of my last interview with the coma survivor, she told me she wanted to try to write a true story of her own, about paralysis and despair and recovery—something she knew more about than she could say in a couple of hours of talking to me.

"How do you start to write?" she had asked me when we were finishing up.

"You read," I told her. "You read as much as you can, then you write a little, then you read some more."

"Then what?"

"You do it all over again. You keep at it till you are not ashamed of what you get on the page."

She had laughed at me, but I had been serious. The books were meant to kick start her in the right direction, or just say thank you. I owed her that for letting me look out of her eyes for a few hours.

Max has no way of knowing about my helpful young woman. He just

. . . .

hates memoirs. He is convinced they endanger the novel, and Max loves novels the way I do. It's why he took this job in the first place, why he is always suggesting titles or commenting on the ones you carry up to the cash register. Max is almost a friend—a big burly man, all shaggy-faced with a thick beard and a club of gray-streaked curly hair tied at the back of his collar. I have come to know him a bit over the years, mostly through the comments he has made on books I pile up on his counter. I know he lives with that girlfriend in a rat warren of an apartment building over in the western addition, that he doesn't make much money and doesn't care, and that he loves to read but has no ambition to write. Most importantly, ours is a relationship that deepened, not when my first novel became a bestseller, but when Max saw that I was always buying new copies of old books by Russell Banks and Larry Brown.

"My icons," he told me. "You see a book by either of them here, you know I already got two copies at home—one mint condition and one all soggy with sweat and tears."

"Where are you from, then?" I asked him.

"Oh, hell! Texas. But don't hold that against me. My daddy brought me to California before any of that cowshit stuck. I'm a redneck, but I'm a San Francisco redneck."

I had laughed then. I liked the notion of a guy who looked like Max and wept over *Father and Son* or *The Sweet Hereafter*.

2

I am a not-private person. It is the curse of being a writer, particularly a writer who is believed to have written a biographical novel. It never makes any difference when I insist my first novel, *Bastard Out of Carolina,* was not biography. I always wind up caught in the conflict of acknowledging that I am Southern and an incest survivor. And yeah, the book was about a young girl who grows up in an enormous Southern working-class family that is unable to do anything about the fact that she is being abused and raped by her stepfather.

"Were you raped?" I am asked.

"Yes," I always say, with my matter-of-fact attitude and no secrets implied.

"By your stepfather?"

"Yes." Again, matter-of-fact and bluntly to the point.

"Did your mother know?"

"Now, that is complicated," I say, and even as I speak, I feel layers of my skin peeling away, leaving me naked and ashamed before I can begin to explain just how complicated.

I wrote a novel trying to put fully on the page a very complicated story, and I hate to see it made simple. Worst of all, I know there is no winning for me in this discussion. I know how it will go. I will tell the scrupulous truth because I need to for my own sake. I will have no way to control what people will think as I say these things. Most terribly, I will know that we are having this conversation in part because they have not read the book. If they had read the book, I would have made some impact on how they think about rape and poverty and incest and Southern families—not as much as I had hoped, but some. They would not ask me these questions if they had read my book—at least I hope they would not.

I try very hard not to be defensive or strident when I tell people that the novel I wrote was not an autobiography. People always smile at me, a smile that widens when I admit how many of my real experiences got translated in some form into my fiction. That's how it works, I say, and watch people try to be polite. This is not a conversation that can have any easy or ready conclusion.

The reality is that I am not to be trusted. Novelists are liars. That is a fact. We make up stories and try to tell them so well that people will fall under our spell and believe what we say absolutely. We work hard so that the reader will believe our fictional creations, believe all that stuff really happened—had to have happened. How, doing that, can we make so strong a claim to truth? More importantly, how, having written a novel that makes such terrible use of our own reality, can we claim a right to say what about our lives is now off-limits for public discussion? Do we get to hold anything back?

Are we allowed to say what about our lives is now private and not for public discussion? Rarely, it seems, very rarely. Every time we do, there will be someone to argue us down and demand that we explain explicitly and in great detail why we are willing to tell this truth and not that one. I, for one, have never gotten over a conversation I had with a reporter many years ago. I hadn't had much experience with interviewers who did not write for the book pages, and he did not want to talk about books or writing. He wanted to talk about my life.

"You always talk about yourself as a lesbian," the reporter said to me. "You act as if it were the most important thing in the world."

"Some days it is," I told him. It is the most important thing when it is

. . . .

used to dismiss my work or to shore up more contempt for people like me, or to refute what is useful in what I have to say.

"What about your sisters," he asked me. "Are your sisters lesbians?"

No.

"Were they raped as children?"

I was still.

"Like you," he asked. "Did they get fucked like you?"

I remember the feel of the enamel of my teeth, my tongue pressing so hard that an ache seemed to slowly climb from my palate up to behind my eyes. I took my time and looked into his face, into his bland smile. He was wearing a charcoal suit and a gray-blue tie. The suit made his skin look sallow, but it made his eyes seem bright and soft, a brown as golden as a tub of dark honey. Too much honey and your teeth rot, I thought. I kept my mouth closed, my tongue clamped to the back of my teeth.

"Come on." He pushed his little tape recorder across toward me. "Don't you have anything more to say?"

Nothing. Not a damn thing.

They want to get a response, I had been warned. Keep that in mind and always think before you speak. I thought. I wondered if he really believed I would answer him. I wondered if he was talking to me that way because I was a lesbian. I wondered if he had read my book. I wondered why he did not become ashamed as I sat there, not speaking, just looking at him. After far too long, I stood up very carefully. I waited for him to make an excuse, to say he hadn't meant to offend me, but he did not.

He shrugged. He smiled. He said, "I guess we are done."

I said nothing. To say anything would have been to scream.

I have always loved the poetry of Sharon Olds, just as I have loved the very matter-of-fact way she has resisted making any simple or direct links between the events described in her poems and the actual lives of her family. I heard her read once and loved the droll way she replied to questions about a series of poems by saying, "Yes, I have children," and adding nothing more. It was not as if we could resist the notion that the girl in the poem she was describing was her girl, but she was not going to give us any further peek into that girl's life. You don't get everything, her manner seemed to say. You get just this much, this that I made deliberately. But when I made it, I moved it away from the child that I birthed, the life she lives that you are not entitled to intrude upon.

That is the way to do it, I thought. That is the only defense. When I am my strongest self, I can make these distinctions.

Making art is about choosing and constructing, then editing and refining. It is not just giving over everything and letting the audience sort it out. To make a good book, you have to hold back as much as you give over—regardless of whether the book you are making is a memoir, a novel, or a cycle of poems. This is true even though the position the writer takes in addressing the art is entirely about fearlessness, self-revelation, and telling a true story. Maybe it is even most true in that situation. In our long happy discussions of Russell Banks and Larry Brown, Max and I have agreed that what we most passionately adore is the way they make men we know real on the page.

"Sonsabitches!" Max would boom. "The real deal."

That is the key. We want the real on the page—the true, what we know that we want the world to know. I want my uncles. Max wants his dad. More than that, I want my stepfather and Max wants himself—what we know and fear and try with our whole soul to sort out.

"Large as life," I told Max once. Large as life and twice as heartbreaking would barely do justice to the people we have known. Nor does the fact that they might not recognize themselves have much impact on the worth of the story. I have put Max into three stories and one novel, and he seems to have no inkling that is the case. Of course, I deleted the beard, the girlfriend, and the bookstore. Like I have tried to explain, I don't write biography. I tell lies.

3

What is the thing that must remain secret and private?
What is the thing that you find shameful?
What would you never tell?

I have a talent that goes far beyond the ability to write. It is the gift to which I can credit everything I have done in my life. Both my survival and my education have been based upon it. I can make a quiet inside my head. I can shut the world out and be still inside. It is a genius. It may be the only kind of genius I truly believe we need to have to write. It is the quality that makes some of us able to think and work in the middle of confusion, violence, uncertainty, and upheaval. That gift is a quality of privacy, a sense of being safe and intact inside. It was the only kind of privacy I had as a

. . . .

girl, and it was entirely a matter of what I was able to make in my own head.

There was always noise in our house, noise and violence and confusion. If no one was shouting, then music was playing or the television was booming. Often both the radio and television were playing at the same time—one in the living room, one in the kitchen—almost never turned off and only rarely turned down. People were always talking. My sisters and I argued passionately and angrily. My mama would retell what had happened while she was at work. My stepfather cursed—us, Mama, the fools he had to face at work, the newsman on the television—everyone. Normal conversation was at high decibels, violent and full of shouted threats.

When there was quiet it was terrifying.

SHUT UP! SHUT UP! SHUT UP!

My stepfather would storm through the house like a bantam rooster with spurs out. We would be directed to shut up and sit down, to sit in a line on the couch or get the hell out of the living room. Go clean the kitchen. Go clean the bathroom, the bedrooms, pick up the trash in the yard. *I want you to get down on your knees and pick up every rock in that grass. If I find a stone when I go to cut that yard, you'll wish you'd never been born.* He would strut, back and forth, arms up, fists tight. Sometimes his rage would spill out. Sometimes we would be dragged up the halls. Sometimes we would be pushed away and he would glare up at the ceiling as if he wanted to get a grip on God. He would flail and sputter, call our names and curse. He would strike out at anything near, anything that dared his temper. He had a habit of kicking doors. The cheap pasteboard doors in our rented houses would split or crack. The next day my sisters and I would try to peel the edges out and tape them to disguise the damage. My stepfather's black eyes would slip over the cracks as if he had nothing to do with them.

One more thing I got to pay for! Goddamn it, one more thing!

Making a quiet inside was my path to sanity. I buried myself in books and stories. I was never without a book in my hand. *What the hell are you doing? Get your head out of that damn book and go help your mother!* I would jump up, run, and then go back to the book as soon as it was safe to do so. I pretended I lived in the stories I read, or I told myself stories in which I could live. At some point the roar around me receded. I could do nothing about it, do nothing with it—there was, after all, no real way of pleasing my stepfather or changing the poverty in which we lived. I could only do one thing. I could put my stepfather, my sisters, even my beloved mother—all of it—aside. I could shut out the noise.

I developed my talent so early and gradually that I cannot pinpoint the date at which it became my reality. Early on, very early on, I simply developed a skill for going deaf to everything that was around me. I could bury myself in a book and not see or hear anything that did not actually slap me in the face or dump me onto the floor. It was a lifesaving ability, and I suspect that it preceded my other invention—the storytelling, though that is hard to say for sure. What is certain is that they fed each other. Going away in my head gave me time and distance to make up stories. Making up stories gave me a reason to pull back up into my head.

4

Everyone recognizes storytellers. They are great baby-sitters, engrossing gossips, artists of the anecdote. I was all of those from an early age, but I was also one other thing and that was a thing I tried hard to obscure. It seemed to me dangerous to have people know how much I was not present in my own life, how far I disappeared into the story in my head. The one thing I had to keep safe and private was that, how much I lived in my head. For my mother's sake, I did not want her to know how much I hated our life. For my own, I did not want to admit it.

This too is a complicated story, not one that has an obvious plot, no simple, easily explainable cause-and-effect factor. There is not one cause. There are endless effects.

An insomniac from an early age, I would lie in bed with my sisters and listen to the night noises. There was snoring from my parents' bedroom, and sometimes grunts or unintelligible mutters. There were the whispered and hoarse sounds of sex, the creak of the mattress springs, or the thud that might have been the bed frame against the wall and might have been something worse. There was the swish of the omnipresent fans in summer, and the clank-clanking furnace in winter, or my stepfather's angry, "Goddamn it, turn that down!"

We lived in close quarters, my sisters and I, for many years in one bed, for almost my entire childhood—one bedroom. Living close is noisy and never private. If you wiggle, someone feels you move. If you sigh or sob, you do so in company. My sisters and I developed a capacity for pretending we were not lying close, for not hearing what we did not want to have to acknowledge. If my sister was squirming, I would not sit up and ask her what she was doing. She might tell me. If my other sister was crying quietly, I might roll over and try to comfort her, but it was all too likely that she would push me away.

Anyone who has lain in bed sure she would die before morning knows what that was like. What astonishes me is the many people I meet who know exactly what that was like—even people who were never slapped in daylight or screamed at by someone who was supposed to take care of them. I meet those people all the time, and they tell me about their own nights of living nightmare—lying rigid on the mattress waiting for madness to come through the door. Even if the door is never forced open, even if the madman never comes storming into the room, you are defined by that fear.

You have to do something to save yourself. You cannot lie awake every night of your childhood waiting for your own destruction. Was that when I learned to go away? Was that when I began to tell myself a story so engrossing or distracting that I would forget that I was afraid and disappear into the story itself? What if there was a staircase in the closet? What if we could go down and into a land where children have their own nation—not a safe place, but one where the dangers were somehow more bearable, less life-threatening, or just less monstrous. I imagined there was such a place. I made myself another country. Through most of my adolescence, I lived in that country.

I don't think this is entirely what is meant by the storytelling impulse—at least not that impulse that is so often mentioned in writing manuals or workshops. I am sure the country I made in my imagination was a place where I could go to be safe. However, the existence of that imaginary territory made me implicitly less safe in the world. There is something wrong, I feared, with people who lived more in their heads than in the real world. Was I told that or did I figure it out on my own? There is no way to know, but it was something that became more and more of a concern to me as I got older. That private place I had created in my mind became a matter of concern to my family and neighbors.

"She lives in her head," they said of me.
"She almost ain't here."
"Earth to Dorothy, come in, Dorothy."

I would come back, but reluctantly, embarrassed to be re-awakened to the mundane reality of dishes to be washed, trash to be hauled out, or questions to be answered in school. What was truly embarrassing was the implied weirdness. Living in your head was a sign of being crazy. Too much daydreaming was evidence of something wrong at home, and the fact that there were terrible things wrong in my home was no comfort. It was perfectly obvious to me as a girl that there was no rescue outside the circle of my mama's family. We were people who had to take care of our own problems, not go to outsiders for help. We were people who had to hold to the myth of self-sufficiency, to blend in and protect one another from the dangerous attentions of the outside world—the sheriff or child welfare. The child of a waitress who wanted to go to college had better not stand out too much or in the wrong way. It was better to seem absentminded than abused, to appear a parody of the bright bookish shy girl.

"Not tied too tightly, is she?" people would say to my mama with a laugh. Mama would smile, as if it were all a familiar joke. It was a joke we all acknowledged, though I knew she was genuinely frightened. What I could not talk about was how much I suspected there was to fear.

Could a person go away in their imagination so often that they didn't come back? Was that what it meant to be crazy? I think everyone who learns to live in their head—upstairs, I used to call it—knows that concern. Maybe you're crazy. Or maybe this is how you manage not to be crazy. What is fearful is thinking that "normal people" are fully present in their own lives, and you are not normal. Maybe "normal people" tell stories, maybe they even tell themselves stories. What I could not know was if "normal people" fell into the stories so deeply that they fell out of their everyday lives. What I wondered was did other people wait for the moments when they could finally have some peace and quiet, to get away and retreat into their imaginary world? Did they keep a running narrative going for months?

In time, I decided there was a kind of negotiated silence about all this stuff—it was not to be talked about. Perhaps everyone had an alternative life in their heads where they retreated when their daily lives became either unendurable or simply boring. There was Thurber's Walter Mitty after all, and the way people talked about daydreaming. It would be humiliating or worse to have one's daydreaming exposed, and I was smart enough to imagine what people would say about my stories.

Imagine me in my daydreams, in an alternate life. There I might be an

. . . .

orphan in a nation of orphans, maybe even a mutant with the ability to read minds—or maybe not. Imagine I broke into an old abandoned house and discovered it was full of books and stuff I never had in my real life. Imagine that every time I lay down, I went to that house, decorated it, wandered its halls, met others like me who had also sneaked away. Maybe I had sex there, or did not and it did not matter. Maybe I was beautiful there, or was not but it did not matter. Say that every time I was alone for a moment, I resumed the unbroken narrative or replayed earlier inventions with new variations. I could be happy there in ways I could not be in my daily life. Would that not be wonderful? Would it not be terrible to imagine having that exposed or stolen? The fantasy was infinitely precious, and completely fragile. It had to be kept safe, and secret.

Where have you been, did you not hear a word I said?
No mama, I didn't.
I swear I don't know what's wrong with you!

If anyone ever penetrated my secret world, looked into my mind the way I imagined looking into theirs, they would see how small and desperate I was. Teachers, doctors, and ministers, with the best intentions in the world, would try to help me. They would shake me out of my daydreams. They would drag me back into my unendurable daily life—the one I dared not let them know too much about. How would I survive if I had to be fully awake and present in my stepfather's house? It would be impossible. For the sake of my own survival I had to hide my imaginary world. I had to pretend in order to shield my true self.

Did I begin to write stories to have a justification for living in story? When did writing the stories become more what I did than dreaming up the stories? When did obscuring the origins of those stories begin to shape the kinds of stories I could tell? These are the questions I ask myself now. These are the puzzles that shape how I look at my own construction as a storyteller and a writer.

5

I sometimes imagine that I crawled out of my childhood like a baby turtle pulling myself out of the sucking mud, astonished at my fortune and in love with the natural world I see around me. Of course, I pulled a few things along with me out of that mud. I learned to use my storytelling talent but never to entirely trust what had produced it.

I know that normal is a construct. I know that average is an invention. I also know that the imagination is a complicated and deeply layered territory, and that most of my sense of shame and fear about my girlish fantasies were baseless. Yes, I dreamed lesbian dreams, a whole planet of girls like me. Yes, I daydreamed love and sex, and passionate escapes. But most of my narratives were stunningly commonplace—a house where no one shouted, a secret place where I was not afraid, or not alone, a place where I could do things people had told me I could not do—nothing so extraordinary as elaborate erotic adventures, just everyday simple things like read books for hours, or learn to play music, or sing, or wrestle happily with people I could trust. Of course, sometimes there were elaborate erotic adventures. Perhaps that is the origin of some of the uncertainty people feel about confessing daydream narratives—the sexual content, or the humiliating details. It is hard to translate one's secret fantasies into acceptable public narratives. Some details must always be obscured, or hidden completely. We know what we risk. The secret story is a window into the soul. The story reveals us in ways we are not always prepared to acknowledge.

From my adult perspective, all my girlish fears have assumed different proportions. Nothing I daydreamed was as scary as I imagined it, or as humiliating. Some things, however, would have put me at risk if I had revealed them in full. For example, I daydreamed my stepfather's murder. Perhaps it was my Baptist influences that made me attribute his death to accident or the intervention of some other person. In my stories, someone was always killing him for me. It was, it seemed, hard for me to admit even to myself that I wanted him dead. From my perspective all these years down, I now believe it was only reasonable that I dreamed that man dead. That I did not try to kill him in my real life is another issue. Sometimes I tell myself that the sane thing to do when you are being slowly murdered is to fight back or run away. Then I have to admit to myself that I did neither. I merely endured.

Why?

All these years later, I look back and think that the girl I was did the right thing. I play the imaginary game of What If and I see all the ways she could have gone mad or died or been destroyed. She took a lot of damage but came out of it a person capable of recovery. She dreamed survival and managed it. Perhaps that is enough to have accomplished.

Madness is real, there is no other way for me to explain my childhood, to explain to myself a man who would beat and rape a child. Having known genuine evil, I am both less afraid of my imagination and more careful of it. This secret private country in my head is very precious, and evidence that I need a place to hide and recover. It makes no difference that I created it when I was a child in genuine danger, subject to my violent stepfather's bullying contempt. The private sanctuary of my own mind was both a sustaining necessity and a secret respite—a place I needed to keep secret.

I wonder sometimes if those who were never beaten as children, who never retreated "upstairs" to avoid an unendurable present, have the same quality of daydreams as those of us who retreated to save our lives? Might that not be the thing we were given in compensation? Of course, to believe that I would have to believe in a rational system of horrors, cause and effect on some scale I prefer remain immeasurable.

I have made peace with not being normal. I have made myself a life that does not tolerate shame or denial. I am who I am, and I tell people that rather flatly. Yes, I am a lesbian. You got that right. Don't know what made me this way and don't particularly care. It is true, my stepfather could put you off men forever, but I don't choose to credit him with the whole of my identity. Maybe I would be who I am now even if he had never been in my life. For me the issue is how I live my life now. Having been so frightened as a girl, I have worked hard to be not so frightened as an adult, to be peaceable and matter-of-fact about my choices.

Doesn't everyone want to come to a place of acceptance? Doesn't everyone have deep and complicated issues to resolve in the process of growing up and building a life they can enjoy? I think they do, even if they have never believed themselves outside the norm. Certainly the evidence I have from those I love indicates that is so—my sisters with their multiple marriages and hard-loved children, my cousins scattered across every corner of this nation, and all my old girlfriends who check in every few years with stories more astonishing all the time. It's interesting being this particular kind of adult—a lesbian woman at midlife who genuinely believes that her sexual preference is not the most exotic or dangerous thing about her, a writer who wants most of all to put on the page versions of the people I have most loved, most feared, and had to work the hardest to understand.

6

I am never matter-of-fact about the people I create on the page. About this I do not lie. I create my family over and over, and I know it. It is where the sweat is for me, the terror and the passion. Women staggering with exhaustion but going on anyway, girl-children with no notion of how they will survive, men who despise themselves and struggle valiantly to not be what they have been made, and always the unique and embattled emotional lives of the working poor—disenfranchised, queer, and desperate. These are my people. This is my subject. I take them seriously, and God knows, I tell a mean story.

"Nobody's going to quit writing fiction," I tell Max at the bookstore. "And people still keep secrets, lots of secrets."

"Only the dangerous ones," he says. He drags my stack of books to his side of the counter. "You know, secrets like the ones get you sent to jail, or get you sued. Everything else they tell. It's become a Goddamned telling society." He snorts through his beard and shoots a quick glance out at the sidewalk. Last year there was some trouble about a man who slipped and fell at the entrance. There had been a few weeks there when Max had complained endlessly about lawyers and insurance and how small bookstores barely survive as it is. Now he tallies my purchases and checks the total off against my credit slip. When Max slides the receipt across the counter, he looks at me directly for the first time. His eyes startle me. Usually hazel dark, they are suddenly a peculiar muddy green.

"What?" he asks me. "What would you never tell?"

I think about it.

There are a number of things I would never tell Max. I would never say to him that his girlfriend can't write a lick. I would never tell him that his beard always smells to me like salty peanuts and marijuana. Most of all, I would never tell him that he reminds me of one of the few men I ever found genuinely sexually interesting. It would change everything if I admitted that fact was also part of what has made our conversations about Larry Brown so poignant. Now only one of those is secret because it might be dangerous. The other two are simply rude. All are private. They reveal more about me than Max.

. . . .

"I don't know," I say to him.

Max shakes his head at me. "You know." He nods emphatically. "You know and you won't say. That's what I like about you."

I am completely taken by surprise, so much so that I leave without arguing with him, though I find myself arguing with him for days afterward—every time I imagine again the expression on his face when he got me so completely wrong. The fact is that I will say anything, tell anything, and have done so in essays, poems, and fiction. I have always known that writing was an act of revelation, writing fiction perhaps most of all. But then I read memoirs like novels—as windows into other people's lives. There is so much that I do not know and want passionately to understand, so much that I am sure is misrepresented, lied about, or hidden. I want to know it all, and I want a world in which it is safe to know it all. That is why I try so hard to be matter-of-fact about the hard truths of my own life. That is why I so rarely speak of the private or the unspeakable. I have never felt that I had a right to name anything unspeakable, to declare any part of my life as private.

As I finish up these notes, I can look over and see the stack of books Max hated. I have added another pile to the ones I got from him, assembling an argument of sorts for myself as much as for the young woman to whom I first planned to give them. On top I have put Mark Doty's *Firebird* (a poet's memoir) and below that Michael Patrick MacDonald's *All Souls* (a family history that explores the origins of violence in South Boston). I am going to add a copy of June Jordan's *Soldier* (a wonderful book in which she explores how her father's life shaped her poet's story). I have already written a letter to accompany the books, a letter in which I explain how much I like the way poets approach the understanding of culture.

What I did not say in my letter is that I am working on something else by putting all these books together. I am planning a way to talk to Max again, to try to get him to think about what it is that our lived experience has to do with our imagination. I am beginning with what is dangerous in separating our secrets, lies, and revelatory truths.

For some of us, the most fearful landscape we can portray is the one in which we were made—our own families and those like our own. I chose to write fiction rather than memoir because it is easier for me to do so. Writing a fiction, I am not bound by the real, or my own sense of responsibility to leave nothing out. A novel leaves a lot out. In a good novel, it doesn't matter if what is being told ever really happened in the "real" world. I have read far too many "true" narratives that I did not believe for a minute, or couldn't finish at all.

What other people seemed to me to have, I have had to work to acquire— a sense of worth. This is the great secret of my life, and no secret at all.

On the Question of Invaded Privacy in Memoir Writing

. . . .

by
VIVIAN GORNICK

One day fifteen years ago I began writing a memoir about my mother, my-self, and a woman who lived next door to us when I was a child. A week later, in a benign mood, my mother said to me, "What an interesting idea you have there." A week after that, in a foul mood, she said to me, "Why are you writing this? So the *whole* world will know you hate me?"

In the first instance I smiled with relief, in the second I went home and quailed. Either way I felt undone, and for three or four days afterward did no work. I'd sit down at the desk and my mother's image would float up between me and the page, blotting out thought.

"What are you doing?" I'd say to myself. "What *are* you doing?"

On the fourth or fifth day the image wasn't there. All I saw when I sat down at the desk was the story I was trying to release from the welter of words looking up at me. I went back to work.

"Don't worry about it," I said to myself once I was thinking again. "She's smart, she'll get it."

What I meant by "She'll get it" was that my mother would see that I wasn't writing to trash her or to aggrandize myself; that I was writing to tell a story in which we both figured equally; a story being told in a spirit that could be trusted; and, moreover, one in whose deeper interest I'd be giving her everything she had—all her wisdom as well as all her madness; that, in fact, giving her everything she had would, I knew, keep me honest in the ways that counted.

Those words—"Don't worry, she'll get it"—were my salvation. They became a kind of mantra, a necessary repetition invoked often in the years

· · · · · · · · · · ·

ahead. They were able to remind me when I needed reminding that every word I wrote was in service to a story that was its own justification.

This story—the one about my mother, myself, and the woman next door—was based on an early insight I'd had that these two women between them had made me a woman. Each had been widowed young, each had fallen into despair; one devoted the rest of her life to the worship of lost love, the other became the Whore of Babylon. No matter. In each case the lesson being taught was that a man was the most important thing in a woman's life. I hated the lesson from early on, had resolved to get out and leave both it and the women behind. I did get out but as time went on I discovered that I couldn't leave any of it behind. Especially not the women. Most especially not my mother. I had determined to separate myself from her theatrical self-absorption but now, as the years accumulated, I saw that my hot-tempered and cutting ways were, indeed, only another version of her needy dramatics. I saw further that for both of us the self-dramatization was a substitute for action: a piece of Chekhovian unresolve raging in me as well as in her. It flashed on me that I could not leave my mother because I had become my mother.

This was the story I was bent on telling; the one I wanted to tell without sentiment or cynicism; the one I thought justified speaking hard truths. The flash of insight I'd had—that I could not leave my mother because I'd become my mother—was my wisdom: a tale of psychological embroilment I wanted badly to trace out.

But, of course, my mother was frightened—who, after all, was I to "expose" her, as she said repeatedly, to the judgment of strangers—and, of course, her fear infected me.

So I wrote my book, concentrating for all I was worth on what I saw as the larger intention—"Don't worry, she'll get it"—adhering religiously to a promise I'd made myself early on that no anecdote, no plot turn, no narrative device was ever to conclude itself with me in a self-serving position or Mama in a defensive one. None. Ever. Not once. And the book came out well, with all the parts in place, the scope of its insight proportionate to the shape of its composition, each accounting adequately for itself to the other. The story had, I think it safe to say, won the day.

As for my mother getting it, this is what happened: she read the book and she came to my house, walked into my living room, sat down in my chair, and said, "It took a lot of courage and some nerve for you to write this book."

. . . .

I burst out laughing and we embraced.

"You told the truth," she added generously. "Nothing but the truth."

A week later, in the middle of an argument, she lashed out, "That's some book you wrote! You've held me up to ridicule!"

A week after that, she wept, "You made my life larger than it is."

A day later she murmured, "I see what an effect I've had on you . . . what an awful effect."

When even more time had passed—and the shock of print had softened—she began receiving praise for the book as if it were meant for her. Eventually she walked around New York signing it. By that time she thought she'd written it.

In short, my mother remained her volatile and impassioned self from beginning to end: essentially a bystander, innocent or not, to the enterprise at hand.

From all of which I learned: the model's response to the written work is not the writer's business. And that is what my mother was while I was writing this book: my model. Exactly as was I myself, and the woman who lived next door. Just as we might have been had I been writing an autobiographical novel or a narrative poem or a tale based on events at which we'd all simply been present. Because my book was not a transcript of our lives. Nor was it a confession or a judgment or an eyewitness testimonial. It was a piece of writing. The distinction is crucial.

We live in an age of testament: more of it written than spoken. Everywhere in the western world, women and men, moved by the now commonly held belief that every life signifies, are sitting down at a computer to bear witness to themselves. This powerful impulse that has overtaken the talented and the untalented alike is, I think, not difficult to trace.

To begin with, modernism has run its course, thereby returning readers to an old-fashioned, perhaps retrograde, hunger for the "personal" story. For many years now our novels have been all voice: a voice speaking to us from out there, anchored neither in plot nor circumstance, hanging out in emotional space. To be sure, this voice has spoken the history of our time—of lives ungrounded, trapped in interiority—well enough to impose meaning and create literature. It has also driven the storytelling impulse underground. That impulse—to tell a tale rich in context, alive to situation, shot through with event and perspective—is as strong in human beings as the need to eat food and breathe air: it may be suppressed but it cannot be destroyed. As the century has worn on, and the sound of voice alone has grown less and less compelling—its insights repetitive, its wisdom now wearisome—the longing for narration has risen up again, asserting the oldest of claims on the reading heart.

To the death of modernism add the concentrated influence of the therapeutic culture, long trained on the dramatic value of the emergent self. And then add the rise of the liberation movements of the last forty years, persuading millions that merely to "speak out" is to perform an act of consequence. In this country alone, thirty years of politics in the street has produced an outpouring of testament from women, blacks, and gays that is truly astonishing. Paradoxically, as the power of voice alone has dwindled, a mass culture has emerged, on a plane unparalleled in history, urging Everywoman and Everyman to tell The Story of My Life.

But a memoir is neither testament nor fable nor analytic transcription. A memoir is a work of sustained narrative prose that bears the same responsibility as does all writing: to lift from the raw material of life a tale that will shape experience, transform event, deliver wisdom. It *does* differ from fiction writing in the way it approaches the task, the chief difference being that a fictional "I" can be, and often is, an unreliable narrator whereas the nonfictional "I" can never be. In memoir, the reader must be persuaded that the narrator is speaking truth. Truth in a memoir is achieved not through a faithful recital of actual events; it is achieved when the reader comes to believe that the writer is working hard to engage with the experience at hand. What happened to the writer is not what matters; what matters is the large sense that the writer is able to *make* of what happened. For that, the power and intention of a writing imagination is required.

From St. Augustine on, the memoir is controlled by an idea of self that is being worked out on the page. That idea, almost always, is served through a piece of self-awareness that clarifies only slowly in the writer, gaining strength and definition as the narrative progresses. In a bad memoir the line of clarification remains muddy, uncertain, indistinct. In a good one, it becomes the organizing principle; the thing that lends shape and texture to the writing, drives the narrative forward, provides direction and unity of purpose. St. Augustine himself, in telling the story of his conversion, sees himself as a man who needs badly to pass out of his own inner darkness: that is the man who gets converted. J. R. Ackerley, on the other hand, writing *My Father and Myself* in the last half of the twentieth century, is discovering that it is precisely himself he does *not* want to

.   .   .   .

know: and that is the man telling *his* story. As for Marguerite Duras, the knowledge she gains at fifteen of a gift for sexual abandon will become the organizing principle of *The Lover,* one of the most remarkable memoirs ever written. From St. Augustine to Rousseau, from Edmund Gosse to Ackerley and Duras, the question clearly being asked in an exemplary memoir, regardless of the situation, is "Who am I?" Who, exactly, is this "I" upon whom turns the significance of this story-taken-directly-from-life? On that question the writer of memoir must deliver. Not with an answer but with depth of inquiry.

Thousands of people are now writing a memoir under the mistaken notion that a situation is a story—my cancer, his heart attack, the children died, the house burned down—which is somewhat like thinking that a novel is "about" young marrieds on the Upper West Side, a year in the White House, a plane wreck in the Sahara. It is not. The situation is not the story. The story is the wisdom, the insight, the thing the writer has come to say.

Because the memoir enterprise is so imperfectly understood, the wrong considerations often fill the would-be memoirist's head. Do I dare tell this or that about mama or papa? Will my sister's feelings be hurt? Is my cousin's privacy being invaded? These questions loom large for people who don't know why they're writing. People who think the situation is the story.

I honestly believe that if a writer sets out to tell a story informed by an intention independent of the situation, these anxieties resolve themselves decently. When some "flash of insight" equal to the kind that triggers a poem or a fiction dominates the prose of a memoir the writer's obligation comes clear. Then every character in the experience being recounted has a shot at becoming a believable—that is, an understandable—human being. More a writer does not owe the models for those characters; and more is not required in the matter of deciding what to "reveal," what to "conceal," whether one is invading, betraying, or exposing.

In short, as the transplanted South African writer Lynn Freed, whose novels are sometimes nakedly autobiographical, observed in a recent interview, "[Y]ou write as if everyone is dead. Then you face the music. I don't know any other way to keep the teeth sharp and the spirit alive."

What more is there to say?

Intentionality is everything.

The obligation of the writer—fictional as well as nonfictional—is to deliver oneself as honestly as possible of what the writer thinks is the truth;

that is, as D. H. Lawrence said, the truth of the truth not of the facts. If that obligation is undertaken in a spirit sufficiently large all will go well. The narrator in a memoir then becomes only an instrument of illumination; it's the writing itself that provides revelation. Exactly as it should. As V. S. Pritchett once said of the genre, "It's all in the art. You get no credit for living."

Privacy in Bloom

.   .   .   .

by
MICHAEL GRODEN

Ever since I first read James Joyce's *Ulysses* almost thirty-five years ago, its main character Leopold Bloom has supplied me with my clearest and most dependable image of the kind of person I'd like to be, someone who lives an ordinary life and survives it with optimism, good humor, integrity, and dignity. A thirty-eight-year-old canvasser for ads, a graduate of the "university of life" (Bloom's phrase), a Jewish outsider in lower-middle-class Catholic Dublin, Bloom lives through one day in *Ulysses* in all its twists and turns and ups and downs. In many ways June 16, 1904, is an ordinary day—"the dailiest of days," one critic called it—but Bloom does attend the funeral of an acquaintance who died suddenly a few days earlier from an alcohol-induced heart attack and, most important, goes through the day knowing that at 4:30 his wife Molly will be unfaithful to him (and, in the second half of the book, has cuckolded him) with her concert manager Blazes Boylan. From the outside, and to his fellow Dubliners, Bloom is practically invisible and silent—they acknowledge him only to scorn him. But Joyce gives us access to Bloom's inner life, and it is his thoughts, responses, reactions, daydreams, and fantasies that make him, for me, a figure of great sympathy, even of heroism.

Joyce gives us access to a full range of Bloom's thoughts as he lives through his day—serious thoughts, trivial ones, happy, sad, generous, selfish, licit, illicit. We eavesdrop on Bloom's plans for his own life and his ideas for improving Dublin civic life (bury people vertically to save space in cemeteries), and on his attempts to recall poems and plays he has read and seen, often with mistakes. We also accompany Bloom into his outhouse where we watch him and read his thoughts as he defecates ("Hope it's not too big bring on piles again. No, just right"); later, we observe him masturbating (he's hidden behind a wall, but we can see his face, and we follow his post-orgasmic thoughts); and we follow his recollections of nights of lovemaking with his wife Molly and on his only half-serious plans for his own adulterous affairs. In one of the most extraordinary sections of *Ulysses*, we witness, as if paraded on a stage, Bloom's unconscious mind, the desires and drives, fears and wishes to which he has no conscious access. He would surely be mortified to learn that anyone else knew about this part of his being, or even to know about it himself. If Leopold Bloom is a sympathetic, dignified, and heroic character, he is also one who has had much of what we would consider his privacy ripped from him by his creator.

I've never thought of Leopold Bloom in terms of privacy before. He's a literary character, after all, a creation of words. But my sense of his dignity and heroism is connected to my voyeuristic interest in his inner life, to my access to what, if he were a living human being, he surely would want to keep private. And, of course, the playing field is uneven: I don't have to give anything away, or expose any part of myself, as I read *Ulysses*—except privately. No one knows how much or how little I'm affected by the book, how deeply or shallowly I respond, with how much interest or boredom, sympathy or hostility, unless I choose to make those reactions public.

Because I'm a professional literary critic and scholar, and a university professor, I do reveal at least some of those responses. Like most academics, I have made a tacit deal regarding my privacy. When I write literary criticism or scholarship, I write about an author or a work, not directly about myself. This ensures me a kind of protection, since I communicate through my ideas, my ability to discover and marshal evidence, and my skill at writing clear, relatively neutral, academic prose. I speak to a small audience, in most of my writings to those people interested in *Ulysses*. Within this tiny group I become a semi-public or sometimes public figure. Likewise, at my university, I become a figure of interest and gossip among the students who pass through my department. In these roles I have found that I like being recognized and acknowledged, and I feel stung when I'm not. To the extent that I am a public person at all, it is only within these few narrow worlds. Outside of them, I remain private, and I think I know how my temperament has led me to this position of severely circumscribed celebrity within a much larger anonymity.

I love listening to the NPR show *Car Talk*, even though I have never had the slightest interest in cars. Recently, Tom and Ray mentioned the

Car-o-scope, a survey they offer on their web site that tells you whether your car is the best match for your personality. I get what they're trying to find out from their questions—if the only two jobs in the world were an accountant or a social worker, I'd choose to be an accountant; I like the inside of my car to be tidy; white-water rafting and skydiving hold no appeal whatsoever for me. I felt confident that the Car-o-scope would conclude that my Subaru Forester and I are indeed made for each other. But one question throws the profile out of whack: "It would drive me nuts being married to an artist-type." For not only can I imagine being married to an artist, I am married to one—Molly Peacock, editor of this volume—and without being driven noticeably off the road. (My Forester, after all, has all-wheel drive.) Furthermore, unlike me, Molly is a writer who has often written about very personal aspects of her outer, inner, and sexual life in her poems and prose works.

When Molly and I married in 1992, both of us by then in our mid-forties, she was well established as a poet, and I knew that, by entering her world, I was granting her freedom to write about anything that happened with me and also to write indirectly or even directly about me. I found myself surprisingly unthreatened by this, feeling a kind of protection in knowing that she would never expose anything about me in her poems that I really wanted to keep to myself. I even felt flattered, I realized, when she wrote about me in her poems, whether about ordinary events like eating meals or watching the New York City Marathon together or intimate ones like making love or lying in her mother's bed the night after her mother died. I also got accustomed to the stranger experience of hearing her perform these poems at public readings, feeling a mixture of pride and embarrassment in knowing that the strangers seated around me were learning things about me that I wouldn't have talked about. (I fell into the habit of sitting in the front row so that I couldn't see the rest of the audience and they couldn't see my face.) And I even adjusted to the more bizarre experience of hearing Molly intersperse these poems with others that are about someone else, even though some people in the audience will think they are learning something about me.

Poems are condensations and crystallizations, but prose is usually much more direct. Shortly after we got married, Molly began writing a memoir, a book she published in 1998 as *Paradise, Piece by Piece*. Her focus in the book was her own growth and development and the crucial life decisions she has made, including her choice to became a poet and especially her choice not to have children. But, in addition to being married to her as she was writing the book, I figure into both themes of her book in other ways because Molly and I were high-school sweethearts in suburban Buffalo in the mid-1960s. We dated, "went steady," through a year and a half of high school and one year of college, and were each other's first lover. (And so I knew the living Molly before I met Molly Bloom.) We broke up at the end of our first college year and lost touch for eighteen years, until, reading the *New York Times Book Review* one Sunday morning in December 1984 in London, Ontario, where I had come to live after being hired by the University of Western Ontario's English Department, I saw a review of her second book of poems, *Raw Heaven*. I wrote to her in New York, where she lived, and soon we began meeting for lunch or dinner whenever I visited there. For several years we developed a friendship at this level, and, since we were both deep into psychotherapy and working through various family problems, I was grateful for her firsthand memories of me and my family from so many years ago. She provided me with the only accounts of those years, other than my own memories, that I was able to obtain.

In June 1991 I faced a professional crisis involving a New York publisher. Molly was the only person I knew who had a writer's experience with publishers, and I phoned her for advice. She couldn't help me much with my canceled contract, but as we talked on the phone evening after evening for a couple of weeks, our talk became less professional and more personal and then romantic. I invited her to visit London, Ontario, and, even though we had never done more than give each other a hug as we met or departed over the past seven years, she said she'd come. Within hours of her arrival we were lovers again, and within six months, even though we had jobs in different cities, we decided to get married. We married the next summer, eloping to a small town in Washington State for a combined wedding-honeymoon. (Completing another circle, the publisher that cancelled my contract in 1991 offered it to me again in 2000.)

A few months after our wedding, Molly's mother died, and she began to talk more and more about her life as a story she had to tell. I encouraged her to write her memoir, but as she began to work on it, I found myself in an unexpected position in relation to my privacy. I was surprised and, I realized, pleased to see that she was including parts of my life in her story, not poetically but narratively, not veiled but undisguised. However, I was being written about solely as I appeared to someone else and as I figured in someone else's life. I was a subsidiary figure, a secondary character, in someone else's story.

.   .   .   .

Trust was essential. I knew Molly to be a decent, honest person who wrote to explore her own inner and outer life, not to depict others badly or cruelly, to seek revenge, or to boost herself at someone else's expense. But she is, after all, a writer, and can you ever really trust a writer? She gets the last word. I had to learn to treat some details from my life as interesting anecdotes that I would enjoy making public, and so I got prepared for the world to learn about the time in 1964 when I went to Molly's house and found a note on an unlocked door instructing me to go into the living room, take off all my clothes, and go into the bathroom. I found her there in a bubble bath, where she invited my seventeen-year-old eyes to feast on the sight of her naked body for the first time. I almost forgot my panic about her parents suddenly coming home as I tripped on the edge of the tub in my eagerness to join her. (They did return, but we were out of the tub, drying off, and managed to escape.) Or about our first weeks as college undergraduates, three hundred miles apart from each other, when she visited me at Dartmouth and we made love for the first time, not as in the glow of a romantic Hollywood movie but in a freezing room in an empty motel twenty hitchhiked miles out of town. She wanted to recount these events, and details about me entered and left her book as she reworked her story for her own purposes over six years.

As I read the drafts that Molly showed me, I sometimes seemed to be mainly a pawn in Molly's story. Incidents from my life got shortened or dropped because they didn't fit the book's evolving narrative arc. I wondered whether readers would see me as a figure who in any way resembles the person I think I am. For the first time I thought sympathetically about Richard Best, a minor character in *Ulysses* who listens, unconvinced, to Stephen Dedalus's theory that Shakespeare based his plays on barely transformed events in his life. Best was also a historically real person (Joyce used his actual name) who became a translator, scholar, and director of the National Library of Ireland. He did not share the unflattering mannerisms and verbal tics that Joyce, partly to revenge himself on the literary figures who had snubbed him years earlier, gave him in print. Fiction and reality blended uncomfortably in Best's life, as he made clear when he responded with annoyance to a BBC interviewer that he was *not* a fictional character but a living being. Of course, Best's protests were hopeless: readers of *Ulysses* who know his story may feel a moment's sympathy for him, but any interest they have is in the character and not the flesh-and-blood person. Was I about to become a Richard Best—were readers going to respond to and even analyze someone else's written portrait of me?

I came to see that a distinction has to be made between exposure, which is against a person's will, and disclosure, which isn't. It made me uncomfortable to realize that the world would know things about my illnesses, professional setbacks, and smaller moments of vulnerability, especially since I don't have the kind of personality that easily reveals such information. But that's not the same as having your towel suddenly swiped away—an involuntary full monty. I felt more like an actor justifying a nude scene in a film. I used to think that beautiful stars were just showing off their perfect bodies. But as I had to think about my life in its nakedness—with all the anxieties that provoked—I came to understand the insecurity that these actors must feel but also to know that, sometimes, the story simply won't work unless the players are fully disrobed.

Letting someone write about that first delicious sight of nakedness or the near comic (we can now admit) loss of virginity is one thing, but illness and family complications seemed like another matter. In the early 1980s I suffered through two bouts of melanoma, and, in fact, when I first wrote to Molly after I saw the review of *Raw Heaven,* she had just learned about my cancer from a friend of mine whom she had recently met, and she thought that I was dying and writing to say good-bye to everyone I knew. When the cancer was new and I was terrified, I told anyone who would listen about it, but most people didn't want to hear, and I gradually stopped talking much about it. Many people who know me now don't know about it at all. But it seemed essential to Molly's story about our reunion: when we re-met, she had to meet me and my illness, and when we decided to marry, she had to take the cancer along with the rest of me. Janna Malamud Smith claims in her book *Private Matters* that knowing another person "depends on a safe place, a wish to tell honestly, and a listener who can bear to hear." Molly became that listener for me, and since she felt her story wasn't complete without the melanoma, it became part of her memoir.

My family is a different matter. I gave Molly a release, first informally and eventually legally, to write about my life undisguised and uncensored, but I didn't give her the same right to use my family's private lives. (My living family consists of my mother, brother, and sister; my father died thirty years ago.) To tell the complex family stories, even though my story is incomplete without them, would involve crucial violations of privacy. This is the one aspect of my life that I asked Molly to omit from her book, and she agreed to do that.

In the years since Molly wrote *Paradise, Piece by Piece,* though, I've often thought about this omission. Molly has written about her mother's odd combination of neglect and encouragement toward her: in order to push her away and keep her at a safe distance, her mother encouraged her to write or paint or do anything creative, as long as she did it independently. As a result, Molly learned quickly that artistic expression was a positive thing and also that she had an audience, and she has often said that she thinks she first began to write in order to reach her mother. Whenever she talks about this, or I read one of her written accounts of it, I envy her: if you have to grow up in a neurotic household, you're not often lucky enough to come out of it with your creative instincts encouraged.

I remember weekly visits to my paternal grandmother when I was seven or eight—my father packed my brother, sister, and me into the car and took us to visit her apartment, where we all sat uncomfortably while she asked perfunctorily about my mother and then went on to various bits of small talk. My mother was the kind of person who never expressed anger, but, in the earliest memories I have, she wasn't speaking to her mother-in-law or even to her own brother. Over the years, she extended the cutoff list to her sister, my grandmother's entire family, every good friend she ever had, and her son (she stopped talking to my brother for about twenty years, reconciling with him in the mid-1990s). Over fifty years later, she never has reconciled with her brother. I never knew what caused any of these rifts. My sister has remained in touch and loyal to our mother over all the years, although she and my brother became estranged in the early 1970s and refused to see each other until they agreed to meet at a dinner for our mother's eightieth birthday in the summer of 2000. But I have continued to speak to everyone, though at the distance of at least 150 miles ever since I left Buffalo for college in New Hampshire when I was eighteen.

If Molly learned to create in the hopes of breaking through her mother's wall, I learned to play it very safe in, I eventually saw, a desperate attempt to avoid doing anything that would cause my mother to close the window in her wall and shut me out. I was well trained: I was in my mid-thirties, several years into psychotherapy for what I thought was help in adjusting to my cancer, before I even began to see that there was any problem with my family (never mind that I was already divorced and severed from several formerly close friends), and older still before I began to get even the small degree of control that I have now over my responses to these ruptures.

I'm interested here, finally, in how my family situation relates to the career I chose as a literary scholar and English professor and to the public-private roles I outlined earlier. I went to Dartmouth to be a math major—I was very good at math in high school, but the utter psychological neutrality of math makes the choice seem very appropriate for me. But I got deflected by literature, and specifically by *Ulysses,* which I read at the start of my sophomore year and fell in love with almost instantly. (Three months after Molly Peacock and I broke up, still on the rebound, I met Molly Bloom.) I wasn't too attracted to the character of Stephen Dedalus, even though he was close to my age and, in his own way, just as lost and struggling as I was—I didn't think I was lost, I wasn't particularly rebellious, I was Jewish and not Catholic, I wasn't feeling especially stifled by the environment I grew up in (although, obviously, I should have been). It was the older father figure, Leopold Bloom, who hooked me, even though he is thirty-eight in *Ulysses* and I was nineteen, and from my fascination with Bloom I came to love everything else in *Ulysses*: its other characters, its exuberance, its wordplay, its games and puzzles, and especially its view of humanity and of how to live in a modern world. Novels, I was discovering, were saying things to me that no living person ever said, even things I would have run away from had anyone said them aloud to me. No other book spoke to me, or has ever spoken to me, in the way that *Ulysses* does, and in its wonderful and beautiful way, about life's setbacks and tragedies but also about its basic comedy, about how to live and to react to setbacks and betrayals, about the inner strength, dignity, and heroism of an outwardly unassuming and unnoticeable person, and about the sheer exuberance and joy of communicating through language.

"It really makes sense you left math for literature," Molly wrote about me in her poem "The Wheel," and of course it does, even though, when I changed my major, I had shown no aptitude for literature or desire to work with it in any of the psychological or vocational tests I was given in high school and college. Literature gave me access to a world I needed to enter, and talking and writing about it provides both the outlet and the safety of relative anonymity that I have to accept as the legacy of my upbringing. Although I've taught a wide range of courses in twentieth-century literature, textual criticism and scholarly editing, hypertext, and film, it is always *Ulysses,* and with it Leopold Bloom, that I come back to, my own Ithaca. I was about eighteen years younger than Bloom when I first read his story, and I'm about eighteen years older than him now—the book has changed very much for me over the years, but my love for it re-

. . . .

mains as strong as ever. I practically stopped teaching it for several years in the 1980s: students found the book too long, too hard, too male, and I found the struggle to convince them of its worth too discouraging. But in the mid-1990s I started worked on a huge project, "James Joyce's *Ulysses* in Hypermedia," and I found myself re-energized. I threw away all my lecture notes and started teaching without the security I thought they provided me—a major act for someone both as anal retentive and as shy as I am. Students still resist the book more than I would wish, but when one or two people in a class of twenty or thirty begin to get hooked, I feel that I have succeeded in my job as a teacher, and also I see a new version of myself as I was when I discovered the book in 1966.

So can a choice to live a life of writing about and teaching the creative works of other people be related to issues of privacy? For me, literary scholarship and teaching seem like a calling, not so much because of the poetry and fiction itself (although I am happy to play my small part in promoting an awareness of and love for literature in an age when it needs all the advocates it can find) as because of the balances they provide me between privacy and disclosure, safety and risk, criticism and creativity. I'm lucky to have found *Ulysses*—a book that for me is about balancing opposites—when I did, just as I am lucky to have twice found the living Molly. Near the end of *Ulysses,* we are given a report of Leopold Bloom's assessment of his day: "He had not risked, he did not expect, he had not been disappointed, he was satisfied." What satisfies him are "To have sustained no positive loss. To have brought a positive gain to others. Light to the gentiles." I'm not a gentile, but Bloom and *Ulysses* have repeatedly given me much more than this assessment suggests. For this to happen, I had to follow Joyce and violate Bloom's privacy and, in the process, to reconsider and maybe open the doors a little on my own—through Leopold Bloom to let my privacy bloom.

Sweet Uses of Adversity

. . . .

by
MOLLY PEACOCK

Just a piece of privacy lattice away, my maniac neighbor is attacking two-by-fours with a buzzsaw. I would be happier hearing birdsong, but that savage is not interrupting me. I have turned my back to him. I have gone through the mirror. I am out to sea. Nothing is going to stop me from whispering what I have to say to you:

I learned privacy at my mother's knee, thinking of the word itself as a participle, derived from her very active verb: *to private*. I should correct myself and say that I learned to private at her *back,* not her knee. Desperate for an emotional life of her own, my mother Polly unpredictably and mystifyingly would turn her back to me, sinking into a sudden current of her own needs. At these moments she seemed to be drowning—or I seemed to be drowning without her. Come *back,* I said, tugging at her sleeve, but inward—or rather, seaward—she went. Years later, when I took Poetry 101, my professor described metaphor as language that "passes through a mirror," and instantly I knew I had found my vocation as a poet. I realized Polly had disappeared through her own reflection.

Writing poetry requires huge amounts of privacy.

Mere being requires huge amounts of privacy, my mother felt, and passed on a fortune of privacy skills to me.

Yet when she crossed the boundary of death, she suddenly felt free to intrude on my solitude. One time she popped up as a ghostly six-year-old with shiny dark bangs and a Buster Brown haircut, what used to be called in novels for girls, "a tanned hoyden." She romped through a meadow near a creek, her pony tethered nearby, waiting for her grandparents to come back from town with their team of horses and wagon, bringing her

. . . .

a book. The year seemed to be 1925, three years before the poet Anne Sexton, whom she vaguely resembled physically, was born. Polly faced me obliviously, not recognizing me in my twenty-first-century clothes (or perhaps I was invisible). Certainly she didn't know that she would become my mother. She was busy becoming herself. She was completely inside her own privacy, in a pleasure of becoming.

The process of becoming is a basic act of privacy, and a cornerstone of life. Developing a room of your own in your head leads to a delicious and necessary distance from any intrusive environment, and it provides as well a blueprint for existence because, in the privacy of your own mind, you always know who you are.

For several years I held a position at Friends Seminary School in Manhattan called "learning disabilities specialist," teaching reading, writing, and study skills, but the fact was that I was employed teaching my adolescent charges how to pilot emotional waters and pirate their identities, indeed, to private. By the time kids are juniors or seniors in high school, they attain Olympic levels of daydreaming. But the ones I taught had somehow been prevented from finding this out for themselves, probably because they had parents who watched them every minute, who never turned their backs on them because their children were not high achievers and were, therefore, in the parlance of achievement, "disabled." One exasperating day I found myself teaching them how to daydream by extorting daydreaming instructions from them for use by an extraterrestrial who suddenly had to attend Friends Seminary. How was the being to sit? What expression was it to form on its so-called face? They humored me by answering that it was to stare at a place a little bit above and behind the teacher's head, half close its eyes, but not all the way, let its mind go blank, let sounds filter out as if a big fan was whirring in its head.

If your mind is a pie, they told it (the invisible extraterrestrial was one of us now; we were sharing our thoughts with a blank chair), save one piece, about one-eighth, to listen to the teacher. Then let the rest of your whole mind wander, like to a place where you can French kiss your girl/boyfriend.

These are instructions for the kind of relaxed interior wandering that promotes mental and imaginative growth, allowing you to come into a loose contact with who you are. De-focusing on the outside world through the construction of interior walls paradoxically creates an atmosphere for creative focus, or concentration. My students took to their list of instructions, originally the property of my mother Polly, the back turner.

Polly grew up as a kind of child barbarian, indulged in her privacy. She was allowed to spend every weekend on her grandpa's farm, even going to school on Monday morning from the farm, spending the weekday nights ruefully at her parents' home, the house, general store, and gas station called "La Grange Garage." Her independence was legendary, both in my family and in the hamlet of La Grange where she grew up as a teetotaling Baptist. On the eve of the American entry into World War II she left home for Buffalo, the nearest city.

There she became intoxicated by the glamorous Anchor Bar where Ted, her future husband, had begun drinking boilermakers when he was twelve. I think now my father may have fallen in love with her because she treated him with the casual egalitarianism with which those who have developed a truly private inviolate self treat others. But the farm girl he loved didn't have a clue about how alcoholism worked, nor did she have a clue about the wild alcoholic family she would marry into—and live with in a small side-by-side duplex. In that house, where I was born, the former tanned hoyden had no room of her own, no meadow, no farm, no horse, only a pleasantly drunk father-in-law, a happily drunk brother-in-law, a warily drunk mother-in-law, and a weepingly drunk husband who had a sexy aura of frustrated violence about him.

How would she create a mental room of her own? Fortunately and unfortunately, she would turn her back on it all.

Both my parents were the less preferred of their siblings, and each was a middle child. My father's older brother died in infancy, and my dad took on the terrible burden of carrying his brother's exact name. He never could measure up to the divine dead other Edward. Whereas my mother was ignored by her mother, but cherished by her grandparents, my father was actively blamed by his mother and father. He never had any privacy. My grandmother judged, disapproved, and interfered with every decision he made, and he lusted for her approval with such a deep child's desire that he never gave up hope of making her happy. Just as his mother could not work her way through the loss of her first baby, he could not work his way through the loss of her fond gaze. (This focus on her led to a profound spiritual neglect of himself, just as my learning-disabled students profoundly neglected themselves in the atmospheres of intrusive supervision in which they lived.)

When I imagine the first kiss shared by my mother and father, it burns with the intensity of two neglected beings who have found each other. Yet how would each of them create the intimately distant space to make a sanctuary of their marriage? "So," John Bayley says in his memoir, *Elegy for*

. . . .

Iris, "married life began. And the joys of solitude. No contradiction was involved. The one went perfectly with the other. To feel oneself held and cherished and accompanied, and yet to be alone. To be closely and physically entwined, and yet feel solitude's friendly presence, as warm and undesolating as contiguity itself." (123) Neither of my parents knew how to cherish the other by granting one another solitude. My dad had nowhere to turn for a moment to himself except to the glow of Black Velvet in a shot glass. (I think of his bartenders as the benign parents who did not intrude or interfere, leaving the patron-child to his own inner resources.)

Every third week my dad left for his job at four in the afternoon. On this shift my mother, sister, and I entered a peaceable kingdom of dinnertimes. We each sat in front of our Melmac plates, then, in imitation of our mother, we turned our chairs to the side. Polly did this so she could read and smoke while she dabbled at her food. She was teaching us to sit at the side of the main activity, to establish, even at a blessedly quiet mealtime, even more privacy. We turned our chairs as she did, trying to continue to cut out paper dolls or color in coloring books, but we were messy and she made us turn our chairs back to the table. "I'm setting a bad example to you, I know," she said, so of course we knew it was a great example, and aspired to it.

Much later on in life, aspiring to be a poet, I read Emily Dickinson's advice, "tell it slant," and knew that Polly had set up a kind of poetic concentration by turning her chair from its direct relation to the table. And still later on, I taught poetry to seventh graders. Every Friday we disengaged the chairs from the desks, and some kids went to lounge on the wide windowsills with a huge liver-colored stuffed corduroy worm that uncoiled to about fifteen feet. We turned the lights off, got comfortable, and followed this recipe: close your eyes, let your pen fall loosely in your hand, let yourself go blank, or if you can't go blank, watch yourself going toward your thoughts. Keep telling yourself your thoughts until words push through your arms, down into your hands, and through your fingers where the pen will begin to write them.

When Robin Byrd, the Manhattan Sex Channel duchess, repeats the same mantra to her audience every show, "Now get your condoms and dental dams, and get comfortable, and remember, if you don't have a loved one, you always have me, Robin Byrd," I think of it as a variation on the recipe we developed. Ours led to learning, reading, writing, and concentration, and Robin's leads to sex, but sex is a huge part of privacy, and eros drives poetry, as all the kids knew.

Having goals requires you to concentrate. But the ability to concentrate, like sex, takes a certain amount of athleticism.

My mother could cook a meal with her nose in a book while she was tying my sister's shoelaces, pouring my father a beer, putting me on the potty seat, handing the newspaper to my grandmother, laughing at my uncle's dirty joke, taking endless ribbing from them all about her reading habits in a household where no other adult read.

By the time I was twelve I could also cook a meal, do my homework, supervise my sister, be on the lookout for my father, watch TV, and read a novel at the same time. I didn't have the experienced dexterity of my mother, but I'd passed my basic lessons. But wait—where was my mother? She had gotten in her car and gone to the back room of Peacock's Superette, our grocery store, where she spent every day of the week from 10 A.M. to 10 P.M., except Sunday when the store opened at 1. She had physically ensured her privacy. That was her goal, but it might not have been a goal she would have admitted.

About this time, at the age of the learning disabled adolescents I taught years later, I read my first Shakespeare play, *As You Like It,* and loved memorizing the lines from Act II, scene i, that articulated a rescuing motto for living:

> Sweet are the uses of adversity
> Which like the toad, ugly and venomous
> Wears yet a precious jewel in his head.

Much later, in college, when it was dawning on me that one of my goals might be to become a poet, I would hear Marianne Moore's definition of poetry as real toads in imaginary gardens and think of my amateurish, inchoate, toadlike poems as bejeweled attempts. But back in Buffalo I learned that one could use adversity. My father's threats and my mother's abandonment could be put to use: I could generate a precious jewel— something creative—out of it all.

My enthusiasm for generating jewels has never dampened. I am creatively energized all the time, and part of that is simply my personality, but another part is the set of privacy skills that allow for unfocused wandering and its flip side, concentration on one thing to the utter exclusion of all else. My mother concentrated on her goal of removing herself from our house to the utter exclusion of her daughters and husband. That was the point for her, really. Yet in achieving it, she modeled a possibility for me.

.   .   .   .

She was turning the forehead of the toad adversity into a jewel. She was creating a way out when none had seemed possible. Writing a poem requires both this exclusive concentration and the unfocused state that allows you to be surprised by your ideas. It provides a way out of doorless conundrums by becoming, paradoxically, a way in.

After Polly achieved her goal, I had to learn a special trick: to maintain the concentration of daydreamy privacy while being hyperaware of signals that something might be wrong with my father. My dad was capable of sudden violence, but there were a few warning signs that one might heed. He could be headed off with a certain kind of placating. Or you could get far out of his way.

Because my sister and I were all alone with him, and because Polly warned us that he could do something dangerous and we should always be on guard, I had to enter my own world, leaving my eyes turned, as sentinels, toward the source of possible attack. This was complicated by the architecture of our suburban house. My bedroom had no door. If I was sure my father was occupied or passed out, I could leave the living room and go to my room, but only if I was sure. Obviously this was stressful. But what I learned from it, a technique of vigilant privating, also allowed me to write three books of poetry while I was working full-time teaching children as "difficult" as my family was. I got out of that house, and with more than the clothes on my back: I knew how to concentrate, I knew how to create, I knew how to recreate privacy in my head.

I could not now tell you if my neighbor has stopped his vicious saw.

That hypervigilance also provided me with a capacity to notice details around me that hardly anyone else noticed. When a poet describes such details, she can fill her poems with shocks of recognition for readers. Everyone knows what the poet is talking about, yet it all feels original because it is so sharply perceived that the imaginary garden comes to seem as real as the toad squatting in it.

When I have thoughts of privacy deprivation, say, when I imagine myself all alone in a nursing home, helpless against the repeated jabberings of my roommate and the sharing of everything: clothes, teeth, eyeglasses . . . I comfort myself with the knowledge that I might still be able to create a precious jewel in my head. Mental privacy has a spiritual dimension: it is recuperative, and it generates health.

Yet by watching my mother completely turn her back on us, I learned the final, ugly skill of privacy: if she had the capacity to turn away completely, I probably do, too. And what she did was bad. It is immoral to leave your girls with their increasingly dangerous father, fallen prey to the last stages of a terrible disease. My mother overdeveloped her privacy skill the way muscle builders overdevelop their biceps. What she did was immoral, and I felt its injustice just at the point when I was entering that most moral stage of development: adolescence. I was becoming an ethical being, and my father (sometimes I just can't see alcoholism as a disease, no matter how hard I try) did questionable things by verbally abusing us and weeping and demanding a love from us we could not possibly give. I wanted my mother to use that other meaning of back. I wanted her to *come back*.

If my mother could have gone this far, as the inheritor of her privacy treasure chest, could I? My anxiety over becoming a privacy monster has contributed to my lifelong urgency to connect to others. I am afraid of what my mother became, but I love her methodology. As far as creativity is concerned, it suggested that there may be an actual art of neglect.

For the last fifteen years I have worked one-to-one with serious writers needing advice, encouragement, and instruction about their writing. Many of these writers are poets, and to my pleasure most of them are publishing in literary journals and some of them have published remarkable books. I devised this peculiar way of making a living during my years as a learning disabilities specialist when I had a small private practice working with individual students outside the school. This practice imitated the form of psychotherapy, yet it wasn't psychotherapy at all. I shudder at the thought of being a psychotherapist because I personally need too much privacy ever to be on call to patients twenty-four hours a day. I know that therapists take special training to develop boundaries which allow them to handle these occasions, but I run even from the prospect of such training. I do not want a phone call from an emergency room at 3 A.M.

While I do not want to be a psychotherapist, I love the *situation* of intimacy between two individuals, one guiding, the other needing guidance, focusing on a subject at hand that both continue to discover in conversation. *That* is my idea of making a living, and that is just what I do. About ten hours a week I engage in just such conversations. They are too intense for me to do more and still leave time for my writing. My students, for lack of a better word, are often women at crucial junctures in their lives, and one of the issues at hand is how they are going to get the time and privacy to write. Many of the middle-aged students have husbands and children whom they have "put first," but the younger single women also feel challenged at making this time for themselves. And as I think about the

. . . .

men who study with me, I realize that this issue is prominent for them as well. It also has to do with bargaining for time from their families and jobs.

So, with both subtle and obvious means, I model ways to private time and space. Some of this modeling comes in the form of appointments I schedule, sometimes many months in advance, allowing that goal to develop on the horizon in more sophisticated landscape than I inhabited with my learning disabled adolescent students, but similar terrain: you can't develop goals until you claim who you are, and writers know best who they are when they are alone. Somehow they must find hours alone in which to accomplish what they need for that appointment.

The type of privacy I enjoy with my students is a lovely, boundaried intimacy, the focus of hours on a subject that emerges and changes with our wandering glances and thoughts. It is a form of mental writing, a form of concentration, and it has the classic shape of mentoring whether the model is Obi-Wan Kenobi and his student Luke Skywalker or Nadia Boulanger and her student Louise Talma: one experienced person and one less experienced person embark on a private tour of a designated terrain, the experienced one noticing the landscape with a trained eye yet remaining focused on the learner, the learner thriving in the focus and gradually shifting his or her eye to the whole vista. This is the intimacy of Dante and Virgil, or Heidi and her grandfather, or Arthur and Merlin, or Elizabeth Bishop and Marianne Moore. All the Zenlike lessons lead to the moment when the rules no longer apply and the student pulls the sword from the stone. In other words, the student claims her own. The mentoring intimacy then dissolves, although the memory of the private lessons seems lifelong, intensifying as the student turns into the experienced one who must take on that opposite role.

This type of learning is a lush form of privacy because the boundaries are as clear as garden walks and the growth is as measurable—and as ravishing and unpredictable—as the seasonal growth of flora for a knowledgeable gardener. The gardening metaphor is completely apt because once you prepare ground and plant the young plant you have simply got to leave it alone and wait for it to grow. Of course you water and mulch and do the appropriate chores, but your job as the gardener is to watch and wait, to encourage, and *not to interfere*. The student, the flora, must grow in its own private way. That is growth's substance and habit. Intrusion, breaking the privacy, damages the plant. I feel completely responsible toward my students when I turn away from them to do my own writing. I am not simply a teacher. I am, foremost, a writer, with my own books and projects. I do not return phone calls in an instant. I do return them, but after I have finished my creative work. I keep the world out, and my students know that after the lesson they become the world. I turn toward my private world of making just as they must turn toward their own. It is Polly's lesson with the spoiled parts of the peel removed.

Although privacy conjures up an image of sitting in a garden, secrecy provokes an image of overturning a rock, spying on the wet maggotty squirming world of its underside. *The Secret Garden*, most girls remember, was actually a walled garden, locked because of a death. A girl finds the key, after a crow has shown it to her, *unlocks* the garden and begins renewing it with two boys, Colin, an invalid, and Dickon. The minute she unlocks the garden it becomes private. Although walled—if one went in uninvited one would be an intruder—it is no longer secret. The private garden nurtures the souls of the beings inside its walls, to the point of Colin's health returning. Above all it is creative. The children recreate what once was there, and the garden shows a healthy resurgence. Privacy always suggests freedom, while secrecy closes down possibility.

I had a bit of a private garden myself. In the golden summertimes, I went to live with my grandparents in the hamlet of LaGrange, down the road from where my mother grew up. I had no responsibilities, and entered a kind of shock of displacement, which led to that requisite state of childhood growth: boredom. Only privacy can generate the glory of this boredom. One day, lying on my back in an apple orchard, I was too bored even to daydream. Looking up into the tangle of gray branches above me, a word came to me: "latticework." It was a latticework of branches. *Pretty good,* I thought, *better write that down.* Privacy at my grandparents didn't mean shutting out the world as I handled infinite numbers of activities, it meant being all alone in the world, observing it, and taking it in, reforming it, and putting it out again, not a wall, but a lattice between me and the world. Why read a book for escape as my mother did, when you can escape and write a book?

But so much for mental chambers. On to the bedchamber.

Because my parents paid me no mind, I spent hours alone in the house when they weren't there and as I paraded naked in front of the full-length mirror of my doorless room I thought of a new word to write down: "ripe." I lay down and learned to masturbate. When I was fifteen or so I had my first orgasm while my parents were in the living room not twenty feet away, so occupied with themselves that I had no fear, even though

.   .   .   .

I felt for sure the bed was shaking. I thought I was having some sort of heart attack I wouldn't survive. But I did. And I tried it again the next night. And the next. Using the privacy skill—being present without being present—I became a sexual being under their noses.

As I drew a bubble bath for myself and my boyfriend, who became my husband decades later, and with whom I have achieved a blissful state of married solitude, I drew it with the confidence that even if we were to be discovered, my parents were too preoccupied to do much about it. Years later my mother told me that during an argument with my father she reached absently beneath the chair cushion (half turning away again) only to find my bra and underpants buried there. (My boyfriend and I had made a mad dash to the backyard when their car came up the driveway.) She never told. That's part of my privacy legacy, too.

By the time I left for college I had a luxurious sense of my own sexuality, all because I spent so much time in my own head enjoying myself. It's fun to be private! And to have private parts, too.

The up side of not having intrusive sexual value judgments thrown at you is that sex is your own. Your own smell, your own taste, your own touch. I'm not saying I went on to have a perfect sex life. But it had a perfect beginning. And so did my imaginative life. I know I grew up in a so-called domestic hell, but as a sexual being and a writer, I was given an excellent, excellent start.

At college privacy began to play a literary role in my life. The poets in vogue were the Confessionals, Anne Sexton among them. She was the Confessional I liked least, but who, of course, influenced me the most. I detested the way she jumped from metaphor to metaphor, not staying with an image for more than a line or two. I hated the way my professor, the one who defined metaphor as disappearance through a mirror, pointed to her picture and said breathlessly, "She was a model, you know." When Sexton visited our campus, she descended on the party thrown for her and stalked, mockingly, each of the flustered, flattered, uneasy English professors who were her prey. Finally, Bengal-tiger style, she closed her jaws over our local antelope of a novelist who later became famous in another country and is still probably dining out on his Night with Anne. But he was only a throwaway line for her. Her raw need—she was drunk—appalled me. But after I read Diane Wood Middlebrook's *Anne Sexton: A Biography*, I wrote the only letter I've ever written to the *New York Times Book Review*, in complete support of Middlebrook's use of Sexton's psychiatrist's tapes, and in complete support of the psychiatrist for releasing them. That was one biography I felt sure did not invade Sexton's privacy because Sexton was a poet who actually built boundaries by unloosing secrets.

Sexton wrote straight out about subjects that were supposed to be kept under wraps: love affairs, abortions, her loathsome fifties wifehood. In a paradoxical way, by revealing secrets she was protecting her privacy—insofar as privacy creates identity. When I considered what I would take for my subjects as a poet, I knew that my sexuality would be one of them. That, in another way, was what I found beneath the latticework of branches. Why had I never read a poem about masturbating? I would write one. (In fact I must have read such a poem—Anne Sexton had written one, but I conveniently forgot it, as conveniently as I forgot her intense formalism in my hatred of her metaphorical flightiness.) I liked poems with distinctly developed, sustained conceits; Sexton was undeveloped, inchoate, always becoming. The voice kept sliding, disappearing as the speaker slipped behind the mirror of metaphor, like my . . . my . . . oh dear.

Born nine years after my mother, Sexton shared some of Polly's coloring; both had dark hair and a bold, tanned look. Sexton learned to write poetry not at a university, but from watching afternoon television, where a poet came on the local channel and taught how to write a poem, like teaching watercolors to the Sunday-painting crowd. If my mother had ever learned how to write a poem, that would probably have been how she'd have done it, too. Aside from my wanting to distance myself from my mother, I also wanted to "write like a man," which I thought meant from strength, or at least not like a flibbertigibbet, or like a suicide. Yet I pored over *Transformations,* Sexton's book of poem fairy tales, when it came out, connecting intimately with that metamorphosing fairy-tale world, where toads turned back into princes and imaginary jewels became real fortunes.

Why, I wonder, was Sexton called a Confessional poet when Allen Ginsberg could howl out the details of his sex life and be called avant-garde? Why could Frank O'Hara write about a party while sitting at the party itself, naming names, and be called New York School? I didn't get it then, and still don't, except perhaps that Ginsberg and O'Hara, by their homosexuality, had already "trespassed" in critics' views, and Sexton was a traditionalist verse-wise, who trespassed in subject matter only. Sexton had sex built into her very name. Her style, I noticed, as I have noticed about other women poets who use their own experience (whose experiences should they use?), was often preceded by the adverb "merely." Anne Sexton was merely confessional. Great warnings were sent out to me by

.   .   .   .

friends and teachers that merely writing the stories of your life in poetry was not poetry at all. Poetry required transformation of experience, not just blurting it out, unmade as a bed from which you've just leapt. *Don't be like her.* Well! I sniffed, insulted. I never intended to be like her at all. I was going to be like Emily Dickinson, that private poet Polly taught me to be. Or like Marianne Moore, reconstructing a world through shadow, allusion—and illusion.

But a poet's subjects are given to her. Like our bodies our subjects are inherited, genetic, almost on the substance level of biology and fate. Our only choice is how to employ that given, and this is the realm of technique. I think of Sexton's formal style as an answer to the fugue states she is reported to have entered, both on the couch and in the course of daily life. A psychological fugue state is unbounded, one's personality amorphous. A poem, especially the intensely formal poems with rhyme schemes and specified line lengths that Sexton chose to write, supplies boundaries. And boundaries, by surrounding a subject, even a wild one (especially a wild one!), reinforce privacy.

Technique can obscure subject or reveal it. Obscuring techniques never appealed to me personally because I could only learn from what I examined and brought to light. Years later, when I was about the same age as Sexton would have been at that party—thirty-eight—I had an abortion, and I wrote about it, because not to write about it meant keeping it secret, and through writing about it I felt I would understand my action better. Sometimes to expose an intimate detail about your life does not destroy privacy. It builds it. Exposing a secret, coming clean so to speak, allows a subject to step into the light while the former secret keeper steps back, the walls of the self rebuilt, since secrecy tears them down. "The brief pregnancy showed us,/ its father and me, " I wrote in a poem called "The Ghost,"

these choices, not shriveling

but choice alive with choice, for as our brief
parenthood dislodged our parents' anchor
and set us anxiously adrift, more
of our lost natures appeared.

To bring a secret to light is not the same as destroying your privacy. A so-called confession fosters a sense of the personal boundaries that are requisite for a zone of privacy. There is a way in which not speaking about a secret subject comes to feel dishonest. Dishonesty is the corner-stone of secrecy. Forthrightness is freeing—freeing especially because the truth allows the teller truth's integrity. To honor yourself by telling the truth is to make yourself as substantial as telling falsehoods makes you insubstantial, even invisible. This is why, private being that I am, I found my blabbermouth side and became a tell-all poet and memoirist—and I did not find it inconsistent with my privating.

I haven't published anything that I felt intruded on other people's pri-vacy—and haven't heard murmurs to the contrary from my friends or ex-lovers. Forthrightness leads to discovery, and discovery to defining the social boundaries required for privacy—maybe I should call this "trued" privacy. Although my mother developed the habit of depending on her best friend to read my work first and to let my mother know if she could take the shock (something like a queen who employs a poison taster), in the end nothing I said breached our relationship. While Polly did not be-lieve in washing your dirty laundry in public, she believed in truth.

It interests me to note that around the same time Sexton was dragging that novelist off for her late-night snack, I was touring the tables in the college snack bar with an envelope, collecting for a friend's abortion. This was in the days before Roe versus Wade, and Sexton's poem about her abortion, simply called "The Abortion," is about a trip to Pennsylvania to an abortion doctor, also pre-Roe. The legal debates about abortion in this country sparked a new interest in privacy—privacy defining a woman's right to choose.

Confessionalism in poetry—which is substantially composed of the telling of the stories of two women's lives, Sylvia Plath's and Anne Sex-ton's—flourished at the same time as female privacy rights surfaced in the courts. It is the underpinning of women's issues and women's lives that has brought privacy into national and literary discourse. One aspect of this discourse is the pitting of poets who write discreetly or sometimes in disguise against poets who write more nakedly and accessibly. Critics, who are always in disguise because they are always behind a text, tend to mistake those who tell all for slobs who don't know what art really is. Therefore, poets like Sexton get drubbed, even by sympathizers like me. My consciously chosen favorite, a poet both critics and poets adore, was fiercely reticent Elizabeth Bishop. She was an observer, whereas Sexton posed as the one observed. But observers do not break apart worlds as Sexton aesthetically did, breaking subject taboos. Bishop, who protected her lesbian life and the shame of her mother's insanity and institutionali-

. . . .

zation at all costs, lived a lot longer. But interestingly, both Sexton and Bishop shared the same goal (they also shared an addiction, alcohol) and that is accuracy—the discovery of the truth as they deeply perceived it, usually a truth about a situation for Sexton, and about a place or an animal observed for Bishop.

I have the feeling Marianne Moore would have gagged at Anne Sexton's poetry (though I don't know for sure). And Moore's successor, Elizabeth Bishop, would never have dreamed of going to Sexton's territory of menstruation and masturbation. Yet the famously retiring Bishop used the infamously flamboyant Sexton's construction at the end of "The Abortion" at the end of her own magnificent villanelle, "One Art."

Sexton spends six stanzas describing the landscape, suggesting that a pregnancy will be terminated, but never stating so outright. Finally, in the last tercet she writes

> Yes, woman, such logic will lead
> to loss without death. Or say what you meant,
> you coward . . . this baby that I bleed. (1961)

Fifteen years later Bishop writes in her last stanza:

> —Even losing you (the joking voice, a gesture
> I love) I shan't have lied. It's evident
> the art of losing isn't hard to master
> though it may look like (*Write* it!) like disaster. (1976)

Both writers, the inhibitor and the exhibitor, exhort themselves to tell the truth. In both poems the writer is a witness to experience who urges herself as the experiencer to "Write it!" (Bishop) or "say what you meant, you coward," (Sexton). Each poet divides her voice into both mentor and mentee, into teacher and student, guide and innocent, each creating an intimate conversation with herself, and in the privacy of this conversation comes to the same lifesaving conclusion, to write the truth. To state specifically what one really means, according to Sexton and Bishop, germinates poetry itself. Truth always forms its own integrity, separate from whatever emotional and social context that generates it. Truth lifts experience out of the personal into the universal, exploding secrecy, and by doing so grants the personality of the writer her integrity, her privacy, even if she has just used an intimate detail of her own life. This is the age-old concept of everywoman, and it is the thin line that every writer who uses her own

experience in her writing walks, even two poets as utterly at the far ends of
the spectrum as Bishop and Sexton.

Shearing off the secret from the private first exposes deceit, then allows
the subsequent revealed integrity of the truth its modesty. For the truth *is*
modest. However once bold or once buried, one's profoundly held truth
possesses modesty because by its nature it can't be either underestimating
or grandiose. It is itself. It is bounded, and that which is self-contained is
private. This brings me back to *The Secret Garden,* which in fact becomes
a private garden. The sour little protagonist, Mary Lennox, finds the key
that unlocks the garden door, and this opening up of the secret place allows the family secret (the reason it was locked) to be aired. Her cousin
Colin's mother (Mary's aunt) was killed by a falling branch of the tree in
the garden, and his father (Mary's uncle) was cast into such deep mourning that he locked the garden and abandoned his house and his duty toward his infant son, who became chronically ill, virtually locked up in his
bedroom by servants and his doctor.

The banishment of the secret allows the walls of the garden to reas-
sume their relation to a door that opens and closes, balancing interior and
exterior in a well-proportioned privacy. Colin becomes well. Mary becomes a moral being, aware that there are others in the world beside herself—and therefore capable of love. And all this upon learning the truth.
Truth creates privacy, I say to you from behind the lattice that separates
me from my neighbor who has blessedly gone in for lunch, and that provides the entrance to my own garden, my floral ocean, from which I cast
out to sea.

An Inside Story

. . . .

by
CATHLEEN MEDWICK

I am an intruder. I write about people's houses. I make my living by enter-ing private spaces, penetrating rooms furnished to meet personal needs, laying bare secrets of domestic life. The odd thing is, some people are only too happy to let me in. First they show me their "public" rooms, the ones that only blaze with brilliance when other people are there to admire the owners' decorating skills, or their ability to purchase the skills of others. These rooms have no secrets. But then, almost inevitably, the owners take me into the recesses of the house, up winding staircases and down care-fully appointed hallways, until we reach what might be called the "pri-vate" rooms. There, all doors open before me, as in some fairy tale in which the curious child obtains a magic key, or a princess is ushered into the realm of an enchanted prince. I enter bedrooms where a monumental bed with crisp white linens and fluffed pillows retains no imprint of a human form. I examine pristine bathrooms without odors, where not even tiny droplets of water cling to the marble basins. Occasionally, I see a daughter's room with armchairs upholstered to match the draperies, and dolls arranged stiffly, like corpses, on carefully dusted shelves.

I know this bedroom isn't really private. It is, like Cecily's diary in Wilde's *The Importance of Being Earnest,* "simply a very young girl's record of her own thoughts and impressions, and consequently meant for publication." Not her own thoughts and impressions, of course—not yet—but those of her parents, the design equivalent of a perfect childhood. This room, like all the others, is not so much decorated as ordained. Still, I feel vaguely guilty about being here, and not only because I'm trying to sniff out clues—because my job requires me to find out something,

95

anything, about how life is lived in this place. I feel ashamed because I know that somewhere, hidden from my view, are the real rooms this family lives in, rooms soaked and soiled with humanity; and that those are the ones I want to invade.

At the same time, I want to step outside and gently close the doors. I want to hand back whatever secrets I've extracted, with a gentle word of warning about admitting strangers into the home. I can't imagine opening up my own house, the reflection of my chaotic heart, to anyone. I remember being appalled, when I visited my neighbor, to find that her kitchen window afforded a full frontal view of my bedroom. Still, I could hardly blame her for looking in. As a girl I used to peer at night, and from a respectable distance, into lit windows in my neighborhood, and wonder if the people inside were as happy as I imagined they were. But "wonder" is too cool a word. Desire is also present, the urge to enter a forbidden paradise and make a home there. The novelist Michael Cunningham describes this impulse as "a chaos of yearning." How can anyone, much less a restless and lonely child, resist the promise of a locked door?

It's no surprise that people who value their privacy put up walls and fences and banks of shrubbery to block the view of voyeurs like me. What is surprising is how many people open their houses and lives to public scrutiny. A recent article in the *New York Times* described the urban hobby of spying on neighbors who don't bother with window shades, and even place their beds in front of windows, so that their most intimate encounters can be widely shared. So-called "MacMansions" in suburbia, with ample front lawns as flat as airstrips, are fully exposed to passersby. Moguls, hand in hand with their decorators, engage in "shelter porn" by allowing glossy house magazines to display their wealth while coyly concealing their identities. The lure of publicity usually trumps the desire for privacy these days.

But for those of us who want to see what's behind the curtain, such displays are minimally alluring. We long for the unguarded moment when we can see what's not meant to be seen. Vermeer must have felt that way; he painted interiors that looked as pristine as the insides of seashells. These were private rooms where women (men in these paintings generally seem incidental) practiced homely occupations such as writing letters, embroidering, or picking out tunes on a spinet. Vermeer seldom let his models look him in the eye. When he did, they always looked a little surprised. He opened windows, but only enough to let in the light. His subjects are contained, as one critic put it, within "an envelope of quiet air"; it's impossi-

. . . .

ble to imagine street noise, arguments, the cries of children penetrating these hushed rooms. So privacy and tranquillity are allied in Vermeer's paintings, even though they can't have been in the world he represented. What we think we see, when we spy on those painted lives, is frozen moments of private time. What we are more likely seeing is Vermeer's longing for a life he never lived. Citizen of bustling Delft, overworked and debt-ridden father of ten, Vermeer must have relished privacy wherever he found it. And it hardly seems accidental that this yearning manifested itself as art at a time in European history when the very idea of domestic privacy was just beginning to come into focus.

During the middle ages, members of a family usually lived in a single room, along with the servants, the relatives, and sometimes the livestock. In such cramped quarters, and even in the more spacious houses of the aristocracy, it wouldn't have occurred to anyone that a room should be "decorated" with furniture, or contain any more of it than was strictly functional. A table would be moved to the center of the room when it was time to eat; chairs backed against the wall when not in use. A bed would be pulled out when it was time to sleep. Four or more people in a bed was not an anomaly, and it was not unusual for people to curl up at night in a chest, cushioned by the household linens. Sex was more or less public, and so was bathing. Defecation occurred where it would. "As the self-consciousness of medieval people was spare," wrote John Lukacs in an essay called "The Bourgeois Interior," "the interiors of their houses were bare, including the halls of nobles and of kings. The interior furniture of houses appeared together with the interior furniture of minds."

In the Renaissance, when explorers worked not only with telescopes but with mirrors, the works of Erasmus and Montaigne, among others, led to a flowering of interest in the workings of the human spirit and intellect. With that came a new interiority, and a new vocabulary to describe it: words like "conscience," "self-esteem," and "melancholy" became common currency. Religious movements stressing the importance of private prayer, as opposed to public worship, gained strength throughout the European continent. Even in Catholic Spain, spiritual life turned inward, and reformers like Saint Teresa of Avila encouraged nuns to seek enclosure, both within the convent and within the soul. Teresa urged her nuns to imagine the soul as a castle with many rooms that they could enter by working their way inward, through prayer, from the crowded and noisy courtyard to the central room where they could be alone with God.

Secular life afforded less inspiring opportunities for seclusion, though people could take refuge in walled gardens, with their hidden benches and shaded groves. Those who could afford to have more than a single room in their houses might retreat to the chamber, dominated by an impressively curtained bed. Married couples could find some degree of privacy there—though the servants were always nearby (sometimes close enough to hear conversation and more), and the chamber was also a place to entertain company. Life was still lived publicly, and it was some time before a feeling for intimate private spaces—what Mario Praz, in *An Illustrated History of Interior Decoration,* calls *Stimmung*—would be fully realized in the arrangements of domestic life.

By the seventeenth century, especially in the cities of northern Europe, people were beginning to occupy their houses in a different way. The bourgeois home had come unyoked from the workplace and was becoming a place of private recreation and repose. Women deftly managed their households and their children, who no longer went to work at a young age but stayed home and were educated. Couples took pride in acquiring furniture, which signaled prosperity, but also the delights of domesticity. A growing respect for family life created an atmosphere of intimacy—*Stimmung*—that Vermeer could convey as a music lesson, or as a wash of amber light on a woman's brow.

I grew up thinking of privacy as not so much a right as a necessity. My father, though before a fiercely private man, installed intercoms in every room of our house, so he could summon his children and also, if the mood struck him, listen in on our conversations. So I understood early in life that privacy was a rare and desirable state, not easily achieved. I saw the difference between the house I lived in, a ranch with chill, sparsely furnished rooms (the formal living-room sofas had knobs that could cut flesh), and the house of my imagination, a late-Victorian construct stuffed with gently worn furniture of no particular venue or value, and plenty of nooks and alcoves. There were, of course, no picture windows to break the illusion of complete containment. A person could curl up on a window seat and gaze out with pleasure, largely because no one could gaze in. What could be safer than a room with a one-way view?

I understood even then that privacy was not solitude: I could be solitary in the woods behind my house, or on a deserted stretch of beach. A hermit could be solitary on a mountaintop. But privacy required walls, and not just physical barriers like the fortifications surrounding medieval castles. I thought that Proust's fabled cork-lined walls were really fortifications; they provided silence and protection, but not serenity. The walls I needed had to provide comfort and reassurance. "The house, the residence," wrote Immanuel Kant, "is the only rampart against the dread of nothingness, darkness, and the obscurity of the past." One proof of this was that haunted houses were always permeable: Catherine Earnshaw's ghostly hand reaching through the window; that bat flying into Mina's bedroom at Dracula's castle; the Red Death stalking through the hermetically sealed rooms of the palace.

Of course, I knew that walls could also be prisons. Rapunzel's tower. Catherine Sloper's townhouse on Washington Square. Miss Havisham's webby residence. Nora's doll's house. Manderley. It was hard not to notice how the prisoners were usually women, immured within their houses by their fathers, their husbands, or their own intractable misery. Men's imprisonment, it seemed, was usually a kind of exile—the Tower for St. Thomas More, Reading Gaol for Oscar Wilde. But women's prisons were almost invariably domestic, which made them much more frightening. What should have been protection turned out to be incarceration. The beautiful room was revealed to be a torture chamber. This was the kind of imprisonment Virginia Woolf meant when she talked about the long suppression of women. There was no such thing as privacy without freedom. A room of one's own had value because one could leave it at will.

When I was in my late teens, my mother moved into her own bedroom. It was really my sister's room, but my sister had moved out long before in a kind of rage; there had been no containing her. After a while, my mother began to sleep in that room, and then to sit there during the day, reading novels at the desk by the window. I remember her extolling *Howards End*, a book that struck me at the time as irrelevant. She also began to write short stories, beginning the long slow process of extricating herself from a house and a marriage that suffocated her. But her death from cancer, shortly after I graduated from college, botched her escape.

Mine was easier. That house had never really held me, and I never missed it after I left. I moved into a succession of apartments, always gravitating toward whatever interior was smallest and most intimate. I had one apartment that was basement level, with bars on the windows and no way out except through the kitchen. That seemed safe enough, though privacy was occasionally an issue: once I saw two gnarled hands on the sidewalk outside the bay window—the old man who lived upstairs was getting ready to peer beneath the shades.

When I moved to an apartment one flight up, with the man who would become my husband, I had what might be described as a spacial crisis. I didn't mind being on the parlor floor, with it's genteel bay window and view of the other brownstones along the street. But the height of the ceilings threw me; I'd always sensed that somehow I didn't have enough personal gravity to keep me grounded in the world. Because the apartment wasn't large, we used his furniture, which he had acquired in one indifferent swoop: a garden-variety Eames chair, a large brown waffle-weave sofa and, because these were the '70s, an ample, ugly shag rug—all functional and characterless. My furniture, by contrast, had been carefully culled from the basement of a secondhand store, and every piece of it was something I could love. I always chose dark wood, and preferred curvilinear pieces (straight edges made me nervous), small-scaled like me. These objects turned my basement room into something like a turn-of-the-century sitting room. It had been (at least when I remembered to pull the shades) a private place; whereas this apartment, tall and narrow, was almost public. Sitting at the table in the bay window in the evenings was like being in a lighthouse; people on the street below waved to us as they passed by.

Moving to the distant suburbs years later didn't help, even though we had long ago scrapped the Eames chair and the sofa (the rug had been a casualty of our incontinent sheepdog). This place, a Victorian farmhouse on a quiet street, should have offered the consolations I needed. But something was still wrong. For one thing, it wasn't sheltered. Trees and bushes had kept their distance, so by day the sun could invade the bedroom without hindrance, and by night the windows revealed a wall of blackness— the few houses we could see turned their lights out early. I realized that what I missed was the human presence: houses near enough so that the slopes of their roofs and the lamplight behind their shades were visible. To relish my privacy, I needed company. I needed to feel less alone.

Of all the houses I've visited, in my career as a journalist or spy, one stands out as having everything its owner needed to combine privacy and livability, a state that could be described as hominess. She was an eighty-year-old widow whose husband, an artist, had died almost a decade earlier. She had remained alone in what had once been their summerhouse on Long Island, an eighteenth-century gray shingle cottage with no outstanding architectural features, but with pleasantly low ceilings and windows whose wavy glass admitted the light in currents. The downstairs rooms were airy but not bare; the tiny upstairs bedrooms were reached by a narrow stair-

. . . .

way. There was hardly a distinctive piece of furniture in the place, which made it a peculiar choice for the house magazine where I worked. (In fact the owner's husband had tacked cotton fabric around slabs of rubber for the living-room sofa, and jerry-built a lamp from his children's Tinker-toys.) But there was color, a warm yellow painted kitchen floor with a red rocker sitting on it, and here and there ceilings painted the deep azure of a Sicilian sky, which had reminded the artist of home.

What the house contained though, mainly, was presences. Almost every object could tell a story of a friend who had passed through, or a child who had outgrown everything except memory. These things had entered the building over time and wiggled into their places on the walls or countertops, so that nothing had been prearranged. No guests had been expected, because humanity meandered through these rooms in a fairly constant stream. Fewer people visited now, but the owner couldn't look out the window without seeing a tree that someone had planted for her a generation earlier, or the low cinder-block walls her friends would sit on for a barbecue in the garden. People who did come by these days felt instantly at home because the house made room for them. By passing through, they became part of its history, which was not official, as in most historically accurate old houses, but personal. No one could invade the owner's privacy, because she was never alone.

I've always hated houses with signs that said "Private" outside their gates. Those houses seem to dare intruders to violate them: "This way to the pot of gold!" I know one editor of a shelter magazine who has clambered over fences and slinked through carefully planted gardens and clipped front lawns because she had to see what someone meant to hide from her. Privacy can't be achieved through exclusivity; only physical distance can. I don't think it's accidental that so many people who cherish their privacy are intensely sociable. They replenish themselves by going inside their houses, so that they can go back out again. The people with "Private" signs, by contrast, seem blatantly public: why else would they broadcast their inaccessibility to the world? Their houses tend to be decorated with an impersonality that is frightening, as it's meant to be, underscoring the message that the furnishings are off-limits. They are by invitation only, meant to be admired—assessed—but not enjoyed. And it's a waste of time in such surroundings to try to assess the character of the owner, because every emotional fingerprint has been wiped away.

I reported on one house that was decorated almost entirely with precious English and American antiques. It was a house that rewarded every attention with what would could be described, in human terms, as a fixed smile. There was to be no sprawling in the Chippendale side chairs, stiffly backed against the wall. Perching with a glass of water on a silk-upholstered Hepplewhite settee was a profoundly unsettling experience. Eating at the impressively pedigreed dining table was unthinkable; then again, I wasn't invited. The owner was not at home.

"It has been said," writes Praz by way of introduction to his classic, and highly romantic, book on interiors, "that just as the body—according to the Swedenborgian philosophy—is nothing but a projection, an expansion of the soul, so for the soul, the house where it lives is nothing but an expansion of its own body." But some houses are really soulless. It is disturbing to be inside them, even when their furnishings are beautiful, because they have no humanity, which makes them monstrous. "The interior," writes Walter Benjamin, "is the sheath of the private man. To inhabit means to leave traces." Echoes. Fingerprints. I once visited a house whose owner, a canny woman in her late seventies, was a collector of priceless Impressionist paintings. What I liked, though, was the glass jar of cheese sticks by the Bonnard; the packs of Marlboros stockpiled in the end table beneath the Degas; the stack of *TV Guides* beneath the Mary Cassatt. In the private rooms of the heart that I was secretly visiting, the most luxurious objects were the pillows, embroidered with humorous slogans, plumped on a white divan beneath the Renoir.

"The surroundings become a museum of the soul," Praz writes, "an archive of its experiences; it reads in them its own history." In my own house, for ten years now, I've been watching that history develop. Well, I've aged, and the house has, too. A few comfortably used pieces of furniture have crept in unexpectedly and bumped less sturdy pieces away—a kind of Darwinian approach to decorating. Objects have jumped from room to room about as frequently as I've felt restless or energetic: that is, often enough to disorient my husband and children, who are still reasonably comfortable in this floating world. I haven't quite stopped looking into other people's windows. But now and then I see, surprisingly, that amber light in mine.

The Devil's Secretary

. . . .

by

YUSEF KOMUNYAKAA

A year ago, someone broke into my apartment. He left greasy handprints on the door and its metal frame; great effort and violence had been used, which left the frame bent—a template of desperation.

Mentioning the incident to three people, each asked in their own way, "Don't you feel violated?"

"Yes," I said.

The thief had emptied out a small inlaid box that held cuff links I'd collected through the years; a pocket watch, silver buttons, old coins. He also took my laptop: a research tool I'd purchased so my friends, fellow researchers, Raddy and Louise, could enter data on Marcus Christian, a Louisiana writer, archivist, poet, and historian—we were attempting to bring his literary contributions to life.

The thief also appropriated my leather jacket. I could see him wrapping the laptop in the jacket, emerging from the building, and walking out onto the streets—the stage where he was soon to be a different man by appearances, wearing my jacket made in Australia and laying down bucks from the sale of the laptop. He had effectively raided my private goods to effect his persona out there in public.

Don't you feel violated? ran inside my head. Papers and books lay scattered across the apartment. He had taken everything that shines. The door had stood open. Was he drug-crazed, hurting for a fix? Was that it? What had driven him to risk his life? The Devil had been busy.

I was out of town. The residents in the building had noticed the open door and notified the manager and police department. A friend had been called, and she informed me that the police spent hours in my apartment, dusting the place for fingerprints, trying to discern a modus operandi, or were they going through my personal effects?

Violated?

The thief had spent a few minutes there, probably running out of his skin as he ravaged the two small rooms.

Violated? Violence. Violent. In America, at times it seems that violence against property gets more attention than violence against a person.

As the cops sifted through my notes, letters, snapshots, bills, files, resumes, and revised poems, notes in the margins of books, everything in disarray, as they attempted to create some logic to the clutter, who is now violating whom?

I grew up in a place where one's privacy was almost sacred—so much so it was taken for granted.

With four brothers and one sister, in a three-bedroom home, we grew up with a sense of privacy—lines that we couldn't cross: "Always a knock on the door before turning the knob." "Never touch anything that isn't yours, without an okay first." "Don't eavesdrop." "Don't be nosy." "Curiosity killed the cat."

To know is to be responsible: "Boy, you knew and didn't tell me. I'm not going to beat him for what he did, but I am going to wear your hide out for not telling me. You knew."

In retrospect, this issue about privacy seems like a mixed message, or confused.

The busybody or nosy person didn't survive in our neighborhood: "Cora Mae never could mind her own business. There she is kneeling on the floor as if she's at a prayer meeting, peeking through the keyhole of the front door, spying on two jokers arguing in the street. Now, the Lord don't like ugly, but the Devil loves it."

"She's on her knees. One of the jokers pulls out a Colt .45 and fires it at the other and misses. But he shoots Cora Mae dead in the right eye. And she's on the floor dead as a doornail."

Many houses are built like stages. The picture window seems more like a transparent screen. Or, a display case. Mainly, things are envied when seen in the erasure of privacy through display.

Private property defines us; it tells the world who we are. It gives us power. I remember hearing the following statement: "If you shoot a thief outside your door, you better pull him into your house." So, private property can mean the difference between protection and murder. If it possesses such power, logic says that we dream to display it, flaunting its

. . . .

illusion of power. "Do you think she would be wearing that dress if the rest of us couldn't see it?" "Do you think he'd own that house or car if we were blind?"

What is privacy's value? Is it something we humans crave initially? Do children desire privacy when they become conscious of their space as separate human beings, does it define them? Or, is the concept of privacy taught? Are they acculturated into attitudes about privacy?

The scientist reveals. The artist reveals. The prophet reveals. Creativity seems to always involve some form of revelation—a kind of disrobing, a facing up to, and seeing into. Writers reveal. And sometimes those such as family, friends, lovers, fellow workers, and so forth, may feel skittish. They don't want their lives to drive the plot. But nothing's ironclad: there are people who will attempt to insinuate themselves into a painting, a photograph, the block of granite a sculptor works on, the novel, the film, or the poem. Their privacy becomes a commodity: sold for money, the idea of money, or notoriety (which sometimes also translates into dollar signs). No shame.

If privacy didn't exist as a concept, and/or principle, would it still have value? Some go to great limits to protect their privacy. We have heard about Thomas Pynchon and J.D. Salinger. And it seems to mention their names is to invade their privacy. We have terms such as *hermit* and *recluse*. Of course, in western society, both are weird or negative. Yet, solitude seems positive when it is associated with something spiritual in western society. In this sense many of us are in awe of the east.

■ ■ ■

The impingement on privacy pulsates throughout Shakespeare as an act of violence against nature. But we only have to return to his "Dark Lady" sonnet series to see how complicated this is. Consider the mere speculation surrounding the woman's identity (or a young man's). It is like a soap-operaish roll call: some dark-skinned woman in a Clerkenwell brothel; the Moor discussed by Gobbo in *The Merchant of Venice*; "Lucy Negro, Abbess de Clerkenwell" at Gray's Inn on Christmas in 1594; Mary Fitton, or Mall, the pale Maid of Honor to the Queen; or is the Dark Lady an emotional composite, a courtesan of the psyche? In this sense, can literature violate one's privacy through conjecture and guesswork on the part of readers?

In literature (or for its creators), rumors of lust and flesh have long been grist for the mill. And, in some cases, as is true of Alexander Pushkin, rumors have ushered in an author's demise. Like a character in his novel in verse, Eugene Onegin, he was shot in a duel. Before, as Henri Troyot writes in the biography *Pushkin,* "Pushkin received an anonymous letter informing him that his wife had met d'Anthes alone in the home of a friend and that he was now, technically and irrefutably, a cuckold. Pushkin immediately asked Natalya where she had been, and Natalya, panic-stricken and in despair, told him all and wept copiously on his shoulder. . . ." Of course, we know Pushkin's challenge of a duel (not the first) ended his life—an elongated soap opera that snowy day on January 27, 1837, at Chernaya Rechka.

■ ■ ■

There are people who consciously and unconsciously attempt to align themselves with celebrity, often purposefully divulging real and imagined affairs, dreamt-up collisions, or soft torture. Such revelations are, in fact, exhibitionism: all have witnessed the tossing of underwear onto the stage where Elvis Presley and Muddy Waters performed.

When I wrote the poem "1984" (Orwell wanted to call his novel *1948*), I kept erasing the words and putting them back. They sounded weird, though I had heard that the monument to J. Edgar Hoover is one endless system of computer terminals and whatnot. Back then, these lines which began this poem frightened me:

> The year burns an icon
> into the blood. Birdlime
> discolors the glass domes
> & roof beams grow shaky as old men
> in the lobby of Heartbreak Hotel.
> Purple oxide gas lamps light
> the way out of this paradise.
> We laugh behind masks and lip-sync Cobol.
> We're transmitters for pigeons
> with microphones in their heads.

I knew about PsyOps, how this group of military men believe the United States could win a war without rockets, M16s, planes, or throw-away grenade launchers. The media. Technology. Subliminal messages as maps of the future. I was afraid of sounding paranoid, a worshiper of conspiracy theories.

. . . .

Onel de Guzman was seventeen years old in 1984, and could hardly have been daydreaming of writing a program that would: "steal and retrieve Internet accounts of the victim's computer." The Internet didn't seem to exist in the minds of everyday citizens. "E-mail Password Sender Trojan" would have sounded like a line from a language poem back in the Pleistocene mid-1980s. De Guzman's blueprint for the Love Bug Virus may have caused over $15 billion in damages around the world. These college-generated cells of Love Bugs commit electronic vandalism against the industrialized world, creating cybercops who make the lingo of J. Edgar Hoover's era sound like baby talk. Loss of control over money and space is generating some nationalistic tough talk that has little to do with the concept of privacy. This has more to do with the trading of commodities and capital. So, these hackers from the Philippines, China, Serbia, Pakistan, or God only knows where, trying to rise to the middle class and its illusions through "hacktwist," seem not aware that cyber horseplay can turn ugly and murderous. The various names are thinly disguised codes for discontent: "Love Bug," "The Pakistan Hacking Club," "Dr. Nuke," "Kosovo in Serbia," "Hello Kitty," etcetera.

■ ■ ■

When people define themselves by proximity to others, they sometimes reveal intimate details in order to psychologically legitimize their status, and the more intimate the details, the closer they feel to celebrity, "the real thing." Elaborating with sordid details allows one to construct a kind of moral superiority, to outdo the other by increasing his or her own currency—elevated through the reduction of the other. In this sense, the ego is a monster, a chimera that cannot be trusted.

Nietzsche says in "On the Uses and Disadvantages of History for Life" (1874) that, "No one dares to appear as he is, but masks himself as a cultivated man, as a scholar, as a poet, as a politician. . . . Individuality has withdrawn within: from without it has become invisible." (*Untimely Meditations,* trans. R. J. Hollingdale, New York: Cambridge University Press, 1983, p. 84.)

■ ■ ■

After a man attempted to break into my Lower East Side apartment for the third time within a year, the security person talked me into giving her copies of my keys, stating that she wished to enter my apartment in my absence to install a camera, aimed through a peephole in the door to video the intruder-to-be, since he was likely to return. She insisted that he was an amateur, because she, on the other hand, knew how to jimmy in a matter of minutes any lock known to man or woman. She assured me the person who had attempted the break-in was no expert, and that the camera and video gear she bought at an electronics outlet would prove her point.

From this experience, I'd venture to say we don't possess a fullproof means of attaining safety or privacy. Since the eyes in back of our heads really don't protect us, such solutions as security cameras present a whole set of questions centered on the purpose of surveillance and who may use the information that it yields.

■ ■ ■

Some people would have us believe they know things about others they couldn't prove to save their lives. Of course, this is especially true when it comes to ordinary people attracted to celebrities. There are a number of people so out of touch with their own private lives that they delve into the public intimacies of celebrities, and then to the extreme, become obsessed even to the point of stalking the stars. Most people, fortunately, express awe for actors, entertainers, and sports figures in a modest sort of way. If, however, their lives are deemed insignificant compared to celebrities, these individuals may deploy their puny lives to the sidelines to involve themselves vicariously inside the boob tube or on the big screen as if it were life itself.

In such pursuits, who can deny that some horrific crimes have been committed with the objective of gaining instant celebrity, even if it ends up defamatory. This extreme behavior manifests the desire to sacrifice one's privacy for the public spotlight. A life becomes an open book for three minutes on the news, which then feeds the insatiable appetites of a certain kind of audience for private or grotesque details. The quality that immunizes people against becoming involved in these complex behaviors is the ability to feel comfortable with one's own achievements.

■ ■ ■

When Eastman invented the Brownie Kodak camera, many instant photographers began to plague the beaches. Some bathers felt that they didn't

. . . .

want to have their pictures taken with wet cloth clinging to every curve (today it is the opposite). Roland Barthes writes in *Camera Lucida*: "The age of photography corresponds precisely to the irruption of the private into the public, or rather, to the creation of a new social value, which is the publicity of the public: the private is consumed as such, publicly (the incessant aggressions of the press against the privacy of stars and the growing difficulties of legislation to govern them testify to this movement)." (New York: Hill and Wang, 1981)

I remember all those dream gadgets and trinkets for eavesdropping and spying in the back of *Dick Tracy, Flash Gordon,* and *Spiderman* comics. They usually cost ninety-nine cents or one dollar, postage included. They never worked as well as our imagination; we usually felt tricked.

But now if one walks into a Spy Store, he or she expects for the Dan Drew gadget to work. And, it does. It is scary business. How do these spy tricks come about? Who did the research? Has some secret war been going on in front of our eyes? There are cameras that can fit into the eyes of a crystal bird. There are listening devices that use the windowpane as a transmitter. Workers are complaining about video cameras in the rest rooms of the workplace. Customers are being spied on in the elevators. Parents are videotaping the baby-sitter. Orwell's *1984* and Huxley's *Brave New World* are as out-of-step with the glut of electronic thingamajigs as Dick Tracy. If the government has satellites spying from outer space, why not have bosses checking up on the new secretaries? (Eastman of Kodak positioned his office close to the women's rest room so he could see how many treks they took.)

Remember the book called the *Cult of Counterintelligence*? For those of us conscious of the potential incursions of technology in our world and craving privacy, we cannot be the only ones playing the devil's advocate because everyone's privacy is being invaded. In this sense, technology takes us back to the cave, to prehistoric times when a stone could be a tool or a weapon. So much depends on the individual holding it—the state of mind, knowing right from wrong.

The privacy issue is very complex, especially since we live in a society where so many of us are hurting for attention, for acknowledgment. This may have been influenced by the touchy-feely syndrome of the 1960s, the feel-good decade for what has been called the "me" generation. When we began to love our bodies more, to pull away from anything puritanic, did we divest ourselves of a sense of privacy? Is there anywhere left to hide from commerce and the wide gaze of the picture window?

.   .   .   .

■ ■ ■

Maybe the gossip machine was invented in small towns or suburbia, but it seems to have been put in motion in our cities. Small towns still exist in the psyches of people strutting around. Products of this phenomenon are the many music videos featuring half-dressed names who grab their crotches as if they were on back roads deep in the backwoods with nobody watching. Just as it is carefully calculated, everybody who is tuned to that channel is looking. The city is the place where people believe they can reveal anything. Of course, there is the fractured psyche talking to reflections in a shop window, half-lost among shadows and images of blow-up life-size dolls and posters of Ricky Martin. In countless bars, after 5:00 P.M., men in three-piece business suits spill the beans to the Norma Jeane look-alikes about an unfortunate love life, even about business partners.

So many of us seem as if we're on some perpetual talk show. This is now our church, the place to testify, to show off our new wardrobe. When the camera is aimed, the brain seems to close down and the tongue overloads. There must be hundreds who tell their most intimate secrets for payment.

■ ■ ■

"it startled us no more than a blue vase or a red rug." I have been intrigued by the poetry and rage in this phrase from Richard Wright's *Black Boy*. So simple and complex, the words say so much about the idea of privacy and racism in America. The words relate to a white prostitute and her John in Memphis, how the bellhops are summoned to serve the drinks in bed, while the two lie there naked. It is an act centered on reducing the bellhop's humanity: he doesn't own the eyes in his head—to see or not see. The bellhop is invisible to them. A naked man or woman will not pull up a cover when a dog or cat passes by an open bedroom door. Wright's couple belittles the bellhop by the bold display of themselves. Decadent exhibitionism diminishes the servant bellhop. If this is the psychology underlying this fictive situation, does it seem to have reversed itself? Now, persons of power reveal themselves to equals and cover themselves when servants enter the room (not only in the Deep South). Display is now lure as courtship, or the definition of freedom. But some in this dumbshow play blind and are reminded of their status: "What the fuck are you looking at?"

. . .   .

■ ■ ■

After bloody WWI, with the decline of Victorianism and the flourishing of Freudian psychoanalysis, people began to openly express their sexuality, especially artists and so-called free thinkers. Communities of like-minded souls began to spring up in New York City and Paris (as well as in small enclaves of other cities). Ann Douglas's *Terrible Honesty* delves into one scene:

> In Greenwich Village, Manhattan below Fourteenth Street where the avant-garde made its headquarters after the war, the adventurous red-haired Edna St. Vincent Millay of "I Burn My Candle at Both Ends" fame was 'It'; her lovers, male and female, were so numerous, 'Vincent,' or so she liked to be called, generously let two men make love to her at the same time; Edmund Wilson was assigned the top half of her body, John Peale Bishop the lower. Louise Brooks, the "secret bride" of New York, early acquired the nickname of "hellcat," and she referred to herself as "a startling little barbarian." Some thought her full name should read "Louise Brooks No Restraint," for she pursued with avidity what she dubbed "the truth, the full sexual truth." "I like to drink and fuck," she announced, and drink and fuck she did, usually in public places.

Such actions often seem to have been advertisements for the ego. At least with the blues and its sexual innuendo, its bold insinuation, names aren't mentioned (but sometimes first names such as Frankie and Johnny).

In our modern society it seems that many have great difficulty enduring silence, in the same way that some are so easily bored or cannot risk anonymity. Their skins seem not to contain them: the whole content and motion of their lives are on the exterior. Consumer marketing depends on a good number of people buying into playing dress-up for pass and review. Some individuals do not acknowledge their own existence until others validate it. Some people crave that their privacy be violated; they awake to an energy from eyes beholding what was once unseen.

Across the Atlantic, in the Parisian neighborhood of Montparnasse lived Man Ray's photogenic model, Kiki (born Alice Ernestine Prin—a "love baby"), an artist and writer. Writing *Kiki's Paris: Artists and Lovers 1900–1930*, Billy Klüver and Julie Martin divulge,

> Kiki celebrated lovemaking and would announce over morning coffee at the Dôme, "I have been well-laid." She took many lovers and once chastised Julian Levy, who didn't want to sleep with her, "Vous n' êtes pas un homme, mais un hommelette" [You're not a man, but a manlette]: Kiki didn't hesitate

to use her sexuality to help friends in need. She would collect money on the spur of the moment by showing her breasts or lifting her skirts in a bar or restaurant, telling the delighted patrons, "That will cost you a franc or two."

Man Ray almost wore out his camera on Kiki, since it appears that she loved the black box as much as it loved her. Of course, at twenty-eight she wrote a book entitled *Kiki's Memoirs,* making her a forerunner of the present-day memoir industry. It seems that many take risks and create antics to have something to write about. There seems to be a need to testify, people hurting to confess: some are talking to lampposts or to reflections in shop windows and others are wearing out the keys on the computer. Louis Armstrong sings, "I got a memory in Chicago. I got a memory in New Orleans. And, I got a memory in St. Louis, too. . . ." But here the memories remain unnamed; they are a bluesy mystery that seek a basic universality. The personal pronouns become less self-centered or egotistical.

In times of flourishing soap operas and talk shows, privacy has lost its sacredness. Ritual as public unmasking often requires new masks. And sometimes, we doubt if we can trust the masking. Of course this touches art as well. Much negative criticism has been written about the so-called confessional poets. An unholy aping of the confessional sentiment has taken hold over the last five decades.

A friend of mine who taught a poetry-writing workshop related the following story:

> I had a high-school student in my workshop—a good writer who shocked the other members of the class with such compellingly vivid details about rape, incest, and sexual abuse. I didn't know what I'd say to her during our conference. We sat facing each other. I said, "The autobiographical details in your poems are very vivid." She replied, "Autobiographical?" I said, "Your life has been harsh." She said, "Isn't this what poetry is supposed to be about?"

The problem with an example of false witness is that we grow callous and doubtful about real abuses happening around us. We cannot think of them as fictional; our lives cannot accommodate more theater on the latest talk show aiming for bloated ratings.

We live in a time of theater—life as theater. It is like tugging on a bit of thread and the whole garment unravels till we are naked in public.

■ ■ ■

· · · · · · · · · · ·

Many of these antics seem to have been a desperate push at the last walls of Victorianism or as anti-establishment acts, whereby privacy becomes secondary. The mores of the 1920s and '30s with a diminished sense of privacy transfused the literature of the Beat movement even if the other side of the coin offered more freedom to the public. The boldness of such figures as Millay, Brooks, and Kiki permeates the social litany dominant during the 1950s. The contradictions between what is private and privacy compared to public freedom really didn't square off. Instead, the personal pronoun "I" fueled the engine of outpourings. This uncensored telling appears in the beginning of Allen Ginsberg's *Howl*:

"I saw the best minds of my generation destroyed by madness, starving hysterical naked,/dragging themselves through the negro streets at dawn looking for an angry fix . . ." and continues with "angelheaded hipsters . . . who were expelled from the academies for crazy and publishing obscene odes on the windows of the skull. . . . " The trails to the private are not disguised. The insinuation and innuendo are thinly veiled, and we can peer through and see the real characters at play. We know who the "angelheaded hipsters" are, that Ginsberg was suspended from Columbia University for writing a derogatory phrase about Jews on a dusty classroom window with his forefinger. We know all the bad actors in this boys' club: Kerouac, Neil Cassady, Burroughs, Orlovsky, Corso, etcetera. We know that Corso spent time in Dannemora, that he boasted he never combed his hair: "although I guess I'd get the bugs out of it if I did."

Publicity translates into currency, and, as the passage of time has revealed, many of the Beats were keenly aware of the benefits that flow from publicity. It was, and still is, a means of producing capital. But, sometimes the antics almost misfired, though Ginsberg knew the value of an empirical controversy. At the time, however, he would find himself hemmed in by his own design, as depicted in the exchange between him and Britain's Dame Edith Sitwell: "My you *do* smell bad, don't you?" she said upon their introduction. "What was your name again? Are you one of the action poets?" Ginsberg's nervous fingers produced a cigarette, which only made her dig her nails in deeper. "Is that a narcotic one? Does it contain heroin?" "No," he said, "but I've got some here. Do you want a shot?" "Oh, dear no," said Dame Sitwell. "Dope makes me come out all over in spots."

Of course, this moment of playful banter was instant grist for the publicity mill and it lead to Dame Sitwell's rejoinder that appeared in *Life*:

Sirs: My attention has been called to a most disgusting report in your paper—one mass of lies from beginning to end—which pretends to describe my meeting with Mr. Allen Ginsberg . . . There is not one word of truth in a single sentence of it.

Mr. Ginsberg never offered me heroin, and as I have never, in my life, taken heroin, it can scarcely 'bring me out in spots.' (An affliction from which, incidentally, I do not suffer.)

The English upper class do not use the expression "my!" (We leave that to persons of your correspondent's breeding.) Nor do we tell people who are introduced to us they 'smell bad.'

This is the most vulgar attack, actuated evidently by an almost insane malice, probably by some person whom I have refused to receive socially, that I have ever seen.

You had better apologise, publicly, both to Mr. Ginsberg and me immediately."

—February 8, 1960

Life replied, "The anecdote . . . had been widely circulated at Oxford. Mr. Ginsberg joins Dame Edith in denying it and *Life* apologizes to both."

In Jack Kerouac's "Belief and Technique for Modern Prose," published in the *Evergreen Review* in 1959, two items underline this issue about privacy:

24. No fears or shame in the dignity of yr experience, language & knowledge

25. Write for the world to read and see yr exact pictures of it

Before the Beats, there have been numerous persons who walked into literary plots and became thinly disguised characters; hardly has this been more evident than in Richard Bruce Nugent's short story, "Smoke, Lilies and Jade" (1926), where the impressionistic landscape is peopled by drugs, androgyny, and homosexuality. Beauty, its Greenwich Village protagonist, is a dual figure, a composite of Rudolph Valentino and the artist Miguel Cavarrubias; Countee Cullen's lover Harold Jackman; and Langston Hughes. Many felt that Du Bois's prophecy had come true—if the emphasis on culture is diminished by the artistic: "turn the Negro renaissance into decadence."

But Wallace Thurman's *Infants of the Spring* (1932) dismantles and caricatures the entire Harlem Renaissance. All the major players and philosophers are on the scene. In the novel's last chapter, Paul Armstrong, modeled after Thurman's friend Richard Bruce Nugent, is a suicide discovered in Nigeratti Manor (Thurman's rent-free house at 267 West 136th Street in Harlem) by Raymond, who represents Thurman.

. . . .

■ ■ ■

I ride the New Jersey Transit train from New York's Penn Station to Princeton Junction, and am often amazed by the numerous people hollering into their cell phones. These New-Age travelers seem to trust their anonymity, talking at decibels to make the conversations anything but private. Everyone within earshot hears intimate love talk to trading on the stockmarket. There might be an air of keeping up with the Joneses. There's always been the strategy to let others "overhear" the price of their houses and cars. Perhaps the first attempt at name-dropping is when boys and girls drop the names of popular dates.

In Thailand, one can buy cell phones that don't have any guts, just the shell of the thing. Ultimately it suggests that the owner of the mock cell phone is not worth the breath they inhale and exhale. While everyone is getting plugged in, ironically, people are disconnecting from each other.

The technology of illusion seems here to stay, but this is not without some threat to the species. A few years after J. Edgar Hoover died—he's the one who initiated the bugging industry—it was suggested that an appropriate monument to him would be a complex of computers. Hoover specialized in revealing little "dirty" details about the personal lives of those he wanted to discredit. An expert at concealing counterintelligence, he himself diverted any sort of revelations that would divulge some of his personal pastimes including dressing up in black taffeta and pearls. Personal freedom depends on privacy and everyone is entitled to it.

■ ■ ■

In early 1995, I spent a day on a nude beach in Queensland, Australia, near Cairns. My two friends took to this easier than me. The two turned back flips and floated atop the sea, gazing up into the hurting light. I cowered, craving at least a fig leaf. Paradise was twenty yards away, among the trees and ferns, where white-plumed honeyeaters and cockatoos flickered through the green and plagued the salty air like winged sentinels. I wanted to pull my clothes back on, to see if I could find and stare down another four-foot, stout cassowary armored in blue feathers.

I can see that outlandish character aiming his spyglasses at everyone, strutting around the edge of the water in his birthday suit. Even if this joker hadn't been there, making me mindful of why some rejoice in such a display, I would still have been shy—sinking down into the waves, like some nameless bottom fish nudging coral with its bright nose.

I won't claim at that moment I was thinking of A. D. Hope's "The Double Looking Glass" that portrays an apocryphal moment between Susannah and the Elders. Her garden has sprouted out of the imagination, cut off from the larger world; its centralized peace is destroyed by the elders—this garden where the real and imagined merge as one. This place of meditation, silence, and contemplation is a sanctuary for the human imagination where Susannah's sexuality lives: "A mirror for man's images of love." I believe a lack of privacy deadens the imagination and the world of sexual love.

Feeling half-ashamed, not wanting to look at the nude figures displayed on the beach, a dance not unlike the male peacock's flare of many-colored plumage and blazon sexual fanfare, I felt as if all eyes were on me. Maybe this self-consciousness was linked to my childhood back in Bogalusa where a sense of privacy was almost sacred. The knock on a closed door said that the person on the other side belonged to his or her own skin.

On Privacy

. . . .

by
F. GONZALEZ-CRUSSI

First impressions are often indelible. Mine, when I arrived as an immigrant from south of the border to a town in Southwestern United States, proved to be so. I evoke those long departed days, and the vividness of the recollection never fails to amaze me.

Silence was one of the features that impressed me the most. I had come to a town of moderate size and expected greater bustle than I encountered. From the bus window I caught sight of broad, well-kept, wind-swept avenues devoid of pedestrians. Regularly traced streets shot their unswerving perspective into the distance, with no human figures to interrupt the geometrical perfection. Well-manicured lawns, carefully tended façades, immaculate sidewalks, and public works in excellent state of repair: everywhere the marks of an industrious, orderly population. But where were they, the members of this population? A sleepy town south of the border, only half the size of this one, would have manifested greater animation. I concluded that the bus had entered the town through back ways and side roads to avoid traffic jams. A well-planned access made sense in this marvelously well-organized country.

The next day I roamed through the town. Again, I encountered generally deserted, neatly kept streets, and smartly maintained—but lonely—alleys, squares, and plazas. With a map, I made sure I had not missed the hub of the place. I figured I had arrived during a national holiday; it would take me a while to become familiar with the calendar of local festivities. But the experience was repeated again and again. Each time I managed to go out to reconnoiter my neighborhood, it was the same spectacle of urbane, clean surroundings with scarcely any human presence. It finally dawned on me: I saw no people on the streets simply because the natives chose not to be outdoors. I had come to a country with a different style of life altogether. A town with no groups of people strolling aimlessly in the streets, even if the weather allowed it. No idle loiterers here. No collective killing time in cafés or shopping malls: if people went to the shopping mall, it was to shop; if they walked on the streets (an activity they rarely engaged in, for they usually drove their cars), it was in order to reach a specific destination.

This realization gave me, at first, a sense of relief. I had left a country where human contacts were frequent, spontaneous, unregulated, and largely chaotic. I had often deplored the raw, wearisome quality of these encounters. Where people obtrude themselves into your vital sphere—call in unannounced anytime; expose their inner emotional landscape to your contemplation, and expect you to do the same—there is little chance for inner collectedness and reflection, which I valued greatly. Moreover, I always felt somewhat at a disadvantage in that milieu. Frequent and random human interactions place us athwart all manner of personalities and temperaments. The haughty demand your submission; the meek, your protection; some ask for sympathy, others expect neutrality. One must be inordinately flexible and versatile, if one is to thrive in such an environment. I simply lacked the shrewdness, the lissomeness of mind that is required. It was restful to come to a place where interpersonal relations, being less frequent and better regimented, were naturally less demanding.

I then went through an experience that many an immigrant will readily recognize. Those very features that I had deemed irksome were the things that I began missing most. I had complained about never being left alone, suffered from interferences, winced at the intrusiveness and indelicacy of boors who forced themselves into my vital sphere. The pressing of crowds bothered me. The odor of frying meats, of pungent condiments, of sweaty human bodies (all common emanations in my native barrio), sickened me. I was now, at last, free from interferences, exempt from unwanted intrusions, unencumbered by crowds and their array of disagreeable sensations. I was relieved, protected from all that constriction and hardship . . . and I never felt lonelier in my life.

A hand of ice that clasped my heart had descended upon me. How I missed the feeling of community! The penetrating odors, the disagreeable whiffs, the jostling of crowds, the unguarded displays of emotion: all the things that I had thought indecorous, unseemly, or distracting, now were revealed to me under a different light. They were reminders of my humanity, reaffirmations of my condition as a living being, and tokens of my af-

·   ·   ·   ·   ·   ·   ·   ·   ·

filiation to a distinctive human group. I missed the noise, the disorder of crowds. God forgive me, I missed even the disagreeable odor of unwashed bodies. The tranquillity of my new domicile began to crush me, after some time, with the oppressive weight of loneliness. The silent peace I enjoyed felt, at certain hours, like the stillness of the grave. I had been bred in a culture that avidly desired and actively sought human contact, and I had come to one that did not make it a priority. This induced me to reflect on the differences of each milieu.

The Anglo-American culture, like that of Northern European industrialized countries, sets strict limits to encroachments on individual freedom. This outlook is deeply rooted in their libertarian traditions and finds both real and symbolic expressions. In general, one does not call in unannounced, even among friends. One does not easily disclose feelings too spontaneous and unprocessed. The others have the right to be left alone, the right of "privacy." This is a word that has no exact equivalent in Latin-derived languages. Spanish *privacidad,* of recent coinage, is shunned by the purists as an anglicism; and *vida privada,* like the French *vie privée,* is suspicious of scabrous and unconfessable shadiness, and therefore quite different from the utterly honorable "privacy." The *Oxford English Dictionary* defines privacy as "the state or condition of being withdrawn from the society of others, or from public interest." It is to be noted, however, that a second acceptation reads: "being alone, undisturbed or free from public attention as a matter of choice or right; freedom from interference or intrusion." Thus, make no mistake, to be left alone must be counted among individual rights; it is a manner of exerting freedom, one of the ways in which the individual can be free.

The person brought up in the Anglo-American culture confers a high value to being left alone. Such a person suffers in the extreme from the pressure of crowds. He, or she, cannot stand the abrasive, irksome nature of too-close and reiterative human contacts. He needs to be free. He needs space to breathe. This is aptly summarized in W. H. Auden's verse:

> Some thirty inches from my nose
> The frontier of my Person goes
> All the untilled air between
> Is private *pagus* or demesne . . .

Nor is this purely poetical fancy. Anthropologists have studied the matter, with all the scientific rigor of their discipline, and conclude that the amount of space that people need to interpose between themselves and the individual with whom they interact, is "culturally programmed." And since a cryptic, obscure-sounding term is needed to bestow a certificate of authenticity in science, they coined the word "proxemics." Its creator, Edward T. Hall, explained in his book *The Hidden Dimension,* that this term refers to the degree of proximity that people of different cultures are apt to find socially acceptable. For instance, Southern Italians tend to talk to friends and acquaintances separated from each other only by a short space, such as may permit, given even a low degree of familiarity, to pinch the interlocutor's cheeks, or grab his arm, or bring the heads of those conversing into direct contact. Any of which would ipso facto raise the eyebrows and stiffen the backs of Scots or Scandinavians.

Where privacy is highly valued, human interaction is correspondingly decreased. Human beings are by nature curious, meddlesome, inquisitive. Given the chance, there is nothing that they would not scrutinize, turn around, dismantle, and observe. However, in most societies they are taught early on that certain things are to be preserved from exposure; that each individual has a *private* sphere; and that privacy is an imprescriptible right of the individual, much like the pursuit of happiness. Only the magnitude of privacy varies considerably in different cultures.

Diminution of the frequency and intensity of interchanges between humans carries distinct benefits. The opportunities for conflict are minimized. Routines are expedited. I recall my unbounded admiration for the American system when I realized that a person could transact all sorts of businesses, including complex dealings with the government administration, with a minimum of irritation. One could obtain a passport by mail, and also a driver's license. One could settle a complicated business after a single visit to city hall, with a minimum of pertinent documents. Where person-to-person contacts are necessary, and privacy held in relatively low esteem, life is never that simple. Not a few Americans have had occasion to corroborate this—those who attempted simple transactions in the bureaucratic maze of, say, Mediterranean countries.

I saw a couple from Topeka or Tulsa, I don't remember which, standing in line in the ill-ventilated hall of a bank in Southern Italy. "Why does everyone stand crowding this space [in front of the window], when there is enough room to spread out in a line, and we would all be more comfortable?" complained the American man, who was obviously uninformed about "proxemics," and the fact that Southern Italians would have adjudicated Auden's desired breathing space—*Thirty inches from my nose*—an outright anchoritic isolationism. When, about forty-five minutes, the man reached the window, only to be handed a slip that he was supposed to present at a second window (in front of which there was,

. . . .

naturally, another disarrayed crowd), I thought his anger reached an un-
common degree of paroxysm. And when—after the second prolonged
wait, during which he loudly complained of the appalling inefficiency of
the bank, the airline, the hotel, and every local service—the curtain was
lowered for a three-hour lunch break, there being just one customer left
between him and the window, I thought the gentleman would succumb to
apoplexy. I don't know how he fared; I had been among the lucky ones
ahead of the disgruntled tourist and left the place in a hurry. As the vernacular expression puts it, I hate to see a grown man cry.

If a simple transaction, such as the exchange of currency, is fraught
with so much difficulty, imagine what a Herculean task it would be to attempt to move through complicated red tape. How do you manage to live
in this environment? If you reside in a country that places greater value on
person-to-person contacts than on privacy, you must learn the survival
skills. You learn how to cajole, to persuade, to flatter, to intimidate, even
to bribe (for this, too, is an art) if corruption is part of the system, as it
often is. If the person behind the window (or the counter, or the desk, or
any of the symbolic barriers that segregate citizen petitioner from bureaucrat petitioned) is of such age, deportment, and appearance as could be
hypothetically made into a potential sexual partner, you flirt. You flirt
openly, shamelessly. But if your age, mood, gender, or other circumstances
interdict the latter approach, and all others are precluded, you suffer in silence. Or you evince an extraordinary humility, a meekness so abject, so
dismal, that pity may spring in the heart of the dreadful bureaucrat, as did
water from the bare rock when touched by the staff of the prophet.

I am reminded of the opera *The Consul* by Gian Carlo Menotti, with
text by Samuel Barber, composed during the Cold War era, and premiered
in 1950. The wife of a political activist who has fled the country attempts
to obtain a visa to join him. She, and a handful of desperate souls come to
sit every day in the waiting hall of a foreign consulate, hoping for a visa.
They are trapped in the system, frustrated, powerless against an unyield-
ing, insensitive bureaucracy. The consul is never seen. Their pleas, their
desperate entreaties, are stopped cold at the counter of the consulate's reception room, or at the desk of an unfeeling secretary who confronts them
with the arbitrary, senseless, fixed rules of a typical bureaucracy. The main
protagonist, harassed by the secret police that knows of her plans to leave
the country and wants to extract information from her, ends up commit-
ting suicide.

In the performance that I watched, the director arranged a surrealistic
scene in which the waiting applicants are slowly lifted from their seats and

.   .   .   .

appear to float, wafted in the air by some kind of ingenious theatrical device. Those of us who have repined under the absurdity and callousness of a monolithic administration, very much appreciate the rich symbolism of the scene. The waiting applicant is utterly powerless. Hanging on the decisions of some obtuse employee, he is like a leaf tossed about by the winds of circumstance. His being is suspended, disconnected from any former meaning; and he can do nothing but wait for a future that hangs on a signature, a seal, or the whim of some apathetic clerk.

Therefore, the petitioner scrutinizes the face, the gestures, the deportment of the employee who holds his fate in his hands. He must learn the difficult art of interpreting the Other's mien, in order to adjust his behavior to it, if he is to survive in the land of interpersonal contacts. And this explains how privacy can become an instrument of domination. The powerful remove themselves from contact with others. If familiarity breeds contempt, they reason, inaccessibility promotes respect. In this they were not mistaken. Louis XIV of France, who among all rulers most effectively used the royal apparatus designed to impress, understood this well. He wrote in his *Memoirs* (II, 5):

> They are grossly mistaken who imagine that all those things [the proceedings of court's etiquette] are pure ceremonial. The peoples over whom we rule, not being able to penetrate the bottom of things, ordinarily form their judgments based on what they see from outside, and it is most often according to preferments and ranks that they measure their respect and their obedience. Since it is important to the people to be governed by one [man], it is equally important that he who fulfills this function be elevated above all others, in such a way that there be no one else who may be confused or compared with him; and one cannot, lest one injure the whole body of the State, take away from the people's master the slightest mark of the superiority that distinguishes him from the rest.

Thus, for the Sun King, privacy had a political objective; it was one more way to impose the overawing, divinely ordained majesty of absolutism upon people who might have had reasons to question it. In our more democratic times, privacy in the powerful is viewed with considerably less deference. Who has not read, in newspapers and popular magazines, the rhetorical outbursts of outraged editorialists, who lament or lambast the paparazzi that hound the favorites of fortune? The suggestion was made, in the mass media, that photographers doggedly pursuing a shot of Diana, the Princess of Wales, caused the automobile accident that led to her death. And editorialists once again donned the sackcloth of outraged righteous-

. . . .

ness when, in no less pathetic strains, they denounced those who, from the cover of distance and by the use of powerful telescopic lenses, captured and diffused the image of some exalted lady—here a fair princess, there the wife of a revered president—in a state of undignifying undress.

In centuries past, this would have been thought a serious offense. Legend has it that the chamberlain of Margaret of Austria, wife of Phillip III of Spain, was incensed when a guild of weavers wished to offer a pair of stockings to the queen and asked for her measurements. Thinking this an insulting impropriety, the attendant thundered: "The Queen of Spain has no legs!" In like manner, editorialists today fear that the flowers of womanhood of the realm will be somehow demeaned if represented in the popular mind as something other than disembodied creatures.

Today's commentators couch their warnings in terms of the "slippery-slope" metaphor. It is not the modesty of the privileged that ought to concern us, read the editorials, but the implicit danger that disrespect for private space may become the norm. Take away the private realm, the "breathing space" we so diligently carved around each one of us, and soon none of us will enjoy that precious commodity, privacy. Our most secret motions, our most cherished intimacy will lie open in the glare of sunlight, undefended and scorned. Is it not true that already our buying habits, our style of life, and even our dark preferences and proclivities are on file in the computers of powerful corporations? In vain do we withhold personal information. For what the corporations may ignore, the State will find out; and once the data are electronically accessioned, you may as well consider them in the public domain, since computers, diabolical contraptions that they are, "talk to each other," as the technical jargon puts it. Nothing, then, will be held secret; nothing will be private anymore.

What editorialists do not say is that celebrity is, and has always been, bought at the price of privacy. The powerful distance themselves from the plebs, and, more or less advisedly, awe them or intimidate them from their lofty stance. The lesser sorts, in their turn, transform the exalted into Idols of the Tribe. Now, an idol is meant to stand in constant display: in order to be worshiped, it needs to be well visible. High on its pedestal, the idol must be the focal point upon which converge the vows, and the prayers, as well as the anxious glances of its votaries. It is thus that every movement of the famous, every detail of the lives of those in power, is eagerly watched by those beneath them in the social ranking.

Mark the double, paradoxical nature of deliberately contrived privacy. On the one hand, the powerful seclude themselves, remove themselves from contact with the common people. Louis XIV buried himself in the luxury and magnificence of Versailles, where none but a few noblemen could have direct access to him; the Chinese emperors did likewise, in the splendor of a vast realm appropriately named the Forbidden City. On the other hand, deep in their stately grandeur and lavishness, they had to renounce any pretensions of privacy. From morning till night, their most trivial acts, alike with those momentous, were a matter of unflagging observation and fastidious recording. Recently surfaced documents throw light on the daily life in the Forbidden City. Inside this mysterious enclave, secluded behind the high walls of an unattainable imperial court, the Idols of the Tribe lived—paradoxically—in perpetual exposure.

We owe to a low-ranking courtier, a lady attendant of the imperial court, a description of life inside the Forbidden City.[1] Imagine the dowager empress of the Manchu dynasty retiring to her quarters after finishing her daily audiences. She is brought back in a palanquin, borne on the shoulders of attendants who advance slowly through the corridors. She is never alone. This time she is surrounded by a number of eunuchs who form a retinue of serious faces, some level with the palanquin, some preceding it, and some behind: all following a protocol that distributes the members of the retinue according to their rank. The most favored, Li Lian Ying, leans his left arm against the palanquin's bar, while in the right hand he carries a pipe. A small eunuch hurries up ahead to notify the ladies-in-waiting in a building known as "The Palace of Beauties," that the empress is arriving. Then the head "aunt," or attendant lady, claps her hands once, and immediately the sign is passed to all the others, who scurry noiselessly to their respective duties, leaving the room. All is done with remarkable demureness. The silence that prevails is a striking feature of the court's atmosphere, one that would be long remembered by those who knew it. The empress then comes into her chamber, unmindful of the lady servants prosternated before the palanquin, and promptly removes the heavy diadem that is part of her headdress.

At this time, the cooks come in, as is the custom, to offer her little morsels, steamed breads in the Manchu style, and sundry delicate desserts. For the empress, although in no way rotund of body, has nonetheless a hearty appetite. She takes six meals a day: three regular meals and three supplementary ones on her own. After this, she drinks a little tea and leisurely smokes two pipes in a row. Then, she asks for the chamber pot. She is, of course, surrounded all the time by attendants who see to it that all her requests be promptly satisfied.

. . . .

It is necessary to explain that, in the midst of all this magnificence, there are no toilets in the whole palace. Urine is derived into troughs and excavations that the eunuchs dutifully cover with ashes of burnt wood. There is no dearth of ashes in the premises, even though not a single chimney is to be found anywhere in the Forbidden City. This is on account of the prevailing general terror of fires, an attitude that seems justified when one considers that much of the construction is in wood. But the vast expanse of the palace is underlaid by an extraordinary system of caves and tunnels, into which the eunuchs push iron carts full of wood coals, which they keep burning during the winter. Thus, the inhabitants of the constructions above feel, during the cold season, as if they were living on a layer of heated bricks. As for the elimination of feces, the courtiers are obligated to make use of pots, which they cover with ashes to ward off the diffusion of repugnant odors.

Following the Manchu custom, the empress asks for the "House of the Mandarins" to signify that she must make use of the chamber pot. What is then brought to her is a contraption that makes the chronicler rhapsodize: the chamber pot of the empress ought to be regarded as a national treasure! The greatest craftsmen and artists of the realm have used their considerable talents to manufacture this refined, exquisitely conformed object. The "Houses of the Mandarins" of the high-ranking officials were usually made of porcelain and could have various ingenious shapes. But that belonging to the empress tops them all. It is made of solid, fragrant, tropical sandalwood, and shaped like a large gecko, a species of lizard, with artistically stylized features. Its body is incurved and seems full of tension. The head is slightly turned toward the back, almost touching its chine, in such a way as to give the observer the feeling that the beast is about to leap upon its prey. Its claws sink firmly into the ground, and terminate the four legs on which the contraption stands. The tail rolls back, graciously tracing a "figure eight" that may serve as a handle posteriorly; the chin directed frontward places the head in a position parallel to that of the tail, and could equally serve as a handle in front. The mouth is slightly open, just enough to seem to bite the toilet paper that is placed inside. The belly of the beast is rounded and swollen. This, of course, is the receptacle fit to receive the imperial feces. It is full of a pulverulent sawdust of fragrant wood, so that when fecal matter falls in, it is immediately wrapped in a fragrant powdery cover. This exquisitely carved chamber pot is said to have been one of the favorite objects of the empress. When she died, it followed her as a "guest of heaven." According to the Manchu custom, various mementos and belongings of the departed ruler are distributed among the surviving relatives; the rest are burned during certain ritual ceremonies and are said to have become the "guests of heaven."

A charming picture of a vanished world. But where in it was privacy to be found? Curious to tell, not for one second; not even for the performance of those physiological functions during which the humblest person today seeks solitude; *never* could the mighty heads of empire shun the limelight. This, incidentally, could be said also of royalty in the Western world during past ages. There are memoirs of high dignitaries that recount the conversations that kings had, while conspicuously sitting on the toilet, with noblemen of their court. It is a fact that Henry IV of France chatted with his minister Sully and other exalted personages, while sitting on the *chaise percée* in full view of his inerlocutors. The Idol of the Tribe could not be let out of sight at any moment. Equally true is that the parturition of a queen was not a private event, but had to be witnessed by various important persons. This is understandable since the royal succession was such a crucial matter—it had to be verified by ocular witnesses.

In the Chinese imperial court, the call of nature had to be communicated to some of the innumerable attendants in the empress's entourage. "Bring me the House of the Mandarins," was the order. A lady-in-waiting swiftly passed on the command to the eunuch in charge of this function, who had been waiting outside ever since the empress returned from her audiences. It was enough for the lady of the court to nod her head in his direction, and the eunuch would run to the imperial chamber, carrying on top of his head a large bundle wrapped in yellow fabric with embroidered dragon motifs on it. He stopped at the threshold of the chamber and kneeled on the floor: he was excused from kowtowing all the way to the ground, in consideration of the fact that he held a large package on the top his head. The lady of the court would take the package, unbundle it, and carry the contraption into the chamber, where the empress was already waiting with her waist-belt untied and the lower part of her body exposed (hence the prohibition to the eunuch to enter the room). Another lady attendant went to take a large oiled fabric from under a tea table. She extended it on the ground, and placed the toilet paper, whose preparation had been the task of female attendants in the "Palace of Beauties," into the mouth of the beastlike chamber pot, and left the place.

The court ladies withdrew, out of decorousness and politeness, from the immediate proximity of the empress. But the latter was not free from their glances. From a respectful distance, in deferential concealment proper

·   ·   ·   ·   ·   ·   ·   ·   ·   ·

to the delicate manners of one of the most refined imperial courts that has ever existed, the Idol of the Tribe was still the target of the unflinching gaze, and she knew it. Wrote the attendant who chronicled the daily incidents, in a moment of nostalgic evocation: "I see again the empress, riding the 'House of the Mandarins,' and playing with the toilet paper, as if titillating the mouth of the beast. What a remembrance!"[2]

What a remembrance, indeed. The lady-in-waiting wrote that as an expression of tender regard and admiration for her sovereign. Today, most of us would think such a memory unworthy of being treasured. The humblest person would insist that certain acts, such as those connected with the discharge of physiological functions, ought to be private. We may be persuaded that to be made the target of the unrelenting public gaze is part of the price that the powerful pay for the privileges they enjoy. For all of us, regardless of our cultural background, fervently believe that there must be a domain of our lives where no one is allowed to look: a perpetually defended *sanctum sanctorum* of individuality.

We are largely what others think we are. The gaze of the Other shapes the very core of our person. There would be much to say in this regard: some believe that the very consciousness of our existence would be impossible without the realization that others look at us. The Cartesian famous dictum has been reformulated as *l'Autre me voit, donc je suis* (the Other sees me, therefore I am).[3] But there remains an inner region within each one of us—vaster in some cultures, more restricted in others—where the Other must not look. As the gaze of others shapes us in the style of the group, imprints us with the mark of the herd, so the existence of an inner territory secluded from the Other's gaze preserves our unique, irreplaceable individuality. This exclusive territory, bastion of our ego; this region of our inner self that must be tenaciously defended, lest our uniqueness and singularity melt away into the anonymity of the Great Whole; this parcel of our intimate being is called "privacy."

NOTES

1. Jin Yi: *Mémoires d'une Dame de Cour dans la Cité Interdite*. French translation from the Chinese by Dong Qiang (Marseille: Éditions Philippe Picquier, 1993).
2. *Loc. cit.*
3. François George: *Deux Études sur Sartre* (Paris: Christian Bourgois), p. 321.

Two Cartoons

. . . .

by
VICTORIA ROBERTS

HOWARD, YOU'RE ALL FOGGED IN.

Lying to Protect Privacy:
A Walk on the "Wilde" Side

. . . .

by
ANITA L. ALLEN

People lie about sex. Indeed, as the television comedians say, people lie *during* sex. That people lie to avoid disclosure of facts about their sex lives and to enjoy sexual independence is a reality observed in everyday life that psychologists have studied and confirmed. In light of the current diverse mix of sexual mores, public officials may decide that carefully concealing their sex lives is essential to the freedom and intimacy they understandably crave. Immediately after President Clinton confirmed his improper relationship with Monica Lewinsky, Americans were eager to understand two rather remarkable phenomena: that intelligent people, who know they will be scrutinized, undertake the kinds of sex lives about which they will probably have to lie; and that these same intelligent people sometimes lie in such sloppy and public ways that their lies can be uncovered easily and with disastrous consequences.

Before President Clinton scandalized Washington, Oscar Wilde scandalized London.[1] The two men merit comparison. A famous lecturer, wit, and playwright, Oscar Wilde had a complex and troubling sex life. He was married and fathered children by his wife, Constance. While married, he undertook a series of three homosexual relationships with other artists.[2] He also engaged in sex and sex-play (voyeurism) with numerous other male partners.[3] Wilde lied to his wife and many of his associates about his sexual practices. Wilde was remarkably reckless about the lies he told, lies that might otherwise have vouchsafed his identity and freedom. On the one hand, he often made efforts to keep his illicit romantic and sexual affairs secret, particularly from his wife and children. On the other hand, he freely and openly associated with well-known homosexuals, with advocates of homosexual tolerance at Oxford, and with notorious and flamboyant homosexuals and indiscreet young male prostitutes in London and abroad.[4]

That Wilde lied can be looked upon with a certain amount of sympathy given the severe legal penalties for open homosexuality in Wilde's time. Why, however, was Wilde willing to risk criminal prosecution? Why was he not deterred by the harshness of the law? It was fairly safe, if one was discreet, to be an educated, upper-class homosexual. Wilde knew that most homosexuals were not exposed and prosecuted in London. More importantly, Wilde may have felt that sexual risks were worth taking if they allowed him to live more authentically. His identity and freedom were diminished by a life restricted to conventional heterosexual marriage.[5]

While still officially denying homosexuality, Wilde virtually abandoned his wife and children in favor of living with the handsome, petulant, and self-centered poet, Lord Alfred Douglas. Douglas's father, the Marquess of Queensberry, disapproved of his son's relationship with Wilde and demanded in vain that Wilde break things off. Prodded by Lord Douglas, Wilde took lying about sex to extraordinary heights when he brought a defamation action against Queensberry.[6]

Wilde's great folly was to sue a powerful opponent and to bring libel charges that he could only defend by easily disproved lies. The libel allegations focused on a hateful note Douglas's father scrawled on the back of a card left for Wilde at Wilde's club. Queensberry and his lawyers maintained that the Marquess's note described Wilde as a man "posing as a Somdomite [sic]."[7] So far as Wilde and Lord Douglas were concerned, the note condemned Wilde as a sodomite. In defamation actions, truth is an obvious defense. The Marquess's lawyers had no trouble rounding up male prostitutes willing to testify against Wilde. They secured hotel staff willing to testify to finding men in Wilde's bed and fecal stains on Wilde's bedsheets. Thus, Wilde's futile attempt at a face-saving lawsuit against Queensberry led to his conviction for sodomy and sentencing to two grueling years of hard labor, a sentence that broke his health and ruined and shortened his life.[8]

With lies we desperately try to preserve our freedom and our identities—our actual identities rather than the masks we must wear as a price of admission to conventional mainstream society. Wilde went too far in trying to protect his life as an eccentric gay artist, much as President Clinton went too far in trying to protect his life as a daring ladies' man. Clinton recklessly engaged in a clandestine extramarital sexual affair with Lewinsky and then boldly lied about that fact on national television and in private meetings with his closest friends and confidants. Like Wilde, Clinton allowed himself to become smitten with a self-centered young lover and then entrusted his remarkable and historic career to an immature lover's judgment. Like Wilde, Clinton wound up hurting and embarrassing his family by an affair with a beautiful, younger, and less gifted person. Like Wilde, Clinton sought to turn the truth-tellers, whom he regarded as having inappropriately pried and distorted the truth, into moral monsters. Wilde literally put Queensberry on trial, while Clinton tried, with some success, to put Kenneth Starr and the Republican Congress on trial in the minds of the American people. Like Wilde, Clinton temporarily sought refuge in technical definitions of sexual conduct in an effort to escape the law. Clinton denied a "sexual relationship" with "that woman" on national television because he could honestly say he never had experienced full penetration penile-vaginal intercourse with Lewinsky. Wilde denied that he was a sodomite because he could honestly say that he did not practice penile-anal intercourse with Lord Douglas.[9]

To lie about sex in such a fashion, to walk on the "Wilde" side, a person must possess character traits and status not shared by everyone. Perhaps one has to feel and be very powerful, and enjoy taking risks. But, perhaps one need only have a very strong urge to be the genuine person behind the masks donned for public roles and private responsibilities. Wilde emerges as more sympathetic than Clinton because conventional morality increasingly regards legally enforced homophobia as unjust, but continues to regard monogamy as a legitimate requirement of marriage. A recent film version of Wilde's life paints Wilde sympathetically as a tragic hero, a gifted genius in love with someone who did not deserve his love.[10] Similarly, *Primary Colors*, a veiled film version of Clinton's presidential campaign, paints Clinton as a tragic hero, a brilliant communicator with a pathetic weakness for illicit sex and greasy food.[11]

We must grapple with the following question: if you take privacy seriously, as many experts say we ought, don't you have to make a virtue out of telling lies to protect privacy?[12] Shall we ascribe a right to lie in response to prying, snooping, and prejudiced questions; a right to lie to protect information about, and distortions of, the details of our sexual practices? Shall we extend that right to public officials and public figures to the same extent as ordinary citizens and resist the temptation to dismiss the problem

. . . .

quickly with the fiction that public officials and public figures "waive" their rights to privacy by thrusting themselves into the limelight?

A large amount of philosophical, jurisprudential, and psychological literature argues that privacy, including sexual privacy, is important. Philosophers ascribe to privacy a utilitarian and deontic value tied to autonomy, independence, self-expression, love, friendship, bodily integrity, judgment, and democracy. Jurisprudential scholars stress privacy's value as it relates to limiting government and democratic rights. Psychologists say privacy is key to our well-being, which is characterized by the reduction of social anxieties.[13]

Sexual privacy is a vehicle and domain for self-expression. It is a realm in which excessive self-consciousness and conventionality can interfere with the pursuit of intimacy through genuine efforts to please and be pleased; a realm that can be diminished by accountability and ridicule. Imagine having to explain why one is attracted only to blonds or needs to hear gospel music to achieve an orgasm. Imagine trying to explain why you prefer phone sex with a near stranger to spending time with your wife. Sex is an area in which we encounter our desires, prejudices, and shame, and cloak these emotions in privacy. Society can be hypocritical about sex, often criminalizing some of the very things consenting adults find most exciting. Privacy allows us to flout social and legal hypocrisy without paying a penalty. Sex in private is a realm in which we can come to see ourselves as we really are and find greater self-awareness; for achieving intimacy sometimes demands self-revelation and the abandonment of habitual patterns of self-deception.

The tastes, preferences, styles, and habits we exhibit in sexual intimacy will usually deserve the protection of privacy norms and conditions. Sex-related violence and aggression must be brought to light, treated, and punished. At least some of the interest in knowing the details of the Lewinsky affair was prompted by the concern about whether the President was guilty of sexual harassment in the White House or abused the power of his office. It is a shame that we had to find this out through secret tape recordings, forced testimony, and DNA testing.[14]

Sometimes we lie because we do not expect other people to appreciate what we regard as our true identities and the private lives in which our true identities emerge. Sometimes we lie because telling the truth can lead to rejection, ridicule, censure, or punishment. Lying can keep the world out and allow us to escape the offensive meanings others assign to our

conduct. It may be easier to say, "I'm allergic to shellfish," a lie, than to reveal that one belongs to a religious minority reviled as a radical vegetarian
cult. It may be easier to say, "I'm not a lesbian," when one is indeed a lesbian, than to invite disapproval, rejection, or even beatings.[15]

Keeping conduct private is a way to escape having to see oneself in the
shameful, hateful, and ridiculous terms that others may see us. Although
nearly every adult engages in some type of sexual activity, we all have
unique combinations of acts, habits, emotions, language, styles, props,
and tastes that are our own. Disclosure of our sexual selves could under-
cut our ability to be our sexual selves. Disclosure may make the sexual
conduct or partnerships we once enjoyed impractical. Disclosure may
subject us to shame and ridicule or decrease our ability to experience joy
and intimacy our way. After the Starr Report and the impeachment, it is
unlikely that Clinton will ever again enjoy the role of Monica Lewinsky's
cigar-toting lover, "Handsome," without feeling ridiculous.[16]

These considerations about the importance of privacy and sexual expression help explain what is going on when powerful men seek refuge in
technical definitions of sex in lieu of truth-telling. They are trying to fight
off the imposition of others' interpretations of their identities and conduct. Oscar Wilde denied that he was a sodomite because he wanted to
disassociate himself from the negative connotations of homosexuality in
the minds of those who disapproved of it and were disgusted by it. He dis-
liked the derogatory meanings others in his society brought to their un-
derstandings of homosexuality: depravity, filth, frivolity, and godlessness.
In his own mind, he was participating in the "New Aestheticism," a realm
of intellectual and spiritual beauty higher than ethics itself.[17] For him, intimacy with young men was not reducible to particular sexual acts or to
fecal stains on linen. These "Greek" relationships, as he understood them,
were part intellectual, part aesthetic, part pedagogical, part paternal, and
part erotic. The parts formed an inseparable whole. Wilde felt as though
Queensberry, who sought him out at a theater and club, was intentionally
destroying his private life. Wilde wrote to a friend that his "whole life
seems ruined by this man. The tower of ivory is assailed by the foul thing.
On the sand is my life spilt."[18] Wilde lied because he was unable through
force of character and art to persuade an entire society of what he thought
was the true nature and significance of his relationships with men, and unable to get his wife, the world, or Queensberry to see these relationships'
true meaning and his true identity. Wilde lied to keep his private world

and his self-esteem intact. He did not enjoy the lies that he repeated to his own lawyer, but they seemed necessary.[19]

President Clinton lied because he believed there was no postfeminist interpretation of his extramarital affair with a young intern that the public would accept uncritically. His relationship could be construed as the sexual exploitation of a young female subordinate, or worse, as sexual harassment, Paula Jones style.[20] For Clinton, I conjecture, the meaning of his affair was harmless and represented consensual titillation, sexual gratification, fun, diversion, and friendship. Lying was an effort to preserve a private domain in which those meanings of the affair could flourish. I have known nonmonogamous married couples who lied to most acquaintances about their arrangements because they did not expect other people to understand the real meaning of their conduct—whether loyal, liberating, fun, expressive, intimacy-expanding, or experimental. Indeed, despite all the talk of Bill lying to Hillary and betraying her, for all we know, the President and his wife shared a private "meaning community" in which affairs were allowed and not considered a breach of their mutual commitments.

Given the importance of privacy and sexual privacy just described, is it always morally permissible to lie to someone making inquiries about one's sex life? The answer is surely no. Parents, spouses, and partners may, by virtue of their responsibilities and our commitments to them, have a right to know the details of our sex lives. A more plausible principle than "one has a right to lie in response to all inquiries into one's sex life" is the principle that "one has a right to lie in response to all unjustified inquiries into one's sex life." Nonetheless, even this principle seems too strong and too simplistic. What inquiries will be *unjustified*? Consider an example involving sexual harassment. In the context of sexual harassment in the workplace, for example, rebuffing rude, invasive questions with falsifications seems morally acceptable. Are you busy tonight? Is your husband out of town? Do you like dirty movies? You know how to show a guy a good time, right? In the above situation, falsification would seem appropriate and certainly not unethical.

Suppose, however, you are a gay man on an airplane and you strike up a conversation with the stranger next to you who asks if you are gay. Further, suppose you are a straight black woman and the person beside you asks if you date white men, not as a come-on, but because he wants to know more about your social perspectives solely for purposes of the conversation. Perhaps the right thing to do in these cases is to answer honestly, but then explain that you believe posing such questions is akin to prying. From the perspective of progressive liberals, proudly affirming homosexuality and racial tolerance when one can do so safely better serves the truth-teller and his or her society.

What if you are a candidate for a seat on the Supreme Court and you are asked by the Senate Judiciary Committee whether you enjoy viewing sexual pornography? Should you answer truthfully?[21] This highly personal question seems improper when put exclusively to the second black man in history with a chance at a seat on the Supreme Court. Refusal to answer could be read as an admission, equaling "sudden death" for the candidate. Denial may be the ambitious candidate's only practical option. A judicial candidate ought not to have to reveal his or her sexual tastes, particularly lawful ones, to others as a condition of holding a public office. No one has a right to such information. It is not self-evident, however, that one therefore has a right to lie, that one ought to lie, or that lying is more ethical under the circumstances than refusing to answer or telling the truth. Willingness to speak the truth, even when it is embarrassing, damaging, and sought without good cause, may be a self-destructive virtue we expect of public officials.

The morality of the situation is not self-evident; the psychology, however, is. In the past, we were reared to expect that we could properly do certain things in private without public accountability. When the privacy ethics under which we are reared clash with a novel tell-all ethic of hardball politics and mass-media journalism, we are unsettled. We may find ourselves unable to humiliate and shame ourselves with truth-telling. We may lie as a result, and who really can blame us? I believe Justice Clarence Thomas did all of the things Anita Hill alleged; however, I do not entirely blame him for not acknowledging it to the Senate.[22]

It is easy to understand, and, therefore, hard to fault, some lying. Lying is an ordinary strategy. We all know it. This is why the public did not turn *en masse* against President Clinton. He should not have had the affair, but his efforts to cover it up with lies to friends, family, and strangers are what you would expect from someone who stands to lose so much intimacy, self-esteem, and prestige. Regrettably for the President, his transparent lies caused Mr. Starr to seek very intimate details of his sexual habits to disprove his story and, once those details were collected, Starr made the case that they should be revealed to the public. But who among us could

. . . .

easily bear, with grace, having the raw details of his or her sex life exposed for all to read about?

An important issue raised by the Clinton impeachment was whether the President lied under oath. In a secular legal system, oath-taking is symbolic. Few Americans today believe, as their common-law predecessors may have, that they place their mortal souls on the line by making false statements under oath. It should not be surprising then, given the functions of privacy, that people will lie, mislead others, and omit facts to maintain privacy, even under oath. Ironically, a person threatened with having her intimate life scrutinized in an official government forum has the greatest incentive of all to attempt the good lie. We should expect lies, omissions, equivocations, dissembling, and so on of persons rightly or wrongly put in such a situation.

Many legal doctrines recognize that requiring people to be truthful about matters they deem very private compromises privacy interests and invites dissimulation. One of the goals of the Fifth Amendment right against self-incrimination is the protection of privacy. The attorney-client, physician-patient, clergy-penitent, psychotherapist-patient, and spousal privileges all have goals of protecting privacy and intimacy. A few years ago, the Supreme Court narrowed the "exculpatory no" doctrine, which immunized from criminal liability persons who make certain false statements.[23] The surviving doctrine presupposes the temptation to lie when the truth will almost surely lead to prosecution and conviction.

Men and women of special genius or charisma can sometimes get the world to accept their interpretations of reality or to embrace their meanings. Oscar Wilde brought such transformative genius to his stories and plays. Success in one domain, however, does not always translate to success in another. While the impulse to set one's own meanings is as understandable as it is strong, it is not realistic for celebrities to expect that they will be able to do the same. Their lives are scrutinized too closely. Like artists, politicians are creators of meaning. A charismatic political leader can stand before a crowd and say, "Happy days are here again," and begin, by his words, to make it true.[24] For powerful celebrities in every field, the hubris of expecting to impose one's own meanings on morally controversial and intimate behavior is fueled by the expectations of success that have been enjoyed in other domains of life. But in areas of sexual morality, it is hard to succeed if one is ahead of one's time. Such was the case with Wilde, who lived in an era of homosexual repression, facing several harsh criminal libel laws.

Celebrity makes privacy and the strategy of lying to protect privacy less available. It also makes less available the strategy of not talking to avoid the need to lie.[25] Famous politicians and top public officials work and play before the eyes of the media, bodyguards, and staff. They face a variety of people in journalism and law enforcement whose professional duties are to not take anyone's word at face value. Consequently, some political celebrities find it prudent to be squeaky clean or extremely careful and, in doing so, may falsify their actual preferences to fit in.[26]

Trust, "a fragile good," according to Sissela Bok, is an issue for American democracy.[27] The men and women elected to public office are supposed to represent the interests of their constituencies. The public needs to be able to trust elected and appointed officials to do what they are elected to do. The Vietnam War, the Watergate Affair, the Iran-Contra Affair, and the Clinton-Lewinsky Affair all illustrate that the President and his closest advisors cannot be trusted absolutely.[28] They are capable of crimes, cover-ups, omissions, and outright lies. Outside of Washington, politicians and officials disappoint as well. They lie, distort, steal, cheat on their spouses, sexually harass women, demean minorities, abuse drugs and alcohol, evade taxes, accept bribes, hire undocumented workers, and assault, plot to kill and, occasionally, actually kill their adversaries.[29]

It is hard to quantify trust or to say just how much trust the U.S. political order requires to remain effective and legitimate. Ascertaining the amount of trust Americans actually place in officials is not easy. Polls only reach a small segment of the population, and the answers people give to pollsters may overstate or understate their actual feelings. On the one hand, several trends could suggest a perilously low level of trust in government: the tone of political discourse is often cynical; the number of people interested in engaging in serious political discussion is small; voter turnout is low, compared to other democracies; and antigovernment activism is flourishing. On the other hand, I suspect the vast majority of people living in the United States would say that government is legitimate and effective, and that they can rely on it. It does reliably offer them security and services worth having. Although it is commonplace to interpret low voter turnout as a sign of disenchantment and disengagement with politics, one might also read it as evidence that those entitled to vote actually do trust that the candidates will adequately serve their needs. Indeed,

I believe that most people in the United States, despite their sometimes vociferous complaints, feel very secure with their government. They do not necessarily believe all public officials are always ethical and fair, but they do believe that they are, on the whole, mostly ethical and fair enough.

When philosophers assert that lies by public officials erode trust, they are resting on a time-honored axiom that workable cooperative enterprises require participants to be truthful, trustworthy, and reliable. The axiom is doubtless true, but does not entail that workable cooperative enterprises will fall apart if leaders are sometimes not truthful about matters of direct relevance to their official duties.[30] In addition, it certainly does not entail that workable cooperative enterprises must fall apart if leaders are sometimes not truthful about matters that the public may deem tangential to their official duties, such as sex, and that are well-understood as matters in which moral failure and lapses in judgment are ordinary and predictable. I am suggesting that the conclusion that lying about sex erodes trust in public officials overlooks how much the U.S. public of today and yesterday understands and discounts sex and privacy-related deception.[31]

Secrecy and deception about national programs and policies are components of presidential power.[32] Many presidents, including some of the greatest presidents, falsified and concealed important personal facts from the American people during their terms in office. Thomas Jefferson's secret was Sally Hemings, a black slave by whom he bore a child;[33] Grover Cleveland's secret was an out-of-wedlock son named Oscar, whose sane mother Cleveland had committed to an insane asylum;[34] Warren Harding's secret was a mistress smuggled into White House closets for sex, and their daughter, Elizabeth Ann, whom Harding declined ever to see or to support;[35] Woodrow Wilson's secrets were dyslexia, a series of strokes, and an extramarital affair with Mary Peck;[36] Franklin Roosevelt's secrets were a mistress and a bout with polio that left him completely unable to walk;[37] John F. Kennedy's secrets were addictions to drugs and sex;[38] and Ronald Reagan's secret, sadly visible before he left office, was Alzheimer's disease.[39]

Sissela Bok raises the following series of key questions: "Why . . . should lying to the public not be . . . legitimate, in cases of persistent and intrusive probing? What is it that turns an official's lie to the public into a matter of public concern, no matter how rightfully private the subject of the lie itself?" Her answer is that "the credibility of public officials is crucial in a democracy." Bok further states that "[a]ppeals to privacy can be exploited to cover up wrongdoing just as much as national security can. . . ." More-over, she makes the slippery-slope argument that lies lead to further lies, lies by the liar and lies by those who emulate the liar. Bok states finally that "when distrust becomes too overpowering within a family, a commu-nity or a nation, it becomes impossible to meet joint needs." Addressing the duties of public officials in this area, Bok finds that in exchange for the privileges that they have been granted, "public servants, doctors, clergy, lawyers, bankers, journalists and other professionals have a special re-sponsibility" to "consider to what extent their actions erode or help re-store this social good of trust."[40]

Bok's most powerful argument is that, for the sake of trust, public offi-cials have a special obligation to avoid deception regarding their private lives, even when their private lives have been perhaps unjustly probed. Notice that Bok rejects the justice-of-lying-to-the-unjust principle as ap-plied to public officials. She also avoids the fiction that public figures waive privacy and expectations of privacy by thrusting themselves into the limelight. My response to Bok is to agree that trust is vital, but to dis-agree that trust in government hinges crucially on officials never lying to protect privacy. In some contexts, "deliberate deception need not in gen-eral pose a significant threat to trust."[41] This is not to say that we should take pride in lies and liars, particularly those whose reckless behavior greatly affects the efficiency of two branches of the national government, and subject our nation to ridicule. We should, however, take pride in our capacity for empathetic understanding of the realm of sexuality as a realm of propriety and impropriety, of a mixture of communal and self-defined modes of intimacy and expression that may or may not conform to social expectations. A significant segment of the public appears to accept the no-tion that a president is justified in lying to protect the privacy of his or her family.[42]

I defend the right of presidents and other public officials to have pri-vate lives sometimes defended by deception. This is not to advocate lying on national television and under oath without conscience and concern for consequences. Privacy is a context for correcting, as well as making, sexually related mistakes. Suppose an official has an extramarital affair, confesses it to his or her spouse in private, and begins to rebuild their mar-riage in earnest. To deny the affair to the public in an effort to avoid fur-ther damage to a marriage is not plainly immoral, and not plainly the kind of deception that, if found out, would significantly erode public trust in government or invite more lies. In a best-selling practical guide to truth-telling in personal relationships, Dr. Harriet Lerner asserts that people seek privacy primarily to protect their dignity and ultimate separateness as human beings, rather than to fool others or engage in acts of deception.[43] For this reason, she argues, we can proudly speak of and exercise our rights to privacy. When it comes to lying to protect privacy, however, Lerner's neat dichotomy breaks apart, for in these contexts, we seek both to fool and to protect our dignity and separateness.

Adrienne Rich suggests that even lying justified by an appeal to privacy can be a product of cowardice and an attempt to "short-cut through another's personality."[44] Because of his manipulative behavior and his cowardice, I do not defend President Clinton's handling of his private life. In my estimation, Clinton was wrong to involve himself with Lewinsky in the shadow of the Paula Jones case, in the corridors of the White House, and in the context of a very public marriage. Having walked on the "Wilde" side, he was wrong to go further down that road by desperately using the public airways and government employees to further his deception. It was almost as if the President thought he was a private citizen lying to a gullible spouse behind closed doors, circa 1958, rather than the most watched and investigated man on the planet lying to the planet in 1998.

As Leonard Saxe astutely observed, "this seems to have become a society in which lying is endemic, but in which a Victorian-like attitude is also maintained that heavily sanctions those who are caught in prevarication."[45] To this, I might add, that ours seems to be a society in which extramarital sex is endemic, but in which a Victorian-like attitude is maintained that severely sanctions those who are caught in adultery. It is time to embrace openly a less hypocritical, more consistent set of norms that would make lying about sex seem less necessary.

NOTES

1. Richard Ellmann, *Oscar Wilde* (New York: Vintage Books, 1988).
2. Ibid., pp. 307, 355, describing Wilde's early homosexual relationships with John Gray and Andre Gide.
3. Ibid., pp. 389–91.
4. Ibid.
5. Ibid., p. 435 ("[Wilde's] life with Douglas, including the publicity of their romantic passion, reflected his intention to oblige a hypocritical age to take him as he was."). Ellmann speculates that:

The excitement of doing something considered wrong, and the [vices of] faithless boys . . . may have been as important for Wilde as sexual gratification. . . . English society tolerated homosexuality only so long as one was not caught at it. His chances of being caught were enormously increased as he combined casual associations with his more idealized ones. . . . Wilde believed in his star. . . . But he was always bringing himself to the brink. (pp. 390–391).

Michel Foucault observed that "we now know that it is sex itself which hides the most secret parts of the individual: the structure of his fantasies, the roots of his ego, the forms of his relationship to reality. At the bottom of sex, there is truth." Wendy Doniger, "Sex, Lies, and Tall Tales," *Social Research,* p. 664. If there is truth in sex, there is surely the most truth in the sex that is most authentic. But see pp. 665–76 (arguing that sexual love is inherently deluding). The sexual act is the ultimate key to concealed identity. See p. 664 (observing that, according to Bible stories, great literature, and Freud, sex is "the most reliable criterion of personal identity"). The true self is revealed in the physical act of sex and in the spiritual act of falling in love. See p. 664 (noting distinction between physical sex and falling in love).

    6. Ellmann, *op. cit.,* p. 439, describing initiation of libel suit against Marquess of Queensberry and quoting Wilde as saying, " 'What is loathsome to me is the memory of interminable visits paid by me to the solicitor . . . [where] I would sit with [a] serious face[ ] telling serious lies.' "

    7. Ibid., p. 438.

    8. F. G. Bailey, *The Prevalence of Deceit* (Cornell University Press, 1991) p. 37 (stating that "[t]he prospect of losing face is, of course, apt to arouse nonrealistic sentiments, and a man can be moved to cut off his nose to save his face").

    9. See Ellmann, *op. cit.,* p. 461 (stating that Wilde did not practice "buggery" as such).

    10. Renee Graham, "Born to Be Wilde: Stephen Fry Realizes Dream to Play Author," *Boston Globe,* May 31, 1998, p. E11.

    11. See John Walsh, "The Big Picture—All Too Black and White," *The Independent* (London), Oct. 29, 1998, p. 11 (criticizing film and noting instance of political "schmoozing").

    12. Michael J. Chandler & Jamie Afifi, "On Making a Virtue Out of Telling Lies," 63 *Social Research* (1996), pp. 731, 731 (noting that a good lie deserves a certain amount of respect).

    13. Carl D. Schneider, *Shame, Exposure, and Privacy* (New York: W.W. Norton, 1992), p. 41.

    14. Kenneth Starr, Referral to the United States House of Representatives Pursuant to Title 28, United States Code, 595 ©, Submitted by the Office of the Independent Counsel, Sept. 9, 1998, available in 1998 WL 614815 [hereinafter Starr Report]Report, pp. 50, 54 (indicating that DNA tests showed that semen on Monica Lewinsky's dress was President Clinton's).

    15. Ruben Castaneda, "Hate Crimes Laws Rely on Motives, Not Targets: Laurel Slaying Illustrates Fine Line," *Washington Post,* Oct. 26, 1998, p. D1 (noting that anti-gay violence has created call for national hate crime legislation).

    16. Starr Report, pp. 60–61, 93, 107, 139. Ms. Lewinsky testified that she called President Clinton "Handsome," President Clinton inserted cigar into her vagina, and she and President Clinton had phone sex on ten to fifteen occasions.

    17. Ellmann, *op. cit.,* pp. 305–06.

    18. Ibid., pp. 438–39.

    19. Ibid. Wilde wrote to Douglas and stated: "What is loathsome to me is the memory of interminable visits paid by me to the solicitor . . . when you and I would sit with serious faces telling serious lies to a bald man. . . ." (p. 439).

. . . .

20. In early November 1998, without admitting wrongdoing or apologizing, President Clinton settled the lawsuit Paula Jones brought against him alleging sexual harassment.

21. Michael Wines, "The Thomas Nomination: Compelling Evidence on Both Sides, But Only One Can Be Telling Truth," *New York Times*, Oct. 15, 1991, p. 20. A polygraph test bolstered Anita Hill's case, particularly her claim that Thomas talked about pornography and sex acts.

22. Anita Hill, *Speaking Truth to Power* (New York: Anchor Books, 1998), pp. 222–224.

23. See Brogan v. United States, 118 S. Ct. 805, 811–12 (1998).

24. Harold Evans, *The American Century* (New York: Knopf, 1998), pp. 241, 246. "Happy Days are Here Again" was Franklin D. Roosevelt's Depression-busting campaign song.

25. Bailey, *op. cit.*, p. 71 ("Public opinion is not easily avoided. If you . . . try to opt out of the game and be neither a talker nor a listener, the penalty is to be considered . . . not part of the community.").

26. Timur Kuran, *Private Truth, Public Lies: The Social Consequences of Preference Falsification* (Cambridge, MA: Harvard University Press, 1995), p.11 (explaining the dynamics of lying to protect oneself and to fit in). Kuran states:

> Talk being cheap, anyone can claim to be against this lifestyle or that political platform. An effective way of making such a claim credible is to participate in efforts to punish those from whom one is seeking dissociation. A closeted homosexual may become a gay basher to allay suspicions about his own private life. . . . [H]ypocrisy is a universal, and often successful, tactic of self-protection and self-promotion.

27. Sissela Bok, "Lies: They Come with Consequences," *Washington Post*, Aug. 23, 1998, p. C1.

28. John Orman, *Presidential Secrecy and Deception* (Greenwood Publishing Group, 1980), p. 4.

29. See Bruce Frankel & Bill Hewitt, "Only in America What Hath Election Day Wrought? A Wrestler, a Brother Act and a Speaker Made Speechless," *People,* Nov. 23, 1998, p. 61 (explaining that unless Burks's widow ran as a write-in candidate, Looper would win by default). The late Tennessee State Senator Tommy Burks was murdered two weeks before the November 1998 election and police charged Byron "Low Tax" Looper, Burks's opponent in the election, with the murder. To prevent the jailed Looper from winning the election by default, the dead man's widow ran in his place and garnered 96 percent of the vote as a write-in candidate.

30. Mary Mothersill, "Some Questions About Truthfulness and Lying," 63 *Social Research*, (1996), pp. 924–25. Mothersill disagrees that lying causes deception to become "a way of life."

31. Poll, Roper Center at the University of Connecticut, Question No. 005 (1998) (noting that in a recent public opinion poll, 49 percent of respondents said that they thought the President would be justified in lying to protect privacy of his family, 46 percent said he would not be justified in lying and 5 percent said they "did not know").

32. Orman, *op. cit.*, p. 7.

33. Patrick Rogers et al., "All Tom's Children: A President's Presumed Affair with a Slave Gives New Meaning to the Term Jeffersonian," *People,* Nov. 23, 1998, p. 77. A DNA test conducted at Oxford University indicated that Jefferson fathered child with one of his slaves.

34. Evans, *op. cit.*, p. 31. Republicans hoped that the disclosure of Cleveland's out-of-wedlock son would cost him the presidency in 1884.

35. Ibid., p. 201 (describing Harding's secret relationship with Nan Britton and his daughter Elizabeth whom he never saw and how the story was published despite attempts of suppression).

36. See Ford Burkhart, "Edwin A. Weinstein, 89, Neuropsychiatrist Who Studied President Wilson," *New York Times,* Sept. 21, 1998, p. B12. Weinstein believed that President Wilson's denial of his illnesses contributed to his presidential problems.

37. Evans, *op. cit.,* p. 243 ("Few . . . knew how crippled he was. The press respected his privacy. The public did not see pictures. . . .").

38. Seymour M. Hersh, *The Dark Side of Camelot* (Little Brown & Co., 1997), pp. 229–30 (emphasizing President John F. Kennedy's sex-filled private life and its effect on the people around him).

39. Burkhart, *op. cit.,* p. B12 (indicating that the physician who studied Reagan's presidency concluded that he suffered from Alzheimer's symptoms, like loss of memory, that left him frequently unaware of world affairs); see also Melinda Beck, "Alzheimer's Terrible Toll," *Newsweek,* Oct. 2, 1995, p.36. Reagan privately worried about his failing memory and once failed to recognize a member of his own cabinet; M. J. Zuckerman, "Bush: Reagan Wasn't Ill as President," *USA Today,* Nov. 29, 1996, p. 2A. Historians and others wonder whether Reagan's failing memory during his term as president was related to Alzheimer's.

40. Bok, *op. cit.* p. C1.

41. Jennifer Jackson, "Telling the Truth," 17 *Journal of Medical Ethics* (1991), pp. 5–9.

42. For a further review of the results of the poll conducted by the Roper Center at the University of Connecticut on whether a president is justified in lying to protect the privacy of his family, see fn. 31 and accompanying text.

43. Harriet Lerner, *The Dance of Deception* (New York: HarperCollins, 1994), pp. 36–37.

44. Adrienne Rich, *On Lies, Secrets and Silence* (New York: W.W. Norton & Company, 1995).

45. Leonard Saxe, "Thoughts of an Applied Social Psychologist," 46 *American Psychologist* (1991), p. 410. Saxe also states, "A kind of hysteria about dishonesty seems to have permeated our culture. Perhaps stimulated by pervasive mendacity, we are quick to call others liars and frauds." (p. 414).

Imperial Bedroom

. . . .

by
JONATHAN FRANZEN

Privacy, privacy, the new American obsession: espoused as the most fundamental of rights, marketed as the most desirable of commodities, and pronounced dead twice a week. Even before Linda Tripp pressed the "Record" button on her tape recorder, commentators were warning that "privacy is under siege," that "privacy is in a dreadful state," that "privacy as we now know it may not exist in the year 2000." Not just Big Brother but little brother, John Q. Public, too, is shadowing me through networks of computers. Security cameras no bigger than spiders watch from every shaded corner, dour feminists monitor bedroom behavior and water-cooler conversations, genetic sleuths decoct my entire being from a droplet of saliva, and voyeurs can retrofit ordinary camcorders with a filter that lets them *see through people's clothing*. Then comes the flood of dirty suds from the Office of the Independent Counsel, oozing forth through official and commercial channels to saturate the national consciousness. Lewinskygate marks, in the words of the philosopher Thomas Nagel, "the culmination of a disastrous erosion" of privacy; it represents, in the words of the author Wendy Kaminer, "the utter disregard for privacy and individual autonomy that exists in totalitarian regimes." In the person of Kenneth Starr, "the public sphere" has finally overwhelmed—shredded, gored, trampled, invaded, run roughshod over—"the private."

The panic about privacy has all the finger-pointing and paranoia of a good old American scare, but it's missing one vital ingredient: a genuinely alarmed public. Americans care about privacy mainly in the abstract. Sometimes a well-informed community unites to defend itself, as when Net users bombarded the White House with e-mails against the "clipper chip," and sometimes an especially outrageous piece of news provokes a national outcry, as when the Lotus Development Corporation tried to market a CD-ROM containing financial profiles of nearly half the people in the country. By and large, though, even in the face of wholesale infringements like the war on drugs, Americans remain curiously passive. I'm no exception. I read the editorials and try to get excited, but I can't. More often than not, I find myself feeling the opposite of what the commentators want me to. It's happened twice in the last month alone.

On the Saturday morning when the *Times* came carrying the complete text of the Starr report, what I felt as I sat alone in my apartment and tried to eat my breakfast was that my own privacy—not Clinton's, not Lewinsky's—was being violated. I love the distant pageant of public life, both the pageantry and the distance. Now a President was facing impeachment, and, as a good citizen, I had a duty to stay informed about the evidence; but the evidence here consisted of two people's groping, sucking, and mutual self-deception. What I felt, when this evidence landed beside my toast and coffee, wasn't a pretend revulsion to camouflage a secret interest in the dirt; I wasn't offended by the sex qua sex; I wasn't worrying about a potential future erosion of my own rights; I didn't feel the President's pain in the empathic way he'd once claimed to feel mine; I wasn't repelled by the revelation that public officials do bad things; and although I'm a registered Democrat, my disgust was of a different order from my partisan disgust at the news that the Giants have blown a fourth-quarter lead. What I felt I felt personally. I was being intruded on.

A couple of days later, I got a call from one of my credit-card providers, asking me to confirm two recent charges at a gas station and one at a hardware store. Such queries are common nowadays, but this one was my first, and for a moment I felt eerily exposed. At the same time, I was perversely flattered that someone, somewhere, had taken an interest in me and had bothered to phone. Not that the young male operator seemed to care about me personally. He sounded as if he were reading his lines from a laminated booklet. The strain of working hard at a job he almost certainly didn't enjoy seemed to thicken his tongue. He tried to rush his words out, to speed through them as if in embarrassment or vexation at how nearly worthless they were, but they kept bunching up in his teeth, and he had to stop and extract them with his lips, one by one. It was the computer, he said, the computer that routinely, ah, scans the, you know, the pattern of charges . . . and was there something else he could help me with tonight? I decided that if this young person wanted to scroll through

. . . .

my charges and ponder the significance of my two fill-ups and my gallon of latex paint I was fine with it.

So here's the problem. On the Saturday morning the Starr Report came out, my privacy was, in the classic liberal view, absolute. I was alone in my home and unobserved, unbothered by neighbors, unmentioned in the news, and perfectly free, if I chose, to ignore the report and do the pleasantly *al dente* Saturday crossword; yet the report's mere existence so offended my sense of privacy that I could hardly bring myself to touch the thing. Two days later, I was disturbed in my home by a ringing phone, asked to cough up my mother's maiden name, and made aware that the digitized minutiae of my daily life were being scrutinized by strangers; and within five minutes I'd put the entire episode out of my mind. I felt encroached on when I was ostensibly safe, and I felt safe when I was ostensibly encroached on. And I didn't know why.

The right to privacy—defined by Louis Brandeis and Samuel Warren, in 1890, as "the right to be let alone"—seems at first glance to be an elemental principle in American life. It's the rallying cry of activists fighting for reproductive rights, against stalkers, for the right to die, against a national health-care database, for stronger data-encryption standards, against paparazzi, for the sanctity of employee e-mail, and against employee drug testing. On closer examination, though, privacy proves to be the Cheshire cat of values: not much substance, but a very winning smile.

Legally, the concept is a mess. Privacy violation is the emotional core of many crimes, from stalking and rape to Peeping Tommery and trespass, but no criminal statute forbids it in the abstract. Civil law varies from state to state but generally follows a forty-year-old analysis by the legal scholar Dean William Prosser, who dissected the invasion of privacy into four torts: *intrusion* on my solitude; the publishing of *private facts* about me which are not of legitimate public concern; publicity that puts my character in a *false light*; and *appropriation* of my name or likeness without my consent. This is a crumbly set of torts. Intrusion looks like trespass, false light like defamation, and appropriation like theft; and the harm that remains when these extraneous offenses are subtracted is so admirably captured by the phrase "infliction of emotional distress" as to render the tort of privacy invasion all but superfluous. What really undergirds privacy is the classic liberal conception of personal autonomy. In the last few decades, many judges and scholars have chosen to speak of a "zone of privacy," rather than a "sphere of liberty," but this is a shift in emphasis, not in substance: not the making of a new doctrine but the re-marketing of an old one.

Whatever you're trying to sell, whether it's luxury real estate or Esperanto lessons, it helps to have the smiling word "private" on your side. Last winter, as the owner of a Bank One PlatinumVisa card, I was offered enrollment in a program called PrivacyGuard®, which, according to the literature promoting it, *"puts you in the know* about the very personal records available to your employer, insurers, credit card companies, and government agencies." The first three months of PrivacyGuard® were free, so I signed up. What came in the mail then was paperwork: envelopes and request forms for various record searches, also a disappointingly un-deluxe logbook in which to jot down the search results. I realized immediately that I didn't care enough about, say, my driving records to wait a month to get them; it was only when I called PrivacyGuard® to cancel my membership, and was all but begged not to, that I realized that the whole point of this "service" was to harness my time and energy to the task of re-ducing Bank One Visa's fraud losses.

Even issues that legitimately touch on privacy are rarely concerned with the actual emotional harm of unwanted exposure or intrusion. A proposed national Genetic Privacy Act, for example, is premised on the idea that my DNA reveals more about my identity and my future health than other medical data do. In fact, DNA is as yet no more intimately re-vealing than a heart murmur, a family history of diabetes, or an inordinate fondness for Buffalo chicken wings. As with any medical records, the po-tential for abuse of genetic information by employers and insurers is chill-ing, but this is only tangentially a privacy issue; the primary harm consists of things like job discrimination and higher insurance premiums. In a sim-ilar way, the problem of online security is mainly about nuts and bolts. What American activists call "electronic privacy" their European coun-terparts call "data protection." Our term is exciting; theirs is accurate. If someone is out to steal your Amex number and expiration date, or if an evil ex-boyfriend is looking for your new address, or if you're plotting a leveraged buyout of Texaco, you need the kind of hard-core secrecy that encryption seeks to guarantee. If you're talking to a friend on the phone about how much you hate *The English Patient,* however, you need only a *feeling* of privacy (unless you work for Miramax).

The social drama of data protection goes something like this: a hacker or an insurance company or a telemarketer gains access to a sensitive database, public-interest watchdogs bark loudly, and new firewalls go up.

. . . .

Just as most people are moderately afraid of germs but leave virology to the Centers for Disease Control, most Americans take a reasonable interest in privacy issues but leave the serious custodial work to experts. Our problem now is that the custodians have started speaking a language of panic and treating privacy not as one of many competing values but as the one value that trumps all others.

The novelist Richard Powers recently declared in a *Times* Op-Ed piece that privacy is a "vanishing illusion" and that the struggle over the encryption of digital communications is therefore as "great with consequence" as the Cold War. Powers defines "the private" as "that part of life that goes unregistered," and he sees in the digital footprints we leave whenever we charge things the approach of "that moment when each person's every living day will become a Bloomsday, recorded in complete detail and reproducible with a few deft keystrokes." It is scary, of course, to think that the mystery of our identities might be reducible to finite data sequences. That Powers can seriously compare credit-card fraud and intercepted cell-phone calls to the threat of thermonuclear incineration, however, speaks mainly to the infectiousness of privacy panic. Where, after all, is it "registered" what Powers or anybody else is thinking, seeing, saying, wishing, planning, dreaming, or feeling ashamed of? A digital *Ulysses* consisting of nothing but a list of its hero's purchases and other recordable transactions might run, at most, to four pages: was there really nothing more to Bloom's day?

When Americans do genuinely sacrifice privacy, moreover, they do so for tangible gains in health or safety or efficiency. Most legalized infringements—HIV notification, airport X rays, Megan's Law, Breathalyzer roadblocks, the drug-testing of student athletes, laws protecting fetuses, laws protecting the vegetative, remote monitoring of automobile emissions, county-jail strip searches, even Ken Starr's cleansing exposure of Presidential corruption—are essentially public-health measures. I resent the security cameras in Washington Square Park, but I appreciate the ones on a subway platform. The risk that someone is abusing my E-Z Pass toll records seems to me comfortably low in comparison with my gain in convenience. Ditto the risk that someone will make me a victim of the First Amendment; with two hundred and seventy million people in the country, my own chances of being nationally exposed are next to nil.

The legal scholar Lawrence Lessig has characterized Americans as "bovine" for making calculations like this and for thereby acquiescing in what he calls the "Sovietization" of personal life. The curious thing about

·   ·   ·   ·   ·   ·   ·   ·   ·   ·

privacy, though, is that simply by expecting it we can usually achieve it. One of my neighbors in the apartment building across the street spends a lot of time at her mirror examining her pores, and I can see her doing it, just as she can undoubtedly see me sometimes. But our respective privacies remain intact as long as neither of us *feels* seen. When I send a postcard through the U.S. mail, I'm aware in the abstract that mail handlers may be reading it, may be reading it aloud, may even be laughing at it, but I'm safe from all harm, unless, by sheer bad luck, the one handler in the country whom I actually know sees the postcard and slaps his forehead and says, "Oh, jeez, I know this guy."

Our privacy panic isn't merely exaggerated. It's founded on a fallacy. Ellen Alderman and Caroline Kennedy, in *The Right to Privacy*, sum up the conventional wisdom of privacy advocates like this: "There is less privacy than there used to be." The claim has been made or implied so often, in so many books and editorials and talk-show dens, that Americans, no matter how passive they are in their behavior, now dutifully tell pollsters that they're very much worried about privacy. From almost any historical perspective, however, the claim seems bizarre.

In 1890, an American typically lived in a small town under conditions of near-panoptical surveillance. Not only did his every purchase "register" but it registered in the eyes and in the memory of shopkeepers who knew him, his parents, his wife, and his children. He couldn't so much as walk to the post office without having his movements tracked and analyzed by neighbors. Probably he grew up sleeping in a bed with his siblings and possibly with his parents, too. Unless he was well-off, his transportation—a train, a horse, his own two feet—either was communal or exposed him to the public eye.

In the suburbs and exurbs where the typical American lives today, tiny nuclear families inhabit enormous houses, in which each person has his or her own bedroom and, sometimes, bathroom. Compared even with suburbs in the sixties and seventies, when I was growing up, the contemporary condominium development or gated community offers a striking degree of anonymity. It's no longer the rule that you know your neighbors. Communities increasingly tend to be virtual, the participants either faceless or firmly in control of the faces they present. Transportation is largely private: the latest SUVs are the size of living rooms and come with onboard telephones, CD players, and TV screens; behind the tinted windows of one of these high-riding, I-see-you-but-you-can't-see-me mobile Privacy-

Guard® units, a person can be wearing pajamas or a licorice bikini, for all anybody knows or cares. Maybe the government intrudes on the family a little more than it did a hundred years ago (social workers look in on the old and the poor, health officials require inoculations, the police inquire about spousal battery), but from a privacy perspective these intrusions don't begin to make up for the small-town snooping they've replaced.

"The right to be let alone"? Far from disappearing, it's exploding. It's the essence of modern American architecture, landscape, transportation, communications, and mainstream political philosophy. The real reason that Americans are passive about privacy is so big as to be almost invisible: we're flat-out *drowning* in privacy.

What's threatened isn't the private sphere. It's the public sphere. Much has been made of the discouraging effect that the Starr investigation may have on future aspirants to public office (only zealots and zeros need apply), but that's just half of it. The public world of Washington, because it's public, belongs to everyone. We're all invited to participate with our votes, our patriotism, our campaigning, and our opinions. The collective weight of a population makes possible our faith in the public world as something larger and more enduring and more dignified than any messy individual can be in private. But, just as one sniper in a church tower can keep the streets of an entire town empty, one real gross-out scandal can undermine that faith.

If privacy depends upon an expectation of invisibility, the expectation of *visibility* is what defines a public space. My "sense of privacy" functions to keep the public out of the private *and* to keep the private out of the public. A kind of mental Border collie yelps in distress when I feel that the line between the two has been breached. This is why the violation of a public space is so similar, as an experience, to the violation of privacy. I walk past a man taking a leak on a sidewalk in broad daylight (delivery-truck drivers can be especially self-righteous in their "Ya gotta go, ya gotta go" philosophy of bladder management), and although the man with the yawning fly is ostensibly the one whose privacy is compromised by the leak, I'm the one who feels the impingement. Flashers and sexual harassers and fellators on the pier and self-explainers on the crosstown bus all similarly assault our sense of the public by exposing themselves.

Since really serious exposure in public today is assumed to be synonymous with being seen on television, it would seem to follow that televised space is the premier public space. Many things that people say to me on television, however, would never be tolerated in a genuine public space—

in a jury box, for example, or even on a city sidewalk. TV is an enormous, ramified extension of the billion living rooms and bedrooms in which it's consumed. You rarely hear a person on the subway talking loudly about, say, incontinence, but on television it's been happening for years. TV is devoid of shame, and without shame there can be no distinction between public and private. Last winter, an anchorwoman looked me in the eye and, in the tone of a close female relative, referred to a litter of babies in Iowa as "America's seven little darlin's." It was strange enough, twenty-five years ago, to get Dan Rather's reports on Watergate between spots for Geritol and Bayer aspirin, as if Nixon's impending resignation were somehow situated in my medicine chest. Now, shelved between ads for Promise margarine and Celebrity Cruises, the news itself is a soiled cocktail dress— TV the wardrobe and nothing but.

Reticence, meanwhile, has become an almost obsolete virtue. People now readily name their diseases, rents, and antidepressants. Sexual histories get spilled on first dates, Birkenstocks and cutoffs infiltrate the office on casual Fridays, telecommuting puts the boardroom in the bedroom, "softer" modern office design puts the bedroom in the boardroom, salespeople unilaterally address customers by their first names, waiters won't bring me food until I've established a personal relationship with them, voice-mail machinery stresses the "I" in "I'm sorry, but I don't understand what you dialed," and cyberenthusiasts, in a particularly grotesque misnomer, designate as "public forums" pieces of etched silicon with which a forum's unshaved "participant" may communicate while sitting cross-legged in tangled sheets and wearing gym shorts. The networked world as a threat to privacy? It's the ugly spectacle of a privacy triumphant.

A genuine public space is a place where every citizen is welcome to be present, and where the purely private is excluded or restricted. One reason that attendance at art museums has soared in recent years is that museums still feel public in this way. After those tangled sheets, how delicious the enforced decorum and the hush, the absence of in-your-face consumerism. How sweet the promenading, the seeing and being seen. Everybody needs a promenade sometimes—a place to go when you want to announce to the world (not the little world of friends and family but the big world, the real world) that you have a new suit, or are in love, or suddenly realize that you stand a full inch taller when you don't hunch your shoulders.

Unfortunately, the fully public place is a nearly extinct category. We still have courtrooms and the jury pool, commuter trains and bus stations, here and there a small-town Main Street that really is a main street rather than a strip mall, certain coffee bars, and certain city sidewalks. Other-

. . . .

wise, for American adults the only halfway public space is the world of work. Here, especially in the upper echelons of business, codes of dress and behavior are routinely enforced, personal disclosures are penalized, and formality is still the rule. But these rituals extend only to the employees of the firm, and even they, when they become old, disabled, obsolete, or outsourceable, are liable to be expelled and thereby relegated to the tangled sheets.

The last big, steep-walled bastion of public life in America is Washington, D.C. Hence the particular violation I felt when the Starr Report crashed in. Hence the feeling of being intruded on. It was privacy invasion, all right: private life brutally invading the most public of public spaces. I don't want to see sex on the news from Washington. There's sex everywhere else I look—on sitcoms, on the web, on dust jackets, on the billboards in Times Square. Can't there be one thing in the national landscape that isn't about the bedroom? We all know there's sex in the cloak-rooms of power, sex behind the pomp and circumstance, sex beneath the robes of justice; but can't we act like grown-ups and pretend otherwise? Pretend not that "no one is looking" but that *everyone* is looking?

For two decades now, business leaders and politicians across much of the spectrum, both Gingrich Republicans and Clinton Democrats, have extolled the virtues of privatizing public institutions. But what better word can there be for Lewinskygate and the ensuing irruption of disclosures (the infidelities of Helen Chenoweth, of Dan Burton, of Henry Hyde) than "privatization"? Anyone who wondered what a privatized presidency might look like may now, courtesy of Mr. Starr, behold one.

In Denis Johnson's short story "Beverly Home," the young narrator spends his days working at a nursing home for the hopelessly disabled, where there is a particularly unfortunate patient whom no one visits:

> He was only thirty-three, I believe he said, but it was hard to guess what he told about himself because he really couldn't talk anymore, beyond clamping his lips repeatedly around his protruding tongue while groaning.
> No more pretending for him! He was completely and openly a mess. Meanwhile the rest of us go on trying to fool each other.

In a coast-to-coast, shag-carpeted imperial bedroom, we could all just be messes and save ourselves the trouble of pretending. But who wants to live in a pajama-party world? Privacy loses its value unless there's something it can be defined against. "Meanwhile the rest of us go on trying to fool each other"—and a good thing, too. The need to put on a public face is as basic as the need for the privacy in which to take it off. We need both a home that's not like a public space and a public space that's not like home.

Walking up Third Avenue on a Saturday night, I feel bereft. All around me, attractive young people are hunched over their StarTacs and Nokias with preoccupied expressions, as if probing a sore tooth, or adjusting a hearing aid, or squeezing a pulled muscle: personal technology has begun to look like a personal handicap. What I really want from a sidewalk is that people see me and let themselves be seen, but even this modest ideal is thwarted by cell-phone users and their unwelcome privacy. They say things like "Should we have couscous with that?" and "I'm on my way to Blockbuster." They aren't breaking any law by broadcasting these dining-nook conversations. There's no PublicityGuard® that I can buy, no expensive preserve of public life to which I can flee. Seclusion, whether in a suite at The Plaza or in a cabin in the Catskills, is comparatively effortless to achieve. Privacy is protected as both commodity and right; public forums are protected as neither. Like old-growth forests, they're few and irreplaceable and should be held in trust by everyone. The work of maintaining them only gets harder as the private sector grows ever more demanding, distracting, and disheartening. Who has the time and the energy to stand up for the public sphere? What rhetoric can possibly compete with the American love of "privacy"?

When I return to my apartment after dark, I don't immediately turn my lights on. Over the years, it's become a reflexive precaution on my part not to risk spooking exposed neighbors by flooding my living room with light, although the only activity I ever seem to catch them at is watching TV.

My skin-conscious neighbor is home with her husband tonight, and they seem to be dressing for a party. The woman, a vertical strip of whom is visible between the Levolors and the window frame, is wearing a bathrobe and a barrette and sitting in front of a mirror. The man, slick-haired, wearing suit pants and a white T-shirt, stands by a sofa in the other room and watches television in a posture that I recognize as uncommitted. Finally, the woman disappears into the bedroom. The man puts on a white shirt and a necktie and perches sidesaddle on an arm of the sofa, still watching television, more involved with it now. The woman returns wearing a strapless yellow dress and looking like a whole different species of being. Happy the transformation! Happy the distance between private and public! I see a rapid back-and-forth involving jewelry, jackets, and a clutch purse, and then the couple, dressed to the nines, ventures out into the world.

Enter a Murderer

.   .   .   .

by
WENDY LESSER

In 1991, a trial held in San Francisco asked, and temporarily answered, the question of whether a television station should be allowed to record and broadcast the execution of a condemned man in the California gas chamber. That legal case, *KQED v. Daniel B. Vasquez,* will provide the central framework of my discussion here, for in the course of the trial there emerged all sorts of information and ideas about how we respond to murder as spectacle. At present, in America, any state-run execution will be that of a murderer, since murder, for at least the last two decades, has been the only crime for which civilians are put to death. An execution is itself the only kind of murder that is planned and publicly announced in advance, so that we know exactly who the victim will be and when he will die. It is thus the only form of murder that anyone but the murderer and the victim could count on attending. (Come to think of it, anyone but the murderer; the victim always has to be there too, but, except in the case of executions, he won't *count* on it in advance.) As a killing carried out in all our names, an act of the state in which we by proxy participate, it is also the only form of murder that directly implicates even the witnesses, the bystanders.

As you may have gathered, I do not approve of the death penalty, and that attitude will naturally color my coverage of *KQED v. Vasquez.* It will not, however, determine my response to the central question in the case— whether executions should be televised or not—for there were critics of capital punishment on both sides. Some death-penalty opponents insisted that televising executions would cause people to vote against capital punishment, others that these broadcasts would only arouse the population's bloodlust. I don't know which, if either, of these predictions is the correct one; as I said, the effects of art and media on behavior are not my concern here. What I find useful in the legal case is the way it opens up and clarifies some of the other questions that concern me about our interest in murder.

Specifically, the case of *KQED v. Vasquez* points up the crucial connection between murder and theater—between death imposed on a human being by another human being, and dramatic spectacle. This connection is not limited to murder's inclusion as a plot device in theater, though that is importantly there, from Agamemnon's, Clytemnestra's, and Orestes' murders of their various family members, through Shakespeare's tragedies and the bloody Jacobean dramas, to that debased modern version, the murder–mystery play that runs for years if not decades on Broadway or in the West End. Nor am I referring only to the theoretical overlap between theater's way of working on its audience and the fascinations of violent spectacle, though that too is there, in Artaud's elaborations of his Theater of Cruelty, in Brecht's discussions of his "alienation effect," and in other analyses of drama's assaultive function. All the connections remind us that there is a profound and historical link between murder and theater. But what has especially struck me, in thinking about *KQED v. Vasquez*, is the way the murderer takes on the role of the central performer in his plot, converting us by default into audience members. While this figure of speech can be applied to all chronicled or broadcast murders, it is actually true in the case of an execution, where the murderer himself is murdered before the eyes of assembled spectators—where the murderer, for once, becomes a victim as well as a killer.

"The really fine rhetoric of Shakespeare occurs in situations where a character in the play *sees himself* in a dramatic light," T. S. Eliot pointed out in his essay " 'Rhetoric' and Poetic Drama," and went on to remark that "in actual life, in many of those situations in actual life which we enjoy consciously and keenly, we are at times aware of ourselves in this way." So a person who sees himself as performing in a play needn't, by virtue of that alone, strike us as unrealistic. Part of the nature of living in social reality is that we often feel we are performing a role. In *The Presentation of Self in Everyday Life*, Erving Goffman demonstrated in detail how our ordinary behavior resembles the theater, with people as actors or masks, different performances as "truth" or "reality" for different audiences, backstage access versus frontal presentations, and all the other implicit conventions that govern the relationships between audiences and performers. That each of us at various moments can play either audience or performer (or both) is part of Goffman's insight.

Goffman's ideas are particularly applicable to events that are both undeniably real and blatantly theatrical, such as the proceedings of the criminal justice system. Remarking on the "type of scene" that occurs when confrontation is allowed to break out, Goffman observes: "Criminal trials have institutionalized this kind of open discord, as has the last chapter of murder mysteries, where an individual who has theretofore maintained a convincing pose of innocence is confronted in the presence of others with undeniable expressive evidence that his pose is only a pose." The leap from courtroom to murder mystery is instructive: it suggests that the two exist on a continuum of ritual, which incidentally happens to extend from the sphere of the actual into the realm of the fictional. Goffman comes even closer to the nub of *KQED v. Vasquez* when he says, "Whether it is a funeral, a wedding, a bridge party, a one-day sale, a hanging, or a picnic, the director may tend to see the performance in terms of whether or not it went 'smoothly,' 'effectively,' and 'without a hitch,' and whether or not all possible disruptive contingencies were prepared for in advance." Warden Vasquez explicitly addressed this issue when, as the "director" of Robert Alton Harris's execution, he insisted he wanted it to be "carried out with tactfulness and precision." Implicitly, he was also objecting to the alternative "performance" that might be framed from the same material by another director: that is, the television cameraman.

Vasquez's choice of the word "tactfulness" is eerily appropriate here, for "tact" is exactly the word Goffman uses to describe the curious relation between audiences and performers in real-life settings. Tact is what the audience uses to protect the performers from its own spectatorship. "Audiences are motivated to act tactfully because of an immediate identification with the performers," Goffman mentions, "or because of a desire to avoid a scene, or to ingratiate themselves with the performers for purposes of exploitation." An audience's tact, especially when exercised to protect inexperienced or unskilled performers, may extend so far that "these tactful actions on the part of the audience can become more elaborate than is the performance for which they are a response." Tact is the audience's way of acknowledging its own presence in front of the performers; it is a way of making that presence into a role *in* the performance. Tact of this kind inevitably disappears when an in-person performance is converted into something on film or, in the case of *KQED v. Vasquez*, something on television. An event that previously required one's collaboration—or at the very least (if we believe Turgenev's account in his "Execution of Trop-mann") one's participatory shame—now has no role for its audience at all. In a televised execution, the audience is not only mute and paralyzed, but invisible.

Part of what actual, bodily present witnesses to an execution provide for the dying man is the impression that he is surrounded by human eyes. It is an impression that ricochets back on the witnesses themselves, whose stares are returned by the victim. "I was astonished to see him slowly rise and coincidentally happen to stare out the window into which I looked. And so I had this vivid impression of him," the courtroom artist Howard Brodie said of Aaron Mitchell's slow death by cyanide. Dave Lamb, the re-porter from the *Oakland Tribune,* observed the same phenomenon: that of Aaron Mitchell snapping his head around "to stare in wide-eyed terror at the eyewitnesses." The witnesses to an execution are there to be seen as well as to see, and the "tact" in their role—to the extent they are allowed to exercise any—lies in their reversal of that predetermined witnessing. An execution, like all such live performances, makes use of what Goffman calls "a basic social coin, with awe on one side and shame on the other." But when the execution is transferred to film, that coin loses all its cur-rency. The witnessing audience becomes instead a nonexistent presence, an invisible crowd of spectators who yield up nothing on behalf of the per-former. Tact gives way to voyeurism.

Writing about Frederick Wiseman's documentary technique, Bill Nichols praises Wiseman for his "tactlessness," his willingness to pierce through "institutional rhetoric," while simultaneously acknowledging that "this lack of tact also pulls Wiseman's cinema toward the realm of voyeurism." If Goffman is right, though, then his variety of tact, the kind that mediates between live actor and audience, cannot ever exist on film. Wiseman's documentary about the Bridgewater Correctional Facility not only confronts that fact; it is centrally *about* that fact. The legal charge against *Titicut Follies*—a charge finally overturned only in 1991, more than twenty years after the film was made—was that it invaded the pri-vacy of the inmates. The implication behind this charge was that Wiseman conducted his investigation carelessly, or recklessly, or ignorantly, without considering the feelings of the men involved. But when you actually see *Titicut Follies,* you realize that the invasion of these particular men's privacy is one of the primary subjects of the movie; and it is a subject handled, by this beginning filmmaker, with the delicacy and complexity we have now come to expect from the mature Wiseman.

.   .   .   .

One of the subsidiary charges against *Titicut Follies* was that it showed "full frontal nudity." In doing so, the Commonwealth of Massachusetts suggested, Wiseman was exploiting the incapacitated inmates, exposing them to leering gazes, using their nakedness to titillate. But the nudity was not something imposed or inserted by Wiseman; it was the standard dress for a large number of the inmates at Bridgewater. The nudity in *Titicut Follies* is disturbingly casual, routine, uninflected, because the men themselves, like animals in a stable, were routinely kept naked in their cells and herded naked to their showers. If this nudity is an embarrassment to us—and the intervening passage of time, with the increasing use of nudity in commercial films and even on television, has made it less of one—that embarrassment is aesthetically and ethically functional, for it makes us feel, on behalf of these institutionalized men, the shame of which their institution has attempted to deprive them.

Nor are we coincidental recipients of the shame. Our role as witnesses has made us deserve it, just as Turgenev's presence at Tropmann's execution made *him* deserve it. Yet because we are not bodily present, our witnessing is even more culpable than Turgenev's, or Howard Brodie's, or Dave Lamb's. We cannot return the gaze of the person at whom we stare. This is the nature of our "invasion of privacy"; this is the voyeurism built into documentary film. Wiseman's understanding of this fact, his acknowledgment of his and our voyeuristic invasion of these men's lives, is made clearest in the film's framing device, the "Titicut Follies" themselves. The Follies were a theatrical performance, a kind of comic-vaudeville show, put on jointly by staff and inmates every year at Bridgewater. Wiseman uses footage from this performance—a performance in which the sick and the well, the incarcerated and the free, are hard to tell apart—to open and close his documentary film. Watching these sequences as if from the position of the Bridgewater audience, one is made to understand an essential difference between theater and film: the fact that our presence is live and complicitous and acknowledged in the former, hidden and unacknowledged and, yes, voyeuristic in the latter. As viewers of a documentary film, we inevitably commit the sin of allowing someone else to be exposed without being exposed ourselves. We are present through the eye of the camera, but in reality we are safely absent; in the face of the inmates' nakedness, we are fully clothed.

I have said that this quality distinguishes film from theater. But Antonin Artaud, drawing up the list of complaints that would lead him to call for a new Theater of Cruelty, saw voyeurism as one of the central problems of the naturalistic theater. Writing in 1938 in *The Theater and Its Double*, he remarked that "as long as the theater limits itself to showing us intimate scenes from the lives of a few puppets, transforming the public into Peeping Toms, it is no wonder the elite abandon it and the great public looks to the movies, the music hall or the circus for violent satisfactions, whose intentions do not deceive them." If Brecht objected to the theater's desire to coerce us into feeling, Artaud objected to the theater's incapacity to make us feel sufficiently. "The misdeeds of the psychological theater descended from Racine have unaccustomed us to that immediate and violent action which the theater should possess," said Artaud. Nor did he feel that the relatively new film technology was a proper substitute: "Movies in their turn, murdering us with second-hand reproductions which, filtered through machines, cannot *unite with* our sensibility, have maintained us for ten years in an ineffectual torpor, in which all our faculties appear to be foundering." The end result, Artaud complained, is that "the public is no longer shown anything but the mirror of itself."

It seems to me that it took the advent of film—in particular naturalistic film, film with sound—to highlight for theorists like Artaud and Brecht the shortcomings of the naturalistic theater. If one wanted to be voyeuristic, apathetic, and unstimulated, then one could do it with a vengeance using the new technology. Why rely, then, on the tired old forms of psychological theater for a weak version of the same thing? If film was an alienated, distancing, audience-divorcing form, then why not make the new theater *self-consciously* so? And so Brecht invented his "alienation effect." If movies were "murdering us" and "violent satisfactions," why not enable theater to do it even more intensely? This is the impulse behind Artaud's Theater of Cruelty—not, as he put it, about "the cruelty we can exercise upon each other by hacking at each other's bodies . . . but the much more terrible and necessary cruelty which things can exercise against us. We are not free. And the sky can still fall on our heads." (I hear echoes here of Paul Bowles's sensibility: "Let it come down.") Movies, I think, helped give Brecht and Artaud their ideas about new possibilities in theater; film, defining its own relationship to audiences, opened up a new and different relationship for theater.

The influence worked both ways. If theater, after Brecht and Artaud, began to draw on the ways in which it was uniquely "live," then film in turn focused on its own deadness, its own capacity for secondhand, relayed experience. "Peeping Toms . . . murdering us with second-hand reproductions . . . no longer shown anything but the mirror of itself": Artaud's phrases could be a summary of Michael Powell's classic thriller *Peeping Tom,* in which a camera-carrying murderer shows his victims, as their final sight, their own deaths in a mirror. It is this horror of theirs which he catches on film for his own peculiar satisfaction, and as we sit in the darkness of the movie theater watching our own horrors and satisfactions mirrored on the screen, we are not in the best position to fault him.

The relationship between the sadistic moviemaker and the voyeuristic filmgoer becomes a central subject of the murder thriller from Powell onward. This tendency cuts across genres, from the low-budget naturalism of *Henry: Portrait of a Serial Killer* to the high-tech outlandishness of David Cronenberg's *Videodrome.* In *Henry,* the eponymous murderer and his disgusting sidekick Otis videotape their murders as they commit them, and the most distressing scene of the film—the slaughter of a whole family—is shown to us in this secondhand form, as a home movie of death. In *Videodrome,* the James Woods character is driven into homicidal madness by the manipulative sex-and-death films he plays for himself on his videotape machine. You can rent this movie and watch it alone on your own VCR, as I did, in which case you will discover that its most frightening as well as most compelling quality is its self-enclosed circularity, combined with its unbroken continuity with our own world. We too are in that loop. *Peeping Tom, Henry,* and *Videodrome* are the film equivalents of Artaud's Theater of Cruelty. They take as their subject not only the seemingly predetermined cruelties of everyday life—the sense in which "we are not free," as Artaud says—but also the coldness of the rendering medium. They are about our own distance from the events that purportedly horrify us.

The distancing effect of film has begun to influence even our perspective on real life. "It's like you're in a movie all the time," said my student Crip, a self-confessed murderer, speaking about life on the Oakland streets. By which he meant *You're always performing for an imagined but unseen audience* and also *Nothing seems real.* A 1991 documentary, Jenny Livingston's *Paris Is Burning,* takes this street perspective as its subject matter. The transvestite characters in Livingston's film are always looking for "realness," and finding it only in the most elaborate disguises and charades. Like Crip, they contend daily with urban violence and hopelessness, and they too derive their conceptions of reality from movies and television. In *The Executioner's Song,* Gary Gilmore says about the second murder he committed, "I felt like I was watching a movie or, you know, somebody else was perhaps doing this, and I was watching them doing it . . ." The self-conscious distance of movies has become the self-distanced movie of life, and the murderer has become both protagonist and audience: "he *sees himself* in a dramatic light," but also (to borrow another Eliot phrase) manages to preserve his position as spectator "and observe always from the outside."

Our own capacity for sympathy, our ability to be moved, seems to be dependent partly on the acting ability of the victim. "If they want to kill me," said Robert Alton Harris in the KQED documentary *Appealing Death,* "then it's just like them going to a show, a movie, and say, 'Hey, let's watch this. This is something new. Let's try it.'" (Harris said this before the proposal to televise his death even came up; he was just talking about the execution itself.) Yet the noteworthy thing about Robert Alton Harris, in this respect, was that he had *not* mastered the skill of presenting an "appealing" death. Unlike Gary Gilmore, Harris was generally felt to have an ineffective stage manner, and his proposed execution—specially if televised in the cool manner promised by KQED—seemed unlikely to reach the heights of tragedy that Gilmore's death became in Norman Mailer's hands. This is not to say that Harris would be any the less dead when the execution was over; only that we would feel less about him.

Our tendency to notice our own feelings in such a situation may be one of our more reprehensible qualities. Dostoyevsky criticized Turgenev's account of Tropmann's execution by saying that all Turgenev could see was the tear in his own eye. This may not be fair, but it is instructive. The more "thoughtful" and "self-conscious" we are, the more likely we are to evaluate not only our own feelings, but the performance that gives rise to them—a performance which we measure in terms of the feelings it produces in us. So even condemned murderers, like Gilmore and Tropmann, get reviewed as actors by the master-novelists who chronicle their deaths. At its most real, an execution is still a form of theater—as was pointedly demonstrated by the five actors from the Curran Theater in San Francisco who requested, and received, permission to attend an execution at San Quentin in February 1935. All we really know is that their names appear on the witness list, along with their theatrical affiliation; but one assumes they were there to pick up a few tips on how to die a believable death.

Being primarily interested in our own response to murder may be a sign of decadent self-indulgence on our part, but it is a version of self-indulgence that can lead to moral conclusions—the conclusion, for instance, that perhaps executions ought not to be televised. The most

. . . .

persuasive reason I can think of not to televise executions, like the most persuasive reason not to have executions, has to do with the effect on us: the witnesses, bystanders, and tacit permitters. I'm not speaking of the specific emotional effect on each of us—repulsion, sick gratification, or whatever—nor of the larger social or political effect on our collective behavior. I'm thinking of what it would mean about us, the audience, if we allowed someone's actual murder to become our Theater of Cruelty, our self-reflective murder film. No social outcome, however beneficial, would warrant this tactic; no end could justify this means.

I may sound cold-blooded when I say that the reason not to *have* executions is their effect on us. I mean the reason at a minimum, in the abstract, regardless of how we may feel about a particular murderer and his crime. This is what I take Brecht to mean when he insists on the removal of empathy as a preliminary to drawing moral conclusions. I can imagine, though I have never felt myself, that somebody might deserve to die for his crimes; what I cannot imagine is that another person should deserve to kill him. We are not in a position to administer death from on high, "to decide who is to live and who is not to live," as Sonia Marmeladov put it to Raskolnikov. This problem has practical effects—the discriminatory difference between execution rates for blacks and whites, for instance, or the occasional incidents of a convicted "wrong man" like Errol Morris's Randall Adams—but the practical issue is connected to a theological one or, if you prefer a less freighted term, an ethical one. There may be a right to execution, but we do not have it.

Because we have no right to execute, we also have no right to use execution, even as morally instructive theater intended to defeat execution itself. Televising an execution is not, finally, comparable to Wiseman's invading the privacy of the Bridgewater inmates, which can be aesthetically and morally justified as making a point *about* the invasion of privacy. Such justifications need to be made in terms of our willingness to implicate ourselves, "ourselves" in this case including both artist and audience. But we do not have enough self available to risk, to implicate, in a theater of actual murder. Art that puts us at moral risk must draw on what we actually have to lose, if it is not to be false or sophistical or merely sentimental. We do not have enough to cover an execution; we cannot afford to risk what that kind of theater would cost us.

Sex and the (Somewhat) Celibate Prisoner

.   .   .   .

by
EVANS D. HOPKINS

The mail line is extra long today. There is a new female guard in the control room, and I suspect several of the men know damned well they have no mail, but just want to get a good look at her.

To see through the seven- by fourteen-inch slot in the control booth cage, you have to climb two wooden steps. As I address the guard, all I see is her pelvis—a tantalizing eighteen inches or so from my face. The dowdy uniform does not diminish her hourglass figure. I ask her a question so that she'll bend down a bit and I'll be able to see her face and hear her voice. But neither quite live up to that body.

The guard hands me a single manila envelope. It's not the fan mail from female admirers I had been hoping for in the aftermath of my *New Yorker* article, but it is an intriguing offer nonetheless.

"They want you to write an article about sex in prison," says Shorty, reading over my shoulder. "You can interview me for this one." He lowers his voice conspiratorially. "I can tell you about how I screwed that faggot Sweet Tee, you know, the one with the titties? Man, I tell you, after ten years being locked up, it was just like screwing a *real woman*."

I start to tell him that's not what I have in mind, but I can't help but feel sorry for the bro'. He was locked up at such a young age, I'm not sure if he's even had a woman before.

Back in my cell, as I think about the editor's proposal, the old adage "write what you know" comes to mind. Well, sex is a subject I once believed I knew a lot about. Indeed, during the early part of my incarceration, sex was something of an obsession. But after I was transferred to the Nottoway prison several years ago, I worked hard to relegate sexual

. . . .

thoughts to occasional private moments with, shall we say, visual erotica. And for the last few months, I've attempted to completely rout such thinking from my mind. I've served sixteen years of a life sentence for armed robbery (an incident, I'm inclined to add, in which no one was hurt), and as I await word from the parole board, hopeful that I will be released this spring, I've resolved to remain completely celibate. So I don't particularly relish the idea of surveying prison sexuality (which, for the most part, is a solitary affair behind bars). As far as I'm concerned, Portnoy should have kept his complaint to himself.

But there was a time, during my imprisonment, when I was actually, in a sense, sexually active. That period is worth recounting, even if it's still a bit painful.

I. THE VISITING ROOM

"Those definitely were the days," I. B. says to me. "A man could at least try to satisfy his woman with those three visits a week."

I'm talking to a man who was at the Virginia State Penitentiary with me during the 1980s. We reminisce about the now-demolished maximum-security prison, which was but a stone's throw from downtown Richmond. "The Wall," as it was called because of its fortress-like appearance, had two visiting rooms: one for visitors with children and the other for adults only, where many couples engaged in nonstop necking and *heavy* petting. These rooms looked rather like lunch rooms found in small factories, with vending machines lining the walls. The more daring would actually have intercourse, often by sneaking into the visitors' bathroom, but sometimes, in more remote parts of the visiting room, under the folds of floor-length skirts. Other couples would slip into gaps between vending machines. The guard on duty more often than not turned his head, either out of sympathy, embarrassment, or fear of confrontation.

I tell I. B. that I'm thinking of trying to "pull" again, to seduce a woman, if only for the pleasure of the correspondence, and I show him a letter I've received from a female "fan."

"I remember when you were like I used to be," says I. B. "Homeboy, you *always* had a woman kicking the doors down to see you, *every* visiting day at The Wall. You say you haven't had a woman in what—eight years? Now if you're really getting ready to go home, and you've done without a woman for *that long*, you damn sho' don't need one now."

I. B. tells me that his wife, whom he met when she worked as a guard, has "stuck with me through tick and thin, even though I can't do anything for her sexually these days, with the way they got the video cameras in the visiting room here. And since the last lockdown, you can't even kiss—much less hug and get close—but at the beginning and end of the visit. Let me tell you, homeboy, after all my wife's been through—humiliating herself, cocking her leg up to let me get a quickie, or workin' my joint under the table—she *deserves* my loyalty once I get out. If you get a woman now, no way she can deserve to have you, over all the women you'll have becking at you when you get out."

II. "HO-OLOGY"

Locked in for the night at 8:00 P.M., for a half-hour or so I pace the nine feet between the cast-iron cot and steel door of my cell, trying to quiet my libido for the night's work of writing. I must take care not to knock over all the books and papers stacked on the makeshift shelves along the wall. After a quick series of contained tennis strokes—the only exercise this forty-two-year-old tennis jock enjoys—I sit and smoke a cigarette, thinking about my conversation with I. B.

Contrary to the way he remembers it, I was never the real ladies' man; in fact I was fairly shy at one time. I never got the chance to do much dating during my teenage years. I joined the Black Panther Party when I turned seventeen, and thereafter my days were filled with political work and writing for the party's newspaper. Of course there was an air of sexual freedom in the party during those days in the early 1970s—especially in California, where I joined the newspaper staff. But most of the comrade-sisters were older than me, and a little out of my league. Consequently, despite my brief period of marriage before my incarceration, my courtship skills were limited before I was locked up.

It was in prison that I developed something of a "smooth rap"—though I was hardly on the level of players like I. B. who served as my mentors in "the game." Men like I. B. came from the streets, and being able to "mack" and "play who's" was part of a culture in which it was both a badge of honor and an economic expedient to be able to control women through the combination of psychology and sex (better known as "ho-ology" among practitioners).

While I never was as successful with women as I. B., there was a time when I pursued women with all my wiles. To a man in prison, having a regular female visitor is part and parcel of the code of manhood. It's about

. . . .

exercising one's power despite incarceration, and—more than that— about finding someone to provide emotional comfort, financial help, and those mirages of freedom that hours in the visiting room can bring.

So why have I chosen to do the balance of my time all alone? Partly it has been because dealing with a woman can create more emotional tension and sexual aggravation for a convict than it's worth. But there is a deeper story here, which requires going back eight years or so, back to when I was still at the State Pen. . . .

After the first few years of loneliness, I learned how to attract women by placing classified ads, and wooing those who responded with long romantic letters laced with my poetry and with bits of erotica. No doubt many of these women were attracted to the outlaw/rebel mystique, and the promise of forbidden sex. Frequent short visits create a heightened sexual tension that also seems to be a turn-on for them—at least for a while. I learned the hard way that such relationships were rarely sustainable, usually lasting no more than six months. Therefore, when one began to wane, I'd begin seeking another.

Then, shortly before I was transferred here to Nottoway, a rural prison fifty miles southwest of Richmond, I met Nancy, who began visiting me with such loyalty I believed that she'd be with me "for the duration," as I used to say. However, a month or so after my transfer here, her car broke down as she drove back to Richmond from a visit. The following weekend she decided to travel here, along with her three-year-old son, in one of the transportation vans that a church group sponsored for visitors. The van crashed in a rainstorm, and both Nancy and her son died. I recall watching the tape of the accident's aftermath on the six o'clock news, and recognizing her suede boots, extending from beneath the sheet that covered a lifeless form. With this tragic turn of events, the game of prison romance became too serious for me, and my days as a player came to an end.

III. THE FAN LETTER

After receiving cards and letters from women in distant states, I finally get a live one from northern Virginia. She writes that she would like to correspond with a prisoner "because I want to give." While her writing is sharp and effervescent, the tone is that of an ingenue: "Is this your first fan letter?" she asks.

Well, years ago I'd have jumped all over her with the full power of my prose. Instead, I send but a short reply, along with a copy of one of my earlier pieces from the *Washington Post,* and hope that her next letter might reveal that 1) there is some intellectual substance there, and 2) she's above the age of consent, now around twenty-five for me (which is relevant should correspondence lead to something more once I'm released).

Her next letter answers the second question, and makes the first one moot. "I can't believe I'm corresponding with a *real writer!*" the letter begins.

I jot a few words on a postcard, telling her politely that I'm busy with a deadline for an article and will try to write more next time.

■ ■ ■

Have I become a prude, in prison, you may ask? I don't think so. Rather, I have chosen celibacy as an exercise, as a means of withdrawing from the immediacy of the visceral world, in order to see things with greater clarity. Standing at some remove is almost a prerequisite for sanity in prison; the immediate world is one of clanking bars, piercing announcements, echoing shouts. The discipline of celibacy is a means of escape, of transcendence, of maintaining self-control.

So no, I am hardly a prude. Sometimes I want a woman so bad I ache—longing not just for sex but for the feminine voice, the gentle touch, or just the image of someone who cares for me to hang on my wall. But I have come to understand that human sexuality is a precious and powerful force that affects us both in its presence and its absence.

IV. HOME

I'm the lone inmate in the prison van, on my way home to the sleepy mill town of Danville, one hundred miles south of Nottoway, on the North Carolina border. Sixteen years of numbing captivity is finally ending.

The guard turns the radio to a Top 40 station. Amazingly, "Fantasy," the Mariah Carey hit of a few years back, blares out of the radio. The end of the song has a question-and-answer chant that repeats several times: "Watcha gonna do when you get out of jail?" The reply: "I'm going to have some fun."

■ ■ ■

. . . .

I am sitting on the porch of my parents' home in the country, enjoying the night air, the stars, the lawn, and trees bathed in the amber glow of a street lamp.

The desire for sex is often a guise of the broader need for human joy, and sex doesn't always satisfy that need. At the risk of sounding square, my period of celibacy has helped me to call upon that emotional quality referred to by early philosophers as *agape*—love of truth, justice, beauty, and humanity and to ground myself for this greater purpose. I no longer feel in danger of losing moral focus, or relying upon a relationship to define myself. I am by myself beneath these trees and great sky, but I am not alone.

I turn to a fresh page from my notebook, and begin to draft an ad for the personals: *Single Black Male, seeking special lady who wants something real this time . . .*

Privacy in the Films of Lana Turner

. . . .

by
WAYNE KOESTENBAUM

28 JUNE 1999

In *Imitation of Life,* Sandra Dee shouts to Lana Turner, "Stop acting!"

I am trying to learn how to keep my emotions private—even from the reader, whoever you are.

In the photographic series "Lana Backwards," John Waters enjoys the back of Lana Turner's head: its self-sufficient, enigmatic chignon.

Waters certainly knows that *Lana* backwards is *anal.*

I live near an historical Hudson River Valley mansion named Olana.

Frank O'Hara: "oh Lana Turner we love you get up."

Yesterday was the Gay Pride Parade—thirty years' anniversary of the Stonewall uprising. I didn't go. I've run out of gay pride.

Lana Turner has an emotionless face in *Imitation of Life.*

Though retentive, I'm not imitating Lana.

Douglas Sirk's crooked camera gives Lana no privacy: he insists that her every gesture yield its secret.

The décor grows more decadent as the story's tawdriness builds. The more Lana suffers, the richer the rooms, the pinker the walls, the larger her diamonds.

Jean Louis designed Lana's costumes. His name, in the credits, earns fancy cursive. Jean Louis has privacy because I don't know his last name.

Lana died four years ago yesterday: 27 June 1995. I don't remember reading the obituary.

. . . .

14 JULY 1999 (BASTILLE DAY)

Only holidays celebrating revolutionary freedom wake me from torpor.

Landscape was Andy Warhol's euphemism for *nude*.

I want to repeat what Andy told his *Diary* about Lana, because it re-shapes the landscape she drapes around me:

> It was a busy day but I left early to catch Lana Turner at Bloomingdale's ($8).
> Bought one of her books ($16). Then went up to her and she said, "I don't
> think I want to talk to you, I've taken you out of my prayers, you said I was
> better when I hadn't found God, so now I pray for you—*badly*." So I think it
> was something I said in the Faye Dunaway interview in *Interview,* I guess she
> read it. And I didn't know what to do, I was a nervous wreck, I said, "Oh no,
> Lana, you've *got* to pray for me, please put me back in your prayers!" And I
> said, "Oh won't you please autograph your book to me?" And so she finally
> did and wrote "To a Friend" with a question mark and then "God Bless You"
> with another question mark. And Lana and her fairy hairdresser and I were
> all there with the same hair.

Note Andy's lumping Lana, fairy, and himself together—three with du-plicitous hair. Note Andy's wish to enter her factitious prayers. Note his assumption that she reads *Interview.* Note *badly.* What does it mean to pray badly—to pray so incompetently that the plea backfires?

1 AUGUST 1999

John F. Kennedy, Jr.'s plane went into a "graveyard spiral." Then I got sick to my stomach and convalesced for a week, thinking about John's final thirty seconds—plunging downward into the water. No one in the press mentioned that John's half-brother, Alexander Onassis, had also died in a tragic plane crash.

Last night I saw *Madame X,* costumes by Jean Louis. In it, Lana has privacy: she loses her identity, abandons son and husband, and pretends to drown off a yacht—but actually moves incognito to some Nordic coun-try (Denmark?) and then to Mexico.

There, living under an alias in a hovel, she loses privacy, for Burgess Meredith, a con man, finds out her secret, barges into her room while she is showering, and offers her a Christmas bottle of absinthe. Lana has no privacy from literary echo: her desolation recalls the fictive worlds of Jane and Paul Bowles.

Nor does Lana have privacy from the viewer, who knows the Johnny Stompanato scandal (her daughter Cheryl Crane killed Lana's gangster lover on Good Friday, 1958) and who sees the film's courtroom scene as an imitation of Lana's real life: facing trial for murder, the Lana character is defended by her son, played by Keir Dullea, who looks Martian, hand-some, earnest, like someone connected to the Scopes trial, or a religious but hypersexed guy who wipes the wet counter clean with a towel at the gay bar Barracuda. Seeing Madame X confess to the judge, the tabloid-schooled viewer remembers photos of the real Lana at her daughter's trial.

The question to ask of any scene in which Lana Turner appears: *is this scene taking place in a prison, or in a room that Lana has liberty to leave?*

I am tempted to say, *Lana is never at liberty, despite her stardom,* ex-cept this generalization seems true of any star, especially the lasting ones.

The large rooms in which Lana, pre-sin, playing wife, wears Jean Louis gowns while she ministers to her toddler, afford us scopic privacy: advan-taged, we look around Lana's loneliness, scanning and surveying it, mea-suring its resemblance to our unfilmed solitude.

Madame X was released in 1966, the year of *Blow-Up.* And yet this Lana vehicle harks back to bygone women's pictures, such as Joan Crawford's *A Woman's Face* (1941) and Bette Davis's *Now, Voyager* (1942)—films in which a star endures exile from beauty; endures a glacial matriarch's put-downs; endures protracted, oceanic travel from one iden-tity into another; endures love affairs with the wrong men (too old, too medical, too asexual); endures wrongful separation from her children. In women's pictures, the star's real-life travail matches the character's, and the punishing process of becoming-a-star or ceasing-to-be-a-star resembles menarche or menopause stretched to the duration of Götterdämmerung.

2 AUGUST 1999

Kenneth Anger's *Hollywood Babylon* reprints the front page of the *New York Mirror,* Wednesday, April 9, 1958 (at that time I was a six-month fetus in my mother's womb): the headline is "Bare Lana's Love Letters," and beside a photo of Lana in sunglasses is a "burning letter from Lana Turner to Johnny Stompanato, knife-slain by her teen daughter": "Oh darling darling, the letter I wrote you last nite was so much in the same vein as yours I've just received—so you see we certainly are in tune . . ." Contemporary pundits may claim that only recently have celebrities lost their privacy, but Lana's career proves that the secret lives of stars have been public property for at least half a century.

From Lana's courtroom testimony, quoted by Anger:

Everything happened so quickly that I did not even see the knife in my daughter's hand. I thought she had hit him in the stomach with her fist. Mr. Stompanato stumbled forward, turned around and fell on his back. He choked, his hands on his throat. I ran to him and lifted up his sweater. I saw the blood . . . He made a horrible noise in his throat . . .

In *Madame X*, Lana reenacts this real-life episode when she pushes Ricardo Montalban down the stairs to his death, and when she shoots Burgess Meredith point-blank in the gut—both scenes reminiscent of Joan Crawford's *Mildred Pierce*, when the daughter (Ann Blyth) shoots her louche stepfather, and martyr Joan tries to soak up the blame. In life, Joan would be betrayed by her daughter Christina in the tell-all *Mommie Dearest*. Star mothers and their daughters do not, together, create the cloistered privacy of Monterchi, where Piero della Francesca's pregnant fresco greets its few-at-a-time pilgrims.

Am I indirectly telling you about my mother and my sister? I hope not.

3 AUGUST 1999

After the death of John F. Kennedy, Jr., I thought about his sister Caroline and was thankful that his mother wasn't alive to hear about the vanished plane.

It is difficult to get *behind* Lana's beauty—difficult to figure out where, if anywhere, it goes. Beauty, a vector, must have a direction. Where does Lana's travel? Not toward the past or the future. Her beauty, like Kim Novak's, dominates by staying put. *Madame X* proves that the 1950s lasted until 1966, if only in the form of Lana's beauty. The costumes are 1950s. The emotions are 1950s. The expectation that a woman would give up her identity to protect her son's and husband's reputations is 1950s.

The X in *Madame X* suggests the male chromosome, not the female. So Lana might be Madame Male, the woman who masochistically gives up her name and her life so that her son can prosper.

Where, recently, did I read that masochism had its joys? In a Lorrie Moore story about a woman who accidentally killed a baby.

4 AUGUST 1999

I am trying to figure out what Lana's abdomen looks like. The costumes call attention to it and also disguise it. Something is up with the abdomen. I'm convinced the abdomen is a crux of the films.

12 AUGUST 1999

Too much time has passed since I last wrote about Lana. Since then I have become what Lana called a "Lanatic"—her lunatic fan.

I am *awaiting* Lana: as I learned by reading Maurice Blanchot's *Awaiting Oblivion*, the words *latent* and *attentive* and *await* sleep together, and describe a state, mine now, of forward-moving decomposition.

After I saw Lana in *The Bad and the Beautiful* I heard about the death by cancer of Anthony Radziwill (JFK, Jr.'s first cousin and best friend). I tried to imagine Lee Bouvier Canfield Radziwill Ross's grief.

Within *The Bad and the Beautiful*, Lana appears in several screen tests, filmed from the rear; we see only the back of her head, as if a frontal glimpse would scorch us.

20 AUGUST 1999

By now I've read three books about Lana—her autobiography, *Lana: The Lady, the Legend, the Truth*; an exposé by her former escort Eric Root, *The Private Diary of My Life with Lana*; and *Lana: The Public and Private Lives of Miss Turner,* by Joe Morella and Edward Z. Epstein.

Note Lana's piquant candor:

> I'd had my appendix removed back in San Francisco, after an acute attack when I was fourteen. An incompetent surgeon had cut me open from just below the navel to near the pubic hairline, and later inserted tubes when peritonitis developed. Because of that botched operation, I had so much scar tissue that my ovaries and my colon were both affected. I suffered terribly during menstruation. My Los Angeles doctor finally had to operate to clean it up.

Here and elsewhere, Miss Turner is both diffident and exhibitionistic. She wants to conceal, but she must reveal, too, so that fans can gain access to her starry interior.

Eric Root, Lana's hairdresser, shocks us by alleging that Cheryl Crane did *not* murder Johnny Stompanato, but that Lana found the two in bed together, and that she herself stabbed the mobster. Eric Root (his platinum hair in the author photo a deliberate copy of Lana's?) spills many other private details of the star's life. My favorite:

> During one of our many conversations in her twilight years, she told me that "Lex [Barker] was physically the best lover I ever had. Not simply because he was well hung, which, my darling, he was, but because he was incredible at oral sex."

· · · · · · · · ·

That came as no surprise to me. Throughout the many years of our relationship she'd told me many times that she preferred the oral route to conventional sex, "because," she would intimately whisper, "I was always *too
tight.*"

We hear, too, about huge jugs of Chardonnay that Lana kept in her refrigerator. Booze and jewels—twinned gods—shadow her private sphere.

Judy Turner chose for herself the name Lana but she didn't know at the
time that it was Spanish for wool. Alas, *They Won't Forget,* the movie in
which, playing a murdered schoolgirl, she wears the famous tight wool
sweater, earning her the sobriquet "sweater girl," hasn't been released on
video.

21 AUGUST 1999

I know too much about Lana Turner: I might self-combust. I want to
write a novel about the Johnny Stompanato affair, from three points of
view: Lana's, Cheryl's, and Johnny's. (I have already written two novels
about private matters, novels I may never publish, not only because in
their present form they are poorly conceived and therefore not gripping
to a reader, but because their subjects are too intimate and undisguised
for public consumption.)

Harold Robbins wrote a novel based on the Stompanato murder:
Where Love Has Gone. Snob, I don't want my projected novel to fall into
the Robbins pool.

My Lana Turner novel will begin with Cheryl's story (what follows is
not fact but fantasy): I will describe her sexual longings for Lana; Cheryl's
horror and delight at her own developing body; marathon masturbation
sessions; reveries as she stares into the mirror; stashed sweets she feeds
herself; boys and girls whose bodies she craves; her car; what she thinks
when she attends the *Imitation of Life* premiere on her mother's arm (only
a year after the Stompanato murder); Cheryl's attitude toward Lana's
chignon and toward her own imitative upswept coiffure.

Then I will turn to Johnny's story (again, not facts, merely fantasies):
his bisexuality; thuggish childhood; violations he experienced as boy-
victim; penchant for beating girlfriends, and remorse afterward; his love
for Lana's fake blonde tresses; his knowledge of her missing eyebrows,
shaved in 1938 by MGM and never growing back, falsely applied every
morning by vigilant Lana; his love of Lanita's breasts ("dear Lanita," he
says, and she says, in response, "I am your only Lanita, your love, your

dearest Lanita"); stupor as he sunbathes, in Acapulco, beside Lana; fury because she forbids him to escort her to the Academy Awards when she is nominated for *Peyton Place* (he beats her, at home, that night, after she returns from the ceremony); his ruminations as he watches *Peyton Place*; what he hears Lana say about Joanne Woodward's performance in *The Three Faces of Eve,* for which she won the Oscar, trumping Lanita; Johnny's lust for Cheryl; curiosity about how far he can push Cheryl into the incestuous abyss; his certainty that Lana knows about his desire for Cheryl, and Cheryl's desire for him; languor as he takes a bath, water scented by a Portuguese infusion that Lanita bought for him in London, where she flew, trying to excise him from her life.

And then I will tell Lana's story, in Lana's voice—not truly her story, as Cheryl's and Johnny's stories, in my telling, are not truly theirs*: Lana's attitude toward her own stardom; Lana's ambivalence about Mildred, her loyal mother; Lana's love of dark men, also of blondes; Lana's curiosity about the male member, and her indifference to its shenanigans; Lana holding the knife and stabbing Johnny straight in the aorta, lucky plunge; Lana's fit of hysterical blindness as she sees Cheryl and Johnny in bed together, and hears Cheryl's callous laughter; the time Lana slashes her wrists, and then must cover the scars with wide bracelets (no star must seem suicidal, says MGM, and yet many of its stars were forced to that brink, Judy Garland among them, Judy once Lana's bridesmaid and neighbor); Lana's forgiveness of Marilyn Monroe's usurpation, because she knows that Marilyn has bulges, and Lana has none; ritual gaze in the mirror before Lana leaves her house for a public appearance ("I must spend another two hours here, studying my face, because it is imperative I do not appear in public unless I am myself, and I have not yet adequately applied the champagne eyebrows, my hair's peach dye tiring the follicles"); Lana's devotion to the first-person pronoun; Lana's attitude toward her bra, its necessity, its normalcy, its grip on appearances, and its relation to the gaze of Douglas Sirk and the gowns of Jean Louis; devotion to Harriet, who polishes her nails; love for Carmencita, loyal maid; Lana's assumption that Carmencita is not entirely a person, but is merely an appendage, a lumpish solicitous presence holding the TV-dinner tray and the remote control; Lana's shock as she watches, at the premiere, the last seconds of

---

*Indeed, will I be able to write this book without fear of legal action by Cheryl, who is alive and well? Certainly I can't use her name without permission, which she would never grant.

Portrait in Black, in which her character is caught as the murderer and the camera freezes an image of her face, framing her, and then, with electric-chair immediacy, reversing the portrait, turning Lana into her photographic negative, turning white Lana into black Lana, as her surrogate daughter Susan Kohner in *Imitation of Life* had secretly wished *(I want Lana to be black so I can be white, I secretly know that Lana is black and merely passing for white)*; Lana's conviction that she is white and that her race is public knowledge, though also a private cognizance, like a mirror observing itself; delight in lying abed until 3 p.m., sleeping and waking, comfortable because she is not yet made up in Lana drag but is still Judy Turner, the failed Judy who dreams of becoming Lana; remorse as she hears Cheryl say, with disgust, "You are Lana Turner!"; certainty that in a past life she was inside Johnny's body, that the body he possesses and calls "Johnny" is hers by right; her shock when John Steele, the false name he uses for the first months of their courtship, cracks open to give birth to the violent Stompanato.

29 AUGUST 1999

Last week I flew to San Francisco to visit my family—mother, father, stepfather, stepmother, sister, brother, brother. I asked my mother if she remembered the Stompanato murder. She said yes, but she didn't have an emotional reaction to it. It was just another scandal. Somehow I thought she would warm to the word "Stompanato," a sign of quality and difference.

If ever I imagined that my father resembled Johnny, I was wrong: my father looks like a fallen wise man from a lost Israelite tribe.

My sister, however, has Cheryl Crane's poise.

In *Portrait in Black,* Sandra Dee again plays Lana's daughter. Many blondes in the 1950s and 1960s (and thereafter) imitated Lana; and Lana knew it. She taught *temperature* to Diana Dors, Jayne Mansfield, Mamie Van Doren, Marilyn Monroe, and, eventually, Madonna.

30 AUGUST 1999

Another intemperate gem from Lana's autobiography:

> Out of the corner of my eye I saw Cheryl make a sudden movement. Her right arm had shot out and caught John in the stomach. I thought she'd

punched him. There was a strange little moment, locked in time, as each
stood looking at the other.

"Oh, my God, Cheryl," John gasped out. "What have you done?"

I darted forward off the counter, afraid that John was going to punch
Cheryl back. Cheryl was backing up slowly, staring at John. John took three
little circling steps away from her, in slow motion. He didn't clutch his belly;
he didn't cry out.

Conjure Lana's feelings as she says "John," and John's as he says "Cheryl";
picture Cheryl's humiliation. Perhaps Lana shames Cheryl by saying, "You
don't want the world to know that you went to bed with my boyfriend, do
you?" and so murder (justifiable homicide) seems a better rap—better to
be remembered as one who defended her mother against a lover's sadistic
abuse than to be remembered as a teenage tramp.

Find Cheryl Crane's autobiography, *Detour,* and devour it.

31 AUGUST 1999

Can you figure out the difference, physically, between Kim Novak and
Lana Turner? To do so, you would need to explore the metaphorical career of platinum, which is beyond my present scope.

Lana does not appear in *Vertigo,* but she almost does. *Vertigo* was released in 1958, the year of the Stompanato slaying (which Lana and
Cheryl euphemistically refer to as "Good Friday" or "the paragraph"). In
film after film, Lana watches a man fall down the stairs or off a roof—as
if Jimmy Stewart's fear of falling in *Vertigo* re-enacted (or predicted)
Johnny's descent into death.

Last night, I dreamed that I embraced John Ashbery and discovered
that he had written many poems unknown to the public; in a secret, opti-
mistic, seaside house, like Lana's Pacific Heights mansion in *Portrait in
Black,* I found his munificent, endless, uncorrected drafts.

2 SEPTEMBER 1999

I've avoided Lana Turner for a day—too dangerous an immersion. I turn
away from it as I'd shirk a hustler district I'm dying to frequent.

Yesterday, I read *A Consumer's Guide to Male Hustlers,* by Joseph Itiel
(a sober, levelheaded assessment of the art of procuring and vending), and
I saw *By Love Possessed*—not one of Lana's best, though she wears a compelling orange bathrobe while, preparing to abandon her "cripple" hus-

band, she packs a suitcase. Hubby (Jason Robards, Jr.) had an accident, and uses a cane, which signifies, in the movie's dated parlance, impotence. (Why doesn't he go down on Lana?) Unsated, she turns to drink and jewels, and finds momentary relief in the arms of Efrem Zimbalist, Jr. Susan Kohner, who tried to pass as white in *Imitation of Life,* returns, in *By Love Possessed,* as the proper white girl who wants hunk George Hamilton's love. George, predecessor of Burt Reynolds and Tom Selleck in my private brothel, plays the son of Barbara Bel Geddes (privately I call her Barbara Bell Pepper), who ghosted Kim Novak—a Lana simulacrum—in *Vertigo.*

My favorite moment in *By Love Possessed* (a snippet I replayed a dozen times): Lana's husband, self-denigrating, says, "I'm still a cripple," and she responds: "You *are* what you *are*! A strong, moody, complicated man—and you *are* a cripple . . . "

Quickly she says "and you *are* a cripple"—as if rushing to reinstate, under the guise of common sense ("and you *will* need an umbrella"), the insult she'd pretended to revoke.

I want Lana's voice to say, as the outgoing message on my answering machine: "Hello. You are what you are! A strong, moody, complicated man—and you *are* a cripple"—for I love seeing men put in their places by icy important women who might one day appreciate my mind (but never my body).

Lana has privacy in *By Love Possessed*—she spends the night with her lover in a secret playhouse. Millions of viewers see her adulterous act, but no other character in the movie witnesses it, and so Lana seems alone with her error.

10 SEPTEMBER 1999

Last night's Turkish delight: *Peyton Place.* In it, Lana hides her slatternly past with a prudish veneer. Daughter Diane Varsi wants to neck in the dark with a boy: mother Lana turns on the light. Lana is dolled up in a vacuum: no reason she needs to wear such phenomenal dresses, no reason her hair needs to be stretched—punishment coiffure—to breaking point in the back, as if it were Foster's Freeze vanilla, squeezed out in conical swirls.

Turn Lana around, stare at the back of her head, the part without a face, the part without expression or animation, the bun-under-duress, the public bun, the fold on the back of her coiffure, where the real hair and the fake hair meet, or where the hair tucks into itself, resembling the lock or clasp on a ten-year diary: this is the puncture point—Roland Barthes called it a "punctum"—where the camera grows curious, instantaneous, unsure of what to do with the information. The bun is a turnover—where the mind, contemplating Lana, turns over on itself.

La Nature lies inside the artificial name Lana Turner.

A gentleman scholar recently told me, "Lana Turner's only serious film was *Imitation of Life*." Wrong. Lana Turner in *Peyton Place* exerts seriously imperious commentary on the meaning of publicity and privacy. With her star turn's assistance, we may brood about the perversity of *place*—impossible definitively to place Lana within culture's continuum of lows and highs, and impossible to place her platinum hair (the hegemonic no-color of whiteness) within the chromatic spectrum.

Who knows how she kept her hair so freakishly correct. Eventually, conveniently, she took on hairdresser Eric Root as her companion. Maintaining and coloring her hair, Mr. Root preserved her public identity's fraudulent foundation.

14 SEPTEMBER 1999

Some people obsessively reexamine their lives; others straightforwardly endure them. I would rather be one who endures; instead, I am an examiner.

Lana Turner and Cheryl Crane remind me of my mother and my sister battling, and of my mother and her mother battling.

Last night I saw *Where Love Has Gone,* loosely based on the Stompanato scandal. Joey Heatherton, playing delinquent daughter to Susan Hayward, has a butch pointiness to her head; the bouffant, a form of exaggeration, leans away from sense. Why is Joey Heatherton's head always pointing to the side? Why is there so much space between her hairline and her eyebrows? Why does every word she utters interrupt realism? Why does she have a boy's first name?

Susan Hayward's hair, in 1964, is big, and is certainly a wig. It prepares for the later, infamous wig she will wear as Helen Lawson in *Valley of the Dolls*. When Susan Hayward's wig and Joey Heatherton's, in the same frame, attract and repel each other, I want to shout with admiration: *How can your warfare be so perfect*?

In a photo of Lana and Cheryl together on a horse, 1959, the "third meaning" (see Barthes's classic essay, "The Third Meaning: Research Notes on Several Eisenstein Stills") is Lana's cigarette. I will never know

. . . .

why she is smoking while horseback riding. My definition of a star: a person around whom "third meanings" congregate, like mosquitoes.

The third meaning: the extraneous detail in a photograph that captures my attention; the incidental crux I choose to contemplate. Lana Turner is the third meaning of 1950s and 1960s star culture. Cheryl Crane is the third meaning of Lana. Joey Heatherton is the third meaning of *Where Love Has Gone*. I lean too hard on the concept of "third meaning," but I can't let go of it: it explains too much. It explains my love of inessentials and accessories, and my identification with objects that promise a definite significance but blessedly never deliver it—stars on the brink of hardening into fetishes, but never finally gaining location, and languishing, instead, as miasmic, unthematic embers.

The film's climax: we learn that Joey Heatherton, when she killed the boyfriend, had actually been trying to stab the mother. Are we therefore to believe that, in real life, Cheryl intended the knife for Lana, not for Johnny?

If I were a girl, and my mother were a movie star, might I want to kill her?

A star will kill to keep her stardom, even if she doesn't seem to be the one holding the knife. The murder implement, in *Where Love Has Gone*, is Susan Hayward's sculpting knife, which she finally uses to kill herself, after slashing the portrait of her mother, played by Bette Davis—a portrait that hangs, like Dorian Gray's, on the studio wall.

Where does the public's love go? Toward a new, young star like Joey Heatherton, who herself will turn into a legendary has-been.

Three generations of Hollywood disasters—Bette, Susan, and Joey—must share one movie. No wonder they don't get along. Throw men into the mix—and at least one will get murdered. Stardom, a competitive psychological situation, has a built-in "murder" switch, flipped by any imbalance in fame's atmosphere.

Literature is private, and this essay is trying, modestly, to be literature. By writing circuitously, foolishly, with difficulty, I keep the meaning private.

Am I at liberty to leave Lana? Am I at liberty to unlock her significance to me, or will it remain private—incomprehensible even to the writer, who is often the last to know?

18 SEPTEMBER 1999

I've decided to finish this essay on my forty-first birthday, in two days.

Last night, I saw *The Postman Always Rings Twice,* often referred to as Lana's best performance. To offset the sluttishness of the character, she wears white, and dies at the end. At the beginning, a sign on the restaurant lawn advertises "Man Wanted": the joint needs staff, and Lana wants a man. Her restauranteur husband gives her privacy: he tacitly approves of her affair with John Garfield, whose sweat-beaded face, in prison at the end, does not invite a good-night kiss.

The viewer has erotic privacy, because Lana never takes off her clothes. (It's 1946.) At the beginning of the film, she resembles a boneless Jean Harlow; by the end, she resembles mature Lana, fantastically cruel and aesthetic.

During the making of *Postman,* Lana's daughter Cheryl was only two or three years old.

Walking this morning, solitary, I thought, "I need to reread *Walden.* I've forgotten how much I relish complete privacy." I don't like when my next-door neighbor can see me sitting on the porch, eating my pork chop and reading the autobiography of Cheryl Crane, in which she vividly describes seeing *Peyton Place* for the first time. (Heretofore, Lana had not permitted Cheryl to see *any* movies, least of all Lana's own.) The uncanny parallels between Lana's private life and her performance in *Peyton Place* were not lost on the melancholy girl:

> I couldn't get *Peyton Place* out of my mind. As I watched Mother act with Miss Varsi some tiny membrane snapped inside me. They were all too familiar, those icy, dangerous looks Mother gave, the imperial manner and tight-assed way of crossing a room, the way she would turn and punch a line. . . . Now, for the first time, I sat engulfed by her Cinemascope image, watching her scold a tall teenager, one whose soft-voiced manner reminded me of me. With that snap came a moment of realization: the techniques Mother used to intimidate and control me came not from a well of feeling but from her bag of actress tricks. To her, life was a movie. She did not live in reality.

Contradicting herself, however, Cheryl claims, a few pages later, that Lana's performance in *Peyton Place* wasn't acting at all, but a glimpse of Lanita-reality: "and while I resented that our private moments had been used in *Peyton Place,* I was glad she had gotten a nomination for it. Anyway, I knew why her acting was so good. It wasn't acting."

When I was a kid, I wanted a movie-star mother. Now, reading *Detour,*

. . . .

I feel lucky not to have had one. Listen to Cheryl: "I knew never to touch pretty Mommy, her hair, her makeup, her dress. In her commitment to seamless glamour, she kept herself in a perpetual state of camera-readiness, even at home." I misread the phrase "commitment to seamless *glamour*" as "commitment to seamless *clamor.*" I grew up with clamor, not glamour.

Cheryl was molested by one of her mother's many husbands, Lex Barker, who played Tarzan. Other Hollywood households may have heard through the grapevine about the abuse, but they hid it from the press—wanting to keep private a star family's nightmare. Lana, too, wanted to keep it private: she was terrified of scandal's possibly deleterious effect on her career. She threw Barker out, but she didn't report him.

Cheryl destroys her mother's privacy by publishing *Detour*: she "outs" Lana as an unloving and inattentive mother. She "outs" herself, too, as a lesbian, although she does not detail the process by which she came to understand her desires: she simply says, defending herself against the imputation that she and Stompanato were romantically allied, "I had discovered girls and had never known a male lover who was tender. If I flirted with John at all, it was no different from the way I flirted with everyone, just like my mother did." How delicately she dispenses the phrase, "I had discovered girls"! About other erotic matters she is more explicit—for example, the proportions of Johnny Stompanato's penis. Not from experience but from rumor she knows "the Academy-Award size of his phallus, which had earned him the nickname 'Oscar.'" Such candor sits oddly with her erstwhile aversion to public revelation: "When it came to my unhappy past, I had always avoided publicity."

In one photo of Cheryl, post-murder, she resembles Monica Lewinsky: poignant typecast girl with no way of telegraphing desire except through the tired visual cues of "on the make."

For a brief period at the start of Cheryl's puberty, Lana helped out. She showed Cheryl how to overcome personal awkwardness.

> She shared with me the secret of her famous walk, and I was able to copy it. You step one foot just slightly in front of the other, and then, as she advised, "Pretend there's a nickel tucked between your buttocks and you have to hold it there for dear life so it won't fall out."

Now we know what Lana was thinking when she walked. Now we know which muscles she was clenching. An unschooled viewer of *The Postman Always Rings Twice* might think her breasts were the center of the event, but now we know better. We know about the nickel. Why not a dime or a

.   .   .   .

quarter? Perhaps because, in the Depression, a nickel was major money, and young Lana couldn't afford to experiment with higher sums.

Later in life I will be more organized. At the moment I am listening to William Kappel play Prokofiev, which reminds me of my father.

The slow cumulativeness of this diary's procedure defines my current relation to romanticism: distant.

This music isn't Prokofiev—it's Liszt. No wonder my temperature rose.

Chromaticism edges the listener step by step toward the goal, which may be ecstasy, or it may simply be termination.

19 SEPTEMBER 1999

Not yet my birthday—but I want to put a temporary period to this detour.

Finally, at the end of her memoir, Cheryl recounts the moment that her mother admitted gratitude for Johnny's death: " 'Cheryl, have I never told you how much I appreciated what you did for me? How you saved my life?' " Suddenly we understand: Cheryl was a hero! A hero, too, for bravely exploring queer bars in L.A. whilst a teen; inspired by Ann Bannon's novel, *Odd Girl Out,* Cheryl discovered her kind and began to hang out at Dolores's Drive-In.

A year ago I was devouring the autobiography of Judy Garland's second daughter, Lorna Luft; I didn't understand why I was so possessed by it, and I condescended to my own fascination. Now I understand: there is no more reliable pathway into the heart of American fantasy than the recollections of classic Hollywood's disturbed yet lucid offspring.

In the 1950s, Lana's screen mannerisms began infecting her private behavior: in moments of stress, she would behave suddenly like one of her characters. Cheryl referred to these instants as the emergence of "L.T." (Lana Turner): " 'You will stand up when your mother comes to the table,' she said in her best L.T. voice," writes Cheryl.

In the past, I strove to speak with an L.T. voice. At the moment, I prefer Cheryl's voice, although it is less glamorous.

I have long wondered how people whose private lives are public knowledge experience mundane daily consciousness unfolding. What is it like to eat breakfast when millions of people know your intimate affairs? Is the experience of eating breakfast altered?

I have been listening to *Faust* while I write this entry. Flirting with damnation, I vacillate between star grandiosity (the jewel song of L.T.)

. . . .

and unstarlike realism, which demands shedding inflations, mannerisms, and distortions.

I see before me—an apparition—the word *putrid,* and I feel, at once, three putrefactions:

(1) a star's reputation decays;

(2) lives are ruined by nearness to stars;

(3) loss of privacy rots the soul.

Now I sound too holy!

At the moment I don't love Lana; instead, I am curious about Dolores's Drive-In, where Cheryl consorted with gay carhops. Dolores's hamburgers and milk shakes seem more real to me than Lana's hair in *Imitation of Life.*

SOURCES

Anger, Kenneth. *Hollywood Babylon.* New York: Dell, 1981.

Bannon, Ann. *Odd Girl Out.* Tallahassee, Fla.: Naiad Press, 1983.

Barthes, Roland. (Trans. Richard Howard.) *The Responsibility of Forms: Critical Essays on Music, Art, and Representation.* Berkeley and Los Angeles: University of California Press, 1991.

Blanchot, Maurice. (Trans. John Gregg.) *Awaiting Oblivion.* Lincoln and London: University of Nebraska Press, 1999.

Crane, Cheryl. (With Cliff Jahr.) *Detour: A Hollywood Story.* New York: Arbor House, 1988.

Itiel, Joseph. *A Consumer's Guide to Male Hustlers.* Binghamton, N.Y.: Harrington Park Press, 1998.

Luft, Lorna. *Me and My Shadows: A Family Memoir.* New York: Pocket Books, 1998.

Morella, Joe, and Epstein, Edward Z. *Lana: The Public and Private Lives of Miss Turner.* New York: Dell, 1971.

O'Hara, Frank. *The Collected Poems of Frank O'Hara.* New York: Knopf, 1972.

Robbins, Harold. *Where Love Has Gone.* New York: Pocket Books, 1987.

Root, Eric. (With Dale Crawford and Raymond Strait.) *The Private Diary of My Life with Lana.* Beverly Hills: Dove Books, 1996.

Thoreau, Henry David. *Walden.* Princeton, N.J.: Princeton University Press, 1989.

Turner, Lana. *Lana: The Lady, The Legend, The Truth.* New York: E.P. Dutton, 1982.

Warhol, Andy. (Ed. Pat Hackett.) *The Andy Warhol Diaries.* New York: Warner Books, 1989.

Template from a Nightingale

. . . .

by
BARBARA FELDON

> All things are there in order that they may, in some sense, become pictures for us. And they do not suffer from it, for while they are expressing us more and more clearly, our souls close over them in the same measure.
> RAINER MARIA RILKE

My mother prided herself on looking like Joan Blondell. "People tell me I have bedroom eyes just like Joan Blondell," she would say with panache as she drew a cigarette from its silver-plated case, tapped it on the table, lit it between gracefully arranged fingers, crossed her shapely legs (just like Joan's), and enjoyed a languorous inhale. In our drab kitchen she was starring on the silver screen of her life playing Blondell. The star herself couldn't have experienced more intoxicating glamour.

Mother used Joan to release exotic longings buried beneath her own puritan diffidence. Her Blondell moments shone amid dreary hours of bookkeeping for a mayonnaise company during the Depression. Surely mother knew that Joan wasn't that idealized character on the screen; no human could have the goddess quotient plus the exact degree of abstraction that culminated in a Joan Blondell; a creature conjured out of her basic Blondellness enhanced by the fancies of writers who knew how to serve my mother's dreams. A work of art. Even her name, Joan, the shop girl and Blondell, the glamour-puss, was a combination of the earthy and the sophisticated. Penelope Gump would hardly have served.

That her idol was fiction, Mother, no doubt, tacitly accepted, but that pesky complication wasn't useful to her. Blondell's two-dimensionality was the whole point. Her breezy sensuality, exaggerated on the screen, pulsed with Mother's inner reality and ignited that which had lain shyly fallow. Much as a photographic negative develops into a positive image, Mom could exploit Blondell to become a more realized self. That's what heroines are for. I doubt that she would have welcomed the press blowing the sparkle dust off of her dream material.

If mother exploited Joan Blondell, I busily harvested Margaret O'Brien because she often played orphans. I was dying to be an orphan! Probably because it seemed more romantic to own that lonely title than to be merely droopy because Dad traveled and Mom worked. Margaret, so winsome in her Peter Pan collar and Mary Jane shoes, was always rescued by some handsome movie star like Charles Boyer (read my dad). So I larkily donned my own Peter Pan collar, buckled on my Mary Jane's, and prayed a lot (Margaret was always praying). Thus, I imitated her seven-year-old's fortitude and transformed my sulky hours.

Her wistfully brave qualities had little to do with her and everything to do with me. God forbid that her off-camera life might reveal a cowardly brat (unspeakable thought even today)! Then where would I have been? Who could I have dreamed myself onto? As audience, we deserve to escape the ambushes of the real world and enter the sanctuary of art. There we can vacation in dream, explore our covert longings, and practice our secret selves. In my notebook I found a quote I scribbled from the poet Rainer Maria Rilke. "I want to unfold. I do not want to stay folded anywhere, for where I am folded, there I am a lie." Unfolding our secret self is a high adventure worthy of devotion: to weave the strands of a dream into the person one wishes to become, the heroine of one's own life.

I meet women today who say that, as little girls, they used me (that is, their assumption of me through Agent 99, the TV character I played on the spy comedy *Get Smart* during the 1960s) as a role model of a woman who was strong, brave, and capable. At that time the press was fairly benevolent. The illusions of those kids were undisturbed by the facts of my private life that would have belied Agent 99's showy bravado. So they blithely cut their hair in bangs, donned their trench coats, rehearsed and then actually acquired the strength and independence I appeared to own.

Once I was even my own dream stuff. During the years of that same TV series, a local television station came to interview Agent 99 (aka me) and to see how we lived. When they arrived, my house looked splendid—but that's not how I lived. At least not until then. Paralyzed by my shopping phobia, my home looked like the set of *Waiting for Godot* until I was mobilized by the TV deadline. In one week I frantically collected everything as though I were throwing together a production for summer stock. Paintings were hung, bookcases built, furniture placed, the kitchen made proud with shiny cookery.

I was interviewed relaxing in my garden at my new umbrella table surrounded by a confetti of roses and held forth like an unruffled woman who gratefully explored a joyous life. When I saw the interview I stared at the person on the screen and enviously thought, "I wish I were her." I wasn't. Yet. But I'd given myself a larval idea of the woman I wished to be and who, over the years, I have come close to becoming. (Is that narcissistic incest?)

As the public has a right to its fantasy property for the purpose of its own growth, then the celebrity has a right to a private life for the same purpose. Although I hoarded Margaret O'Brien's movie self as fantasy food, I had no claim to her offstage persona. Out of the spotlight she was free to commit all the little-girl embarrassments she wished without being tattled on; free to star in her own story not be a character in mine, and free to be private even when in public. She did her job on the screen, I thanked her at the box office; the score was even. Neither of us would have profited by my imaginings colliding with her realities. (In fact, it can be disconcerting to confuse the two. Rita Hayworth was once said to have commented ruefully, "They go to bed with Gilda, but they wake up with me.")

Personally, I've never felt harassed by befriending fans, in fact they've made the world a charming place in which to wander. But a former TV series co-star isn't as swathed in the smoke of glamour as a major celebrity is. I'm sure that, for them, the public's "hands-on" goodwill can feel like a physical mauling and that media exploitation can feel like a psychological one. That essential cloak of privacy that protected our fantasy objects, once spun by a more disciplined press and reinforced both by the muscular studio system and the manners of the awed public, has become sadly frayed by what I feel is unnecessary disclosure. For most celebrities, it is far too frayed to expect to wear. Once upon a time, in the early 1960s, it seemed different. I remember a prominent actress who was seeing a man whose estranged wife was in a mental hospital. When this information fell into the hands of Hollywood's most notorious gossip columnist, the actress implored her not to reveal the relationship due to the unstable condition of her friend's wife. It was never printed. But now it is nearly impossible for an actor to gather together enough dream material out of which the public can fabricate a healthy, larger-than-life hero or heroine. (Fantasy figures germinate best in the shelter of mystery—not in the banal

. . . .

glare of exposure. In any case, who's to say that by exposing the grit of our role models' lives the media has given us a realistic portrait?)

I think of the celebrity landscape as a pointillist painting that flies apart when we approach it too closely. The media's appetite for negative gossip (is positive gossip an oxymoron?) constantly assaults this painting—and everyone loses. After all, the actor is useful dream stuff onto which the audience can project secret aspects of itself. Therefore, each performer packages her image in such a way as to move the merchandise, selectively revealing and concealing. (Everyone has at least one foot of clay no matter how elegant the deceiving shoe.) Is it helpful to undermine her commodity with the foibles of her personal life? Of course, one might argue that reality is superior to illusion, but the illusion is the point of that painting.

Are the media and the public now collusively crashing through the walls of privacy or does the press keep the public on its leash like a creature whose appetite grows with eating? I find myself standing in the market checkout line guiltily thumbing though racy tabloids (of course, I'm much too high-minded to buy one) imbibing celebrities' classified secrets like a perfect little scandal vacuum. And since I'm not left with a graceful line sketch of the unfortunate subject but a grotesque caricature (they rarely expose the secret generosities of the victim), I've puzzled over my cheerful susceptibility to such ignoble news. What engenders my appetite? Envy? Or is it the moral superiority I can feel, the source of my grandmother's "Did you ever?"

My grandmother, an easily scandalized Baptist who rented out rooms to factory workers, exclaimed, "Did you ever!" when Mr. Kozinski moved out, leaving a stack of girlie magazines in his room. "Did you ever! It took your Aunt Rene and me the whole afternoon to read through them!" Like Grandma, I don't vigorously resist scandal stuff if it's in the vicinity, just as I don't duck junk food if it drifts my way. I'll erode a whole bag of potato chips though sheepishly aware I may be damaging my heart.

Of course, for some celebrities public confession is part of their package and offered willingly. (Imagine the Anaïs Nin phenomenon without her eagerly published diaries.) The operative word is willing, however, and even here emotional shrapnel is hard to control. How many unwitting bystanders have been startled to find themselves "confessed" along with the celebrity?

There is a Zen saying, "When you meet a swordsman on the street, show him your sword. Do not show your poem to a man who is not a poet." If you're famous enough, whom can you trust? Friends are potential informants, your housekeeper an incipient author, and your past a ticking threat. If one night, in a frenzy of despondency, you confide your desolation to your computer, there is probably a wild-eyed youngster out there somewhere hacking away at your heartbreak. Of course, the famous can't edit what's in print and on film. If they want to flourish as humans, they must risk showing their poems to someone. Otherwise, they will be constantly drawing their swords; an arduous lifestyle. But how can they protect themselves and thereby preserve our heroines for us? The celebrity pantheon is especially worthy of sheltering because we dreaming animals are in peril without our fantasy gene to help guide us through the all-too-real world.

Yet not all famous persons are harmless dream objects. In fact, public figures can so disastrously bruise us (millions have perished still doting on their idols), that it's prudent to minimize illusions and cultivate a robust skepticism about celebrities, whether they be teachers, our latest heartthrob, or politicians. But skepticism is not the same as dream destruction. It is a balance to the dream, a cautionary aspect of our healthy internalized heroism.

There is a paradox, of course, in possessing a heroine. Once we have grafted her qualities into our psyches sooner or later our idol will begin to lose potency and topple. Toppling an idol is a sign of growth. In fact, it's essential to eventually divest our heroes of their godly robes in order that we blossom, be they scout leaders, movie stars, gurus, or Nancy Drew. As we, not without guilt, cast away their magic, like jettisoning the training wheels of our first bike, we feel ourselves moving forward. But the timing is important and it is unhelpful for the media to do the deed for us; to prematurely crush our heroes before we've had the good fortune to experience ourselves through them. There should be a line between reverence and destruction, a cultural Maginot Line that the public must help the media draw (or perhaps it's the media that must help the public) if we are to keep the world safe for idols. It is not so much that our idols, as citizens, have a right to privacy. It is that we, as audience, have a right to the fantasies that will promote our own private heroics.

As a child I was thrilled when my mother's best friend, Rita Kerlin, came to visit and brought me a book. I hugged it to myself, ran out the kitchen door, settled onto the back stoop in the sunlight, and eagerly opened *Pete the Parrot*.

It seems that Pete was a derelict little bird who had been discarded in a ditch by its owner. Along came a young boy who plucked Pete out, took

·   ·   ·   ·   ·   ·   ·   ·   ·   ·

him home, scrubbed him down, fluffed him up, and taught him how to speak. Before you knew it, Pete became the most famous bird in history and reporters arrived from all over the world to interview him. "Tell us, Pete, what is the secret of your success?" And the little bird answered, "Give the world the best you have and the best will come back to you."

A huge YES exploded in my kid brain as I recognized that this was the way I wished to live my life.

Of course, *Pete the Parrot* was written in the 1940s; in the 1990s one might imagine the reporters probing into the gruesome circumstances of Pete's being abandoned (did he assault his master's second wife?) and producing an update on his latest misdemeanors (he may be sadistic to kittens). How that breaking news would have tarnished my nine-year-old's philosophy of life!

Long after I internalized the heroism of Pete, I saw a documentary on nightingales and learned that a nightingale can't sing its song unless it hears it first. If it hears robins and wrens it won't chirp a note, but the moment it hears any fragment of a nightingale song, it bursts into its elaborate music as if it had known it all the time. In fact it had. It seems that the nightingale has a template in its brain containing its whole song, but it doesn't know it's there until it's triggered by the example of another nightingale.

I like to think that we, too, have a template containing our unsuspected potential; and that it must be triggered by a sort of human nightingale. Once our exemplars have done the job, they are free to fly away; we've looked into the mirror of them and seen ourselves. But if every nightingale who might unleash our best potential is shot down by the savage press, will we, our dreams wounded by fact, find ourselves unable to sing? Or, worse yet, being natural mimics, will we ape that which is maimed?

Lifting the Veil of the Right to Be Let Alone

. . . .

by
ROBIN WEST

Writing in 1890 in the *Harvard Law Review,* law professors Warren and Brandeis, in one of the most influential law-review articles of the century just ended, opined that the "right to be let alone" is both greatly cherished and often threatened in modern life, and accordingly ought to be made secure against infringement by whatever legal stratagems might be closest to hand. Their words proved prophetic. The impact of that one article on the course of twentieth-century law, both common law and constitutional, was unparalleled. First, their article spawned, and quickly, and as the authors hoped it would, the creation of a common-law tort to protect our desire to be left secure against the prying eyes of others. We can now sue each other for invading our distinctively American and distinctively modern "right to privacy," if certain conditions are met, just as we can sue each other for more ancient and widely recognized wrongs, such as libel, slander, or assault.

More important, however, than this common-law right of action, the authors' argument for the sanctity of the "right to be let alone" prompted the Supreme Court, in the first three decades of the twentieth century, to create a panoply of quite specific constitutional "rights to privacy" protecting individuals—and particularly heads of households—against intrusive *state* action as well. Thus, the Court held, early on, that a household head has a "right" to educate his children in whatever language he desires—and hence that laws requiring education in English were unconstitutional. Similarly, it held that parents have a "right" to send their children to private rather than public schools—and hence, laws requiring attendance in public schools were also found unconstitutional. These household or

. . . .

family rights regarding parental powers—eventually dubbed "privacy rights"—were expanded in the 1960s and '70s, to include the right to decide to have children at all, and hence, the right to use contraception, first inside the privacy of marriage, and then outside of marriage as well. In 1972, of course, the right to privacy was recognized by the Burger Court to also include the right to procure a safe and legal abortion, at least during the first two trimesters of a pregnancy. And finally, in the last twenty years, innumerable contemporary constitutional commentators—although pointedly not the current Supreme Court—have argued that the constitutional "right to privacy" also includes the right to engage in sexual intimacy with partners of one's own choosing. If they are correct, then state laws criminalizing sodomy and same-sex intimacy are unconstitutional. Thus, and despite the no doubt temporary setback of the current Court's opposition to some of the modern expansions of privacy rights, over the course of the century just concluded, the "right to privacy" has fundamentally rewritten not only specific corners of American law, but even our aspirations and hopes for law quite generally.

Such a "right to privacy" is, of course, nowhere to be found in the written Constitution, and constitutional purists have joined forces with social conservatives and organized opponents of legal abortion to oppose the expansion of "privacy" to include reproductive decisions, or at least those decisions which decide the fate of fetal life. Nevertheless, in spite of the ferocity of the opposition to the abortion decisions, the "right to privacy" itself—the moral ideal of a sphere of protected individual privacy, in which a person is free from both the prying eyes (or cameras) of other citizens and the paternalistic intrusions of a "nanny-state"—currently enjoys incredibly widespread support, not only among pro-choice advocates, but among the general public. Almost no one has an unkind word to say for privacy. And, for the vast majority of lawyers, judges, and legal commentators, the existence of a constitutional right to it as well as the moral case for it is virtually beyond criticism. Indeed, for most of the legal establishment, the right to privacy may now be *the* foundational, paradigmatically American, and most defining of all of our rights. It is no stretch at all to say that among lawyers (and maybe for many more of us as well) the modern right to privacy, like the autonomous, iconoclastic, spirited individual the right protects and is intended to produce, is now one of the foundational blocks—comparable in importance, say, to the "separation of powers" (also nowhere mentioned in the Constitution)—of our constitutional form of government, or at least of that part of it—the Bill of Rights—that protects individual freedoms. The "right to be let alone" becomes talis-manic. More than any other ideal, it defines the twentieth-century under-standing of our civic and constitutional liberties.

Some of this is no doubt for the good—healthy individuals do need privacy in order to thrive. It is also true that the constitutional "right to privacy," at least historically, was the vehicle in this society for securing important reproductive rights for women. However, there is surely no warrant for the virtual immunity of the "right to privacy" from open criti-cism. It's just not at all clear, even from a frankly liberal political perspec-tive, that the right to privacy has done us more collective good than harm, or so at least, it seems to me. Let me suggest that the "right to privacy" is rooted in a false or incomplete conception of our nature, and a cramped understanding of our civil ideals. In the hundred years we've lived with it, this notion and its branches have produced some poisoned fruit. We need to rethink its premises, and perhaps reformulate our hopes for it.

THE COSTS OF PRIVACY

First of all, to return to the rhetoric that inspired it, does the state of being "let alone" bear any connection to the ideal of autonomy, or to the dream of a robust individualism, to which privacy rights are so routinely con-joined? Surely not in any literal sense. An infant "let alone" will die, not flourish, and this period of utter dependency, during which solitude is lethal, not precious, persists for several years. Far from being an incidental or marginal attribute, this extended period of infant-maternal dependency is a central part of what makes us human: as developmental psychologists tirelessly remind us, the biologically necessary connection with others who sustain us in infancy both marks our species and leaves its trace in our ma-ture morality. Furthermore, a young child "let alone" might survive, but will not develop or learn a language. This dependancy on community for the development of language is likewise hardly incidental: our linguistic capacity, no less than our extended infancy, also marks and connects our species. An older child or adolescent "let alone" is a victim of neglect and will develop patterns of behavior and thought and feeling we all readily recognize as sociopathic. Finally, even an adult "let alone" might develop a Thoreauvian appreciation of the wilderness, but will more likely be-come, at best, narcissistic and ingrown, and at worst, paranoid, suspi-cious, and a danger to himself and others.

Of course, as its authors would have quickly noted, the "right to be let alone" is not meant to be taken *literally*; what it signifies is not that we value solitude per se, but rather, that we value the autonomous, independent, free-spirited individual the right to privacy protects. But both plain English and the brute facts of life are instructive, here as elsewhere: being "let alone," if we look at the entire course of a life, leads to infant death, stunted language, sociopathology, narcissism, and paranoia, and while these conditions no doubt *isolate* those who are so afflicted, they are not symptoms of healthy, autonomous, independent individuals. Thus, even if the ideal of autonomy is *all we seek*—even if a loose confederation of autonomous beings is our only aspiration of civic life—we will not attain it through protecting privacy rights alone. The nurturance of others, no less than their respect for our privacy, their tolerance of our idiosyncracies, and their celebration of our differences, is absolutely essential to the development of individual spirits. We need rights of connection, of care, of nurturance, and of community, as well as rights of privacy, if we want to be a community, let alone a nation.

Individual autonomy is not all we seek in civil society, however, and the deeper falsehood of the "right to privacy" is that it suggests that it is. We also seek nurturant connections with intimates, loving parental relationships with our children, fraternal friendships within our communities, unalienated work that connects us with our natural and socially constructed world, and political equality and a shared civic mission with our co-citizens. The right to privacy, and its presumed centrality, render these "ideals of connection" either anomalous, or lesser, or indeed suspect: while we may have an *interest* in our connections to our children, parents, neighbors, co-workers, descendants, and co-citizens, we have a *right*—a fundamental guarantee—to privacy; while we may have *desires* to connect with others, we have a right to be "let alone." The implication of this hierarchic ordering—a right to privacy, an interest in connections with others—is clear enough: being let alone, then, must be more important—more central to our identity—than being connected with others. Indeed, we have a right, not to healthy and nurturant connections to others, but a right to be *free* of those ties and the obligations they entail. There is something frankly nightmarish about the social vision these rights of insularity imply: a community that seeks nothing greater than a wall of privacy around every individual is not a community, but a mutual noninterference pact, and perhaps not even that. If its members take their own professed ideals seriously, their lives will be both psychologically and spiritually deformed.

Our century-long exaltation of the value of privacy and neglect of the value of human connection has concrete, if unintended, consequences. First, the "right to privacy" and its animating rhetoric has hugely burdened the effort to create a civil society of political equals. We have not simply permitted, but we have valorized—have rendered "quintessentially American"—the individual who stands apart from public, shared, civic space and institutions, including our public schools, our political life, and our civic obligations. We've romanticized isolationism domestically no less than globally: because we have a right to be let alone, we have the right to isolate our children, to withdraw from public engagement, to arm ourselves against undue governmental intrusion, to run our households as we see fit, to inflict corporeal punishment on our dependents, including, until quite recently, our wives. The exponential growth in home schooling and the school-voucher movement are the relatively benign logical end points of this progression. The continuing prevalence of domestic violence, insulated against intervention by the "privacy" rights of households and particularly the patriarchs within them, the now-popular Second Amendment "right to bear firearms," and indeed the modern militia movement itself, are not so benign, but they are just as direct a consequence.

Second, the rhetorical power of the "right to be let alone" has enormously burdened the task of legislating in such a way as to meet the needs of dependents—those who need care—and those who provide care to dependent others. All of us spend a significant part of our childhood years entirely dependent upon the care of others, and now—in a world in which women are no longer exclusively relegated to the unpaid private world of caregiving—most of us, men and women, can expect to spend a substantial part of our lives tending the needs of fully dependent others. The activity of "caring for" others—not the act of being alone—is a central, defining part of many of our lives, indeed for most of us it is the activity that will more than any other constitute our identity for a substantial portion (not all) of our adult lives. The activity of giving care, however, in turn leaves us vulnerable, particularly in a culture that valorizes and rewards market-based, compensated labors. It is hard, sometimes impossible, to earn a living while caring for the needs of infants or the aged.

How should we, how could we, ameliorate that vulnerability? One possibility, as a growing number of feminists in academia, in law, and in journalism are now urging, would be to recognize "care" as a public value—of comparable or greater importance to public life, for example, than publicly funded art, education, or civic participation. Were it so recognized, greater public support for care and caregiving might follow. If it did not, furthermore, then it might make some sense, in a liberal, rights-based culture, to soften the vulnerability to which those experiences and activities lead, with a regime of counter-majoritarian, care-based rights. If we recognized care as a public value, we might, for example, be prompted to legislate toward the end of protecting the economic security of new parents. A strengthened, bolder version of the Family and Medical Leave Act—the Act passed over Clinton's signature, providing three months' unpaid leave to employees of large companies—might well follow from an acknowledgment of the value of caregiving to public life. Similarly, if we recognized, as we now don't, a "right to care," as well as the public value of care, we might further acknowledge the possible unconstitutionality, as well as the blatant cruelty, of the recent Welfare Reform Act, also signed over Clinton's signature, one term and one impeachment skirmish later. A recognition of either, or both, the public value of caregiving, and the right of individuals to provide care without endangering themselves or their dependents, would deeply transform our politics and our constitutional visions both.

The value that needs to be recognized is the value of nurturant care, not the value of splendid isolation, and likewise, the rights that need to be granted to those shouldering the burdens of dependent others are relational "rights to care," not rights to be let alone. Indeed, a right to be let alone will prove worse than useless to either the political or legal effort to secure greater recognition or well-being for caregivers: the presumed primacy of the "right to be let alone" makes any sort of "relational right"—such as a "right to provide care"—an anomaly or worse. The antipathy runs deep, and has consequences well beyond the possibilities of caregiving rights. In a world that valorizes individual privacy as much as we currently do, any sort of relational right—whether they are construed as welfare rights, parental rights, rights to affordable childcare, rights to decently funded public schools, or rights to health care—are going to be marginalized. A society of self-actualized loners, secure in their right to be let alone, ought not need them.

The exalted right to be let alone stands in considerable and constitutional tension with the attempt to put forward what Rabbi Michael Lerner, editor of *Tikkun Magazine,* has recently called a "politics of meaning." When we are isolated from each other, the "meanings" we create are the spontaneous products of self-generative and noninteractive individual egos; in such a world there can be no "politics of meaning," for the simple reason that in such a world there can be no politics. My privately held values, beliefs, perceptions, feelings, and assertions are all mine, in the same way that my furniture is mine, and with the same consequence: I own them, I caused them, I owe no one any explanation for them or justification of them, and I can use them randomly or in any way I please to assert and insert my own isolated self into and upon the world. Meaning, in a world in which my quintessential right is to be let alone, is not a product of engagement with others, nor is it a means by which I can seek or attain connection with others. Instead it is the right to disengage from politics writ large—to disengage from public space, from political fora, and perhaps foremost, from public meaning. So long as we valorize the right to be let alone against and above all other rights, we will never embrace a politics of meaning; in fact, we will never embrace politics.

REASSESSING PRIVACY

What would we be giving up, were we to abandon or substantially modify our commitment to a foundational constitutional right of privacy? Very little of any value. Current anxieties about privacy, and the felt need for constitutional or legal rights to protect it, I think, stem from three sources: fear of organized conservatism's opposition to women's reproductive rights, and particularly the right to safe and legal abortion services; fear of the powers and readiness of conservative legislators to "legislate morality," and to thereby interfere, and ferociously, with the ability of individuals, particularly but not only gays and lesbians, to form intimate relationships that nurture and enrich their own lives; and third, concerns regarding the powers of Internet service providers to obtain information about our lives without our consent and possibly without our knowledge. But, save the ambiguous case of abortion rights, in none of these areas, has the threat been alleviated by formulation of a "right to privacy," and furthermore, in all three, protecting against such harm through a regime of privacy rights might well do *more* harm.

A number of legal commentators and a growing number of courts have argued that women's reproductive freedom might be better grounded in other, more explicit constitutional guarantees—such as the right to equal protection of the law, or the right to enjoy a measure of liberty without undue infringement by the state—than in the "right to privacy," or its various constitutional correlates. Securing safe and legal abortion might have considerably more to do with the need to secure women's equality, liberty, and physical integrity, than with the need to secure the "privacy" of the doctor-patient relationship, or the privacy of the husband-wife partnership. Reformulating reproductive rights as equality rights or liberty rights, furthermore, would clarify the case for requiring public funding of abortion services for poor women. The privacy-based "right to abortion" we now enjoy secures only a right to privately contract with a private doctor for the sale and delivery of a private commodity—the abortion. It is, at best, a contract right to purchase something free of the moralistic intervention of the state. Such a right is not as robust as it sounds: it does not, importantly, guarantee *access*. The privacy-based right to abortion would be fully met, for example, even were it the case that abortions become so rare a commodity that they were priced outside of the range of virtually all women. That is not so unrealistic a scenario. Today, the right is fully met even though in a growing number of states only relatively privileged women can afford one. The right is fully met even if a woman who has no access to abortion services might *die* from complications from an unwanted pregnancy. It is fully met even if, as in some states, teenagers are not permitted to have one without parental or judicial consent. The right is fully met even if women who are pregnant because they were raped cannot obtain one. And the right is fully met in spite of the current conditions that render its obvious alternative—mothering—so bitterly unpalatable for so many. It is not at all as clear that general access to reproductive decision-making, grounded in a general right to equal protection of laws and a right to personal liberty, would be so cruelly cabined.

Were the Court to recognize (as it is currently disinclined to do) a "right" to same-sex intimacy grounded in a general right to privacy—rather than in equality or liberty—such a right might likewise prove to be less valuable than its proponents might wish. A right to same-sex intimacy rooted in privacy would indeed have the effect of voiding laws that criminalize sodomy or same-sex intimate acts, as its proponents hope. But as with our privacy-based right to abortion, it is not at all clear that it would do any more than that. It would not, for example, pave the way to recognition of same-sex marriage, or entitlement to the privileges marriage bestows: indeed such recognition of the public value of same-sex relationships would require precisely the level, and type, of state, public, and civic recognition that the right to privacy vilifies, and more pointedly, against which the wall of privacy is erected. More importantly, I think, the grounding of same-sex intimacy in the privacy rights of individuals does nothing toward the goal of achieving the social equality or liberty of gay and lesbian citizens, and may actually frustrate those goals: it would insulate acts and choices that are already overly privatized by virtue of social censure. Protecting gay and lesbian identity, in other words, through privacy, rather than through rights of equality or liberty, would, in effect, validate, legitimize, and even constitutionalize, the closet. Privacy rights might well be granted, but at the cost of even greater social stigma.

And what of the explosion, and dissemination, of personal information, made possible through the expanding and unpredictable technologies symbolized by the Internet? Doesn't this phenomenon cry out for legal regulation, and through a regime of privacy rights? These issues are exceedingly complex, and well beyond the scope of this essay, but here again, it's worth noting that we ought to be careful what we wish for.

First of all, the greater harm done by cyberspace technologies might not be occasioned by too little privacy but too much: at least according to the lessons of current research, there is something to the neo-Luddite fear that excessive dependence on our new technologies has left many of us socially isolated, mildly or severely depressed, and even more severed from our real communities of living creatures than did television or radio, and with even greater costs to our civic life and individual mental health. Even if the threat posed by the Internet to the integrity and security of personal information is real, it seems that much of that menace is a function of inequalities between suppliers and consumers of cyberspace-related goods and services—not lack of privacy per se. Those inequalities may indeed "cry out" for legal intervention—without it, the anarchy of cyberspace so loved by its enthusiasts might increasingly resemble the Hobbesian state of nature, albeit without the violence, where the strong simply dictate at will, and without political reprisal, conditions of participation to the weak. What is not at all clear is that a regime of "privacy rights" will correct those inequalities—indeed they may exacerbate them. Privacy rights are by definition universal and neutral—they protect strong and weak alike—and they protect them, fundamentally, against state intervention. Privacy creates a sphere into which the state may not intrude. Fighting the intrusiveness of powerful actors in cyberspace—including their intrusive ability to obtain, use, and disseminate information about less powerful cyber-participants—with a regime of privacy rights, is a classic example of trying to fight fire with fire: it might work, but then again, it might lead to a disastrous conflagration. We might better fight the "power" of Amazon.com to monitor our purchases and hence amass and then market information about us, by turning the computer off, walking to our local independent bookstores, and paying cash for our purchases, than by constructing yet another dubious privacy right—a right that may well have the unintended consequence of further insulating the rights of sellers as well as buyers, in the name of privacy, to construct terms of market transactions free of the meddling intervention of state control.

Where does this leave us? I am not suggesting that we should forgo all privacy in our lives, or that our appreciation of the privacy we enjoy is always misguided. What we do need to rethink, however, is the absolute presumption of value that we have accorded it, in law and particularly in constitutional law, over the last hundred and ten years since the case for it was first put forward. That presumption of absolute value has done considerable harm as well as some good. The "right to privacy," for example, has insulated the right to purchase an abortion, protecting that purchase against undue criminalization by the state, but it has done so at the cost of further burdening the effort to secure a right to actually have one, to say nothing of further burdening the effort to secure the rights of caregivers—especially mothers—and to honor (and compensate for) the value of caregiving labor. This trade-off was unnecessary: we could have better served the needs and interests of women facing unwanted pregnancies through making the case for the necessity of legal and safe abortions as a means of securing women's political equality, liberty, and physical integrity; we did not need to add privacy to the mix. The right to privacy has likewise protected the peaceful, thoughtful, animistic Thoreauvian camped in the wilderness, but at the cost of making more rather than less difficult the identification of the value of civic participation in public life that Thoreau himself so treasured. This too was unnecessary: we could have better secured the interests of naturalists by directly making the case for appreciating the wilderness. Had we done so, it would have underscored, rather than undermined, the case for civic, participatory, environmentally responsible public engagement. We have secured, through privacy rights and rhetoric, the rights of fathers to dictate the terms of their children's education, but at the cost of leaving those children, as well as their mothers, vulnerable to sometimes life-threatening violence—the "right to privacy" protects the violent patriarch's abuse no less than it secures the rights of Amish parents to educate their children as they see fit. This too was unnecessary—we could have protected the integrity of cultural subgroups by affirming the worth of those communities directly and by making the case for the value of cultural diversity, rather than by isolating children and mothers in the dubious "privacy" of hellish upbringings. Likewise, we have secured the privacy of the eccentric, and iconoclast, by

· · · · · · · · · · ·

rendering aid to the militiaman, the Unabomber, and the Second Amendment zealot—and so on. None of these concessions are necessary: we can and should appreciate eccentricity, iconoclasm, and Millian dissent without being "privacy fundamentalists."

One way to reassess privacy, and the constitutional right to it, might be to undertake this thought experiment: we could try to reformulate the values, the choices, the ways of living, and the civic bonds we think our privacy protects, in direct terms unadorned with the insulating rhetoric of privacy and rights. Were we to do so, we could then rethink or sift through various ways to protect those choices, values, and bonds, look more frankly at their costs, and debate whether the case for those protections outweighs them. Were we to attempt this project, we might find that we can do this public deliberative work most readily without, rather than with, the obfuscatory rhetoric of privacy. Indeed, the need to do so is perhaps what becomes most glaring, once the veil of privacy is lifted.

Extravagance on a Small Scale: Gossip and Privacy in a Rural Area

by
KATHLEEN NORRIS

Living in a tiny, farm-to-market town surrounded by many thousands of acres of pastures and fields can feel like being caught inside a sumptuous nineteenth-century novel, complete with characters out of Dickens and plotlines complex enough to suit George Eliot or Jane Austen—love! marriage! bloodlines! money! In a sense, privacy does not exist, because the broad lines of every person's story are exposed, and commonly known. To survive in a small town one must consent to be a public figure, famous not for fifteen minutes, but for several generations. My place here was established in the deep past, and even after my twenty-five years of living in the house where my mother was raised, it is still "Doc Totten's" house, and I am still "Lois Ferne's girl." I refer to the perennials in my backyard garden as "my grandmother's" columbines and daylilies. I merely tend them.

I feel enriched when people tell me they still remember the Bible studies my grandmother conducted at her churchwomen's group. And I am amused by the kinky fondness with which they remember how badly my grandfather drove in his dotage. When you saw his car coming—inevitably it was smack in the middle of the street—you maneuvered to get out of the way. People rush to reassure me that Mrs. Tubbs was far worse because she was so short she could barely see above the steering wheel. She and my grandfather never collided, which may rate as a minor miracle.

Before I returned to my family home, in 1974, I had lived in New York City for six years, long enough to take for granted my sense of anonymity. And to cherish all its shadings. Commuting to work by bus, I did come to know a group of strangers, their faces, wardrobe, and general state of health, as we tended to see one another each weekday morning. I learned to detect subtle changes: a woman who had seemed happy, or at least content, might appear one morning looking careworn and anxious, and I was left to imagine what sort of trouble had arisen in her life.

New Yorkers are expert at protecting their privacy in a crowd of people, developing a finely calibrated sense of when it is acceptable to speak in public, or how much we dare intrude on another person before letting her go back to the newspaper or her private thoughts. But, over time, I found that even the slight familiarity among these bus riders allowed us to speak to one another with relative ease when something out of the ordinary occurred.

One morning it was a minor traffic accident at Broadway and 110th. By the time our bus approached the scene, the drivers involved were engaged in cursing each other with vivid language and vigorously executed gestures. Concerned, we watched from the bus, and listened. But we soon began chuckling, and rolling our eyes, as it was clear that the elaborate obscenities taking place beneath our windows were protective coloration, guaranteeing that no physical violence would ensue. Eventually the street was cleared, and we moved on. On another morning we witnessed the sad evidence of a suicide. Someone had apparently jumped from an elegant apartment building on Fifth Avenue: we glimpsed the flashing lights of an ambulance, a stretcher with a body bag, and police interviewing witnesses, who pointed up at the building's blank windows. Suddenly I knew who the Catholics were among us, because as our bus passed, they made the sign of the cross.

Urban people often say that losing their anonymity is the thing they fear most when considering a move to a small town. But while one is never anonymous when walking down the street—when I was a child, my grandmother would hear of any serious infraction on my part before I arrived at home—one can retain one's sense of privacy. Ironically, the ubiquitous gossip helps, and the more imaginative the better. As the gossips grow content with what they think they know, you find that you can get away with things they would never suspect. Those who assume that they know everything about you do you a favor, because you can feed their rumor mills with insignificant material while keeping to yourself what really matters. Acting as an editor of your own life, you can place in the social notes of the local newspaper mention of your dinner parties, trips to Rapid City, or the visits of relatives, while keeping hidden what seems truly private—your true opinion of the new pastor, for example, or the inner workings of your marriage.

I must admit that I have become enough of a small-town denizen to take some comfort in knowing some share of the narrative that accompanies each face I see. I could tell you why one woman gave up wearing her fancy wardrobe and elaborate wigs, and in fact gave up on men. It's quite a tale, involving a pregnancy, elopement, bigamy, and arson. I find that I now become slightly disoriented in an urban area, because the clerks at the drugstore or supermarket are not personally known to me, and the minor pleasantries we exchange are not informed by the rich compost of narrative and mutual knowledge.

The clerks and shopkeepers in my town could tell stories on me if they so desired. Perhaps I was their hapless Girl Scout troup leader when they were in fourth grade; or they attended a Vacation Bible Study class at which, after much fumbling, I finally abandoned our curriculum with its maddening, tacky crafts projects and bland text. I read the class the Psalms instead, and had them write their own. Cursing psalms were especially popular. Someone else might remember me and my husband as the young couple who held an Easter egg hunt in their home for a church youth group despite the spring blizzard that had dumped nearly three feet of snow the day before. Maybe they recall that the only decorated egg that no one could find, among the dozens we had hidden in our old house, was the one we had placed in the egg drawer of our refrigerator. Perhaps they once overheard me and my husband having a spat in the grocery store, and what they think of us is based on that.

My story has become their story, and I have no idea how they would tell it, just as they can't know how I would interpret their own. I knew I truly belonged in a small town when this mutuality began to seem right. But my inner urbanite can still be shocked by the sheer nosyness that is considered normal where I live. I can usually laugh it off, as when a neighbor asked me, in an exasperated tone, which one of those cars we'd had in front of our house all summer was *ours*. We had inadvertently been providing her with some good telephone gossip, but it was also a chore. She'd grown weary of keeping track of the variety of automobiles—loaners, a few rentals—that we'd been using while looking for something to buy. To the small-town person, nothing is private, and nothing too trivial to merit public comment and speculation.

Having so little privacy can contribute to a simple sense of belonging, which matters more to me as I settle into middle age. I like the way that our knowing so much about one another often forces us to take responsibility for one another as well. When we notice a woman at church who has aged noticeably over the summer, becoming frail, we might take extra time to speak with her and find out how things are going. Delivering Meals on Wheels to a shut-in one day, we find to our surprise that the front door is locked, and call around to relatives or neighbors until we determine that the woman is all right. Her son had taken her to a doctor's appointment, and forgot to tell us not to deliver the meal. But we are to resume service tomorrow.

One of my favorite people in town is a paranoid schizophrenic. Her story is a tragic one, and knowing it helps me to understand the images, symbols, and wild leaps of the imagination she uses to describe her plight. What she'll tell you is that her mother gave her a lobotomy on the kitchen table when she was seventeen; when I repeated this to the court-appointed attorney who had been assigned to represent her at a commital hearing—she had also asked me to attend as a character witness—he sighed and told me that it was a damn good metaphor for what had actually happened. He and I are but two of the many who keep an eye on her, and who will alert her doctor when she stops taking her medication and grows manic.

The fact that everyone is on public display has its uses. It can act to counter the human tendency to put on airs, or indulge in the status symbols that seem to provide so many Americans with a sense of identity and self-worth. In an isolated rural area such as mine, clothes, shoes, and cars—or more likely, pickup trucks—tend to be utilitarian rather than trendy. To dress up for church, you put on your newest blue jeans. An outfit from Prada would be totally wasted here—*Prada, who? Are his people from around here?*—and if people found out how much you had paid for it, you would never live it down.

The status symbols of the television culture are known to us, but rarely appear in our midst. The only Jaguar sedan I have ever seen in North or South Dakota was parked in front of my house for several hours on one fine spring day, occasioning a steady stream of traffic, mostly teenagers and local policemen who stopped to look it over. Some wondered if it were ours, purchased with an unexpected windfall I'd recently made on a book (which, in typical small-town fashion, had been wildly exaggerated). But it was a cop who made the dead-on guess, figuring that the car's presence was related to my new celebrity. Not long before, I had appeared on television, on *CBS Sunday Morning,* and the Jaguar was the car of a

. . . .

fan from the East Coast who was driving to Idaho and had arranged to meet with me en route.

This cop also told me something that brought home the dreary ubiquity of gossip in a town such a mine. The police were all laughing about a local busybody who had asked a policeman's wife what kind of trouble my husband and I were in that a police car was so often parked by our house. The answer was disappointingly simple: one of the cops had recently moved into a house nearby.

But that gossip had no doubt imagined something much more exciting. Perhaps my husband and I had finally been caught at the international drug smuggling we'd been engaged in since we moved to town. The fictional talents of small-town people are nothing to sneeze at, and our coming to town from New York City provided a mother lode of material. Some people romanticized our move from Manhattan, inventing a vast fortune that my grandparents had willed me provided that I leave the sinful city and take up residence in the house they had built here in the 1920s. Others assumed that we were up to no good, some spreading the word that we were drug dealers, others that we were federal narcotics agents.

After twenty-five years, those rumors have finally faded. And we learned to live with them in the meantime, coming to accept that anything we did or said might be hashed over, deconstructed, and reassembled in the most peculiar ways imaginable. In a culture that is resolutely non-literary—few homes here have many books on their shelves, where the Reader's Digest and National Geographic prevail—the sheer inventiveness of gossips helps bolster my faith in the awesome powers of the human imagination. When one set of rumors fades, another soon takes its place. Lately my husband and I have provided grist for the gossip mill by taking extended business trips and also by purchasing the house across the street as a library for our books.

Like most small towns in the western Plains, our town, founded in 1907, began declining in population shortly after the homesteading boom of the early teens. The disastrous farm economy of the last twenty years has accelerated the process, with real estate prices collapsing accordingly. A teacher friend recently purchased a small two-bedroom house, old but livable, for $5,000. The house my grandparents left us is not large, and we had never been able to organize our books properly, or even shelve them all. In recent years, when houses in the neighborhood came up for sale, my husband and I would debate about the wisdom of purchasing one and using the interior walls for shelving. The second time that the house facing ours came up for sale, a 1920s two-story with a large yard, three small bedrooms, one bath, a newly remodeled kitchen, small living and dining rooms, the asking price was $11,500, and we went for it.

This was such an outrageous act that we knew rumors would be forthcoming, and I was curious to see how inventive they would be. The grand prize goes to the one that had us buying the house for my sister and her two children, who would be moving here from Hawaii, banished to South Dakota for some unfathomable and no doubt exotic reason. This was apparently the result of my mentioning to someone that my sister and her children were coming for a visit and might stay across the street during the week they'd be in town. The true story of our purchase seemed so strange that, as my husband and I were toting book boxes across the street, some boys I didn't know pulled their bikes up, and one asked if we had really bought the house for our books. When we said yes, he said, "Wow." And to his companions: "See, I told you!" Shaking their heads, they raced off.

A few rumors floated that we had purchased another house because our marriage was in trouble. My recent success as a writer may have been the root of that, as small-town people are acutely aware of the destructive aspects of success. Over the years we've seen people drink and fumble away an inheritance of 4,000 acres of range and crop land, and others who made—and spent—millions in the oil boom of the early 1980s, having to scramble to avoid bankruptcy in the 1990s. In a small town, when the specter of good fortune rears its head, a kind of tribal wisdom kicks in. The harsh realties of Dakota living teach us that if something good happens, something bad is sure to follow. And we protect ourselves with laconic sayings, describing some enjoyable experience as "better than a poke in the eye with a sharp stick." We protect ourselves, too, with endless gossip and speculation about the calamities of others. Having witnessed the flaming burnouts of those who tried to rise above what is still commonly referred to as "one's station," people here generally prefer to adopt the ghetto mentality of not calling attention to oneself, not succeeding in a way that would be "different," or cause resentment within the group.

My local roots go deep, but as writers, my husband and I were always "different," a catchall term used in our area to cover everything from a homosexual orientation to an inordinate interest in religion, the arts, or visiting any city in which you do not have relatives. When we first came to town, people tended to refer to our writing as a hobby, and after a few polite questions about our publications, they would offer to show us their collection of stamps, guns, beer cans, or old automobile licenses lining the wall of a garage. Now that several of my books have been best-sellers, the questions tend to be less polite and focus on the business aspects of writing. As usual, speculation has outrun reality. One friend who said, "I guess you all are making so much money you travel first-class now," seemed disappointed when I laughed and said no. I told her that even if I had that kind of money, I wouldn't spend it on a first-class seat in a tin can.

Where privacy is concerned, money may be the last great taboo. But in a small town, information about your money is considered fair game for gossip. If you are employed by the school or the city, your salary is printed each year in the local weekly newspaper. In an area where minimum-wage jobs abound, and it is not unusual for a ranch family to net $12,000 in a year, couples who enjoy a double salary from the school or hospital are often resented, and criticized for any perceived lack of sensitivity to the plight of those around them. As for us, people have always overestimated the extent of our worldly fortune, so our relative austerity seems to meet with their approval. It seems right that we keep a car for ten years and dress simply. What we spend on books would appall people, but the only person who knows is our accountant, and he doesn't tell.

My family has always been a good source for gossip about money. My grandfather was a pioneer physician, who practiced medicine here for fifty-five years. He was notoriously lax about billing patients. I recently heard a story about a woman, nearly eight months' pregnant with her third child, who entered his office sometime in the 1950s to request a bill for her previous two deliveries. When my grandfather tried to put her off, she declared that she would not only not leave his office, she would not have the next baby until she had paid for the last two. She got her bill.

While my grandfather seems to have run his medical practice for love, he also liked to dabble in business. He became one of the founders of a local bank, and for several years owned a weekly newspaper. He purchased crop and ranch land, which he leased out. Having been raised on a ranch in Kansas, he was not content until he had also built up a small cattle herd and hired experienced ranchers to manage it. By the time I arrived, much of the land had been rented to the same families for thirty years or more, some going into the second generation. It was this tangle of property and personal relationships that I had to learn to navigate. I named our fledgling family farm corporation, Leaves of Grass., Inc., which I later found had contributed to the rumors about our drug use.

My grandfather's sense of privacy was such that I don't believe he ever let anyone in town know the full extent of his investments. After he died in 1973, both his attorney and his wife of sixty-three years were surprised by the contents of his safety deposit box, which held a bewildering variety of stocks and bonds, and a lovely photograph of my grandmother as a young woman that she had forgotten. She thought it had been taken in the first year of their marriage. The box also contained a small envelope with a scrap of dress fabric and a lock of his mother's hair—she had died when my grandfather was eight years old—and I like to think that it made the battered metal lockbox a private haven, a holy place where my grandfather could come to remember, or gather his thoughts, when as "Doc Totten" he had had to tell another eight-year-old that his mother was dying.

During our summer visits when I was young, my grandparents often admonished me and my siblings not to tell people more than they needed to know, particularly about money or business dealings. They knew, as we soon learned, that some gossips are not above pumping children for information. And when I moved here in 1974, I was grateful for their advice. Not long after we had settled in, someone asked me exactly how many acres the family had inherited, and I knew enough to answer vaguely. I later learned that this is considered an extremely rude question in western South Dakota. Your love life is fair game, and we may speculate wildly— my husband was once informed he was having an affair with a woman he had not met—but to ask how much land you own is stepping over the line.

In a town such as mine, gossip is so much a part of the fabric of life that professionals have a difficult time establishing standards of confidentiality. Attorneys, bankers, clergy, teachers, accountants, and doctors have to spell out norms that would be understood in a place more urban, more urbane. People in my town who want to be more certain of their privacy hire professionals from Rapid City or Bismarck. And even then, one can't be sure. Networks of family and friends extend far and wide in the region, and people talk.

When someone was asked at a local bar, "How did your AIDS test come out?" doctors at the local medical clinic faced a staff that was baffled by their outrage. The idea that a person would be fired if the leak could be traced to them seemed strange and coldhearted. The doctors were castigated for being so testy, for not having recognized that health is not considered a private issue here. For many years, hospital admissions and discharges were routinely broadcast on the local radio. It took the threat of a lawsuit for the hospital to give people an option. And most people still choose to have their name on the list because it's the expected

·   ·   ·   ·   ·   ·   ·   ·   ·

thing. Your friends would be disappointed not to know you had been admitted, because otherwise they would not be able to send a card or make
a visit, or even pray for you as they should. Bad health is not private here
simply because it's so visible. And often, when people ask how you are,
they really want to know. In my church, during the "cares and concerns of
the congregation" section of the worship service, it is common for someone to give a detailed medical report on a friend or spouse: "Well, the hip
replacement went real well. But an infection set in, and now they're treating that, and we don't know when she's coming home." A prominent businessman who developed a severe bipolar disorder helped to dispel the
stigma attached to mental illness by granting the local newspaper an interview about his condition and his experiences in treatment.

In local gossip, any sort of illness is talked about more prayerfully than
not. But money and love are the two great mainstays of talk that is hot,
wild, and mean. They constitute the basis of much of our greatest literature, and in a small town we might come to know Tom Sawyer, Humbert
Humbert, Blanche DuBois, and Anna Karenina in the flesh. Sometimes
they coexist in the same, miserably unhappy family. And their stories seem
as endless as the prairies.

We wonder if a young farm couple will make it, trying to raise their
family in a trailer just a few hundred yards from the main house where his
parents live. It doesn't seem likely, when we hear—it's gossip, but the person speaking knows the family well—that the only face-to-face contact the
wife had with her in-laws for the last six months came when they knocked
on her front door and served her with a summons in a property dispute.
Will she throw herself at that handsome young man she met on the job she
had to take in town to make ends meet? The outcome is surprising and yet
has a certain inevitablity: the marriage held together, but the couple
moved to Denver, forcing the parents to sell their land. They never spoke
to their son again.

We see passionate affairs ignite and burn out, or sometimes even turn
into a love that endures. One day I saw a woman in her late thirties, the
wife of a prominent businessman, breeze down the post-office steps to her
new red sports car, a satisfied smile on her face. Her hair was newly styled
and highlighted, her hem was short, and I wondered if she were having an
affair. I didn't have to wonder for long, as she soon ran off with a younger
man. Some years later, when she developed a terminal illness, he stayed
with her to the end.

In an area where so many live frugally, auction sales, church events, and bridge clubs provide entertainment for those who consider a trip to the theater on Main Street for the weekend movie too expensive or frivolous. Gossip is a frugal extravagance, at least financially. But it can also be extravagantly costly in the private pain that it causes. At the very least, it is odd to consider that one is starring in elaborate fictions. Odd to know that even when I feel as if I am living quietly, going about my business, someone, somewhere is making up an outlandish story, just because this is the sort of town in which you have to make your own fun.

Living well is the best revenge. One can outlive the talk and have the last laugh. My mother created a great scandal when she eloped in the 1930s with another Northwestern student. As the only child of a socially prominent couple, she had long been of major interest to the arbiters of gossip, who found my father less than promising: a Methodist pastor's son, an aspiring musician to boot! Concerning their marriage, one matron intoned, "This bears watching." My family quoted her on the cake with which we recently celebrated my parents' sixty-first wedding anniversary.

Just about anything "bears watching" in a small town, and we have the luxury of time, watching family stories unfold over many generations. But we can shortchange others by pigeonholing them according to what we know of their family history, never quite seeing them as individuals. We also reduce people to their civic roles—the doctor, the lawyer, the teacher, the town drunk, the whore, the druggie. All too often we miss the private people who are hiding in there, behind the public mask.

I had a lesson in this when, shortly after my book *Dakota* was published, I received a letter from a man who had once been my neighbor. He had been a young banker just setting out in his career and beginning a family. Our few exchanges had been of the "hot enough for you?" variety—a question one inevitably hears when it is more than 100 degrees above, or more than 10 degrees below zero. I had thought him dull.

But his letter was full of the pain he had encountered as a banker in hard times on the Plains, having to make hard decisions about whether or not to renew an operating loan for a rancher in the coming year. He gave a brilliant overview of the current conditions here, in which more and more family ranchers are selling out to their neighbors, who are trying to build operations that will be large enough to compete in markets dominated by a handful of giant "ag-biz" conglomerates. He commented that many ranchers and farmers survive in this marginal area only because they are aggressive, shrewd, and greedy for whatever wealth they can wrestle from the land.

. . . .

He said he had seen other ranchers that he would compare to Indians and artists, who wished to live at peace with the environment, whose families were now going into the fifth generation on the land. There are many ranchers who are knowledgeable practicing environmentalists, and who will humbly say of a majestic butte rising out of one of their pastures, "Of course, no one really owns a thing like that." My banker friend said that he hoped, although the first sort of rancher was winning the acreage war, that there would always be a place on the Plains for the other, and for all those others—Indians, artists, writers—who might offer a different perspective from that of greed and exploitation, and help us realize who we are and why we are here.

His letter made me realize how blind and narrow-minded I had been when he lived just across the alley from me. This was a person I might have gotten to know, and I had been too lazy, contenting myself with the superficial familiarities that help us get by in a small town. But all too often they prevent us from getting to know our neighbors as the thoughtful, private people they are. A comment by the first-century Christian theologian Philo of Alexandria has become a kind of mantra for me, a means of avoiding the trap set in any small community, of mistaking a public face for the wondrously complex and private whole: "Be kind, for everyone you meet is fighting a great battle."

.   .   .   .

ANITA L. ALLEN is a professor of law and philosophy at the University of Pennsylvania. She earned her law degree from Harvard and her Ph.D. in philosophy from the University of Michigan. She has written and lectured about the law and the ethics of privacy for more than fifteen years.

DOROTHY ALLISON is the author of *Bastard Out of Carolina*, a finalist for the 1992 National Book Award; *Cavedweller* (Dutton, 1998), a national best-seller and a *New York Times* Notable Book of the Year; as well as the memoir, *Two or Three Things I Know for Sure* (Dutton, 1995). Her poetry *The Women Who Hate Me* (1990), short fiction *Trash* (1989), and essays *Skin: Talking About Sex, Class and Literature* (1995) are available in small press editions from Firebrand Books. Ms. Allison's first novel, *Bastard Out of Carolina*, was made into a highly acclaimed film directed by Angelica Huston. *Two or Three Things I Know for Sure* was translated into a short documentary that took prizes at the Aspen and Toronto film festivals and was an Emmy-nominated feature on PBS's *POV*.

BARBARA FELDON is best known as "99"—the secret agent on the TV series *Get Smart*. She has also appeared in several motion pictures, only one of which she wishes to recall: the Michael Ritchie film *Smile*. Onstage she performed in the Circle in the Square production of *Past Tense*, the Off Broadway musical *Cut the Ribbons*, and her one-woman show, *Love for Better and Verse*. Her involvement in the women's movement led her to host Lifetime Network's *The 80's Woman*, an in-depth look at all aspects of women's lives. Barbara is exceedingly grateful to the voice-over industry for subsidizing her addiction to taxis and books. Over the years she has developed a number of poetry and prose readings: Great Love Poetry, The Poetry of Pablo Neruda, Jane Austen, and Virginia Woolf.

Barbara lectures on women's issues and is a supporter of Girls Incorporated, a national organization devoted to helping underprivileged girls develop options.

JONATHAN FRANZEN is a frequent contributor to *Harper's Magazine* and the *New Yorker*. He is the author of two novels, *The Twenty-Seventh City* (1998) and *Strong Motion* (1992). A new novel, *The Corrections*, will be published by Farrar, Straus & Giroux in 2001.

BRONWYN GARRITY is a freelance writer and producer of web sites and DVD ROMs. She created and produced the entertainment section of Trackers.net, Oxygen Media's web site for teen girls. Bronwyn is currently a producer at Canned Interactive in Los Angeles, California.

F. GONZALEZ-CRUSSI has had a dual career, as physician and writer. Emigrated from his native Mexico in search of postgraduate medical training, he later became professor of pathology at Northwestern University, and director of the Pathology Department of Chicago's Children's Memorial Hospital. His *Notes of an Anatomist* (Harcourt Brace, 1985) was translated into seven languages, and earned him the first prize for nonfiction of the Society of Midland Authors. *Suspended Animation*, (Harcourt Brace, 1995) another book of essays, was nominated for the 1996 Spielvogel-Diamondstein PEN Award for the essay. Dr. Gonzalez-Crussi's work was the subject of a BBC documentary aired in Britain in 1992 (the filming itself was the subject of another book, *Day of the Dead*) and was adapted to the stage by a theatrical company ("LiveBait") of Chicago in 1995.

VIVIAN GORNICK is a critic, essayist, and memoirist. She teaches in the M.F.A. program at Pennsylvania State University and lives in New York City. She has recently completed a book on the personal narrative to be published fall 2001 by Farrar, Straus & Giroux.

MICHAEL GRODEN is professor of English at the University of Western Ontario and director of "James Joyce's *Ulysses* in Hypermedia." He is the author of *"Ulysses" in Progress* (Princeton University Press, 1977); general editor of the 63-volume manuscript facsimile series, *The James Joyce Archive* (Garland Publishing, 1977–79); compiler of *James Joyce's Manu-*

. . . .

scripts: An Index (Garland Publishing, 1980); and co-editor with Martin Kreiswirth of *The Johns Hopkins Guide to Literary Theory and Criticism* (Johns Hopkins University Press, 1994). "James Joyce's *Ulysses* in Hypermedia" will present the text of *Ulysses* in several versions along with a vast array of explanatory and interpretive information—words, photographs, videos, audio version of texts, recordings of songs—in electronic, hyperlinked format. Groden has lectured on the project throughout North America and Europe, and he has taught *Ulysses* at Cooper Union and the 92nd Street Y in New York City as well as at the University of Western Ontario.

EVANS D. HOPKINS has written for the *New Yorker,* the *Washington Post,* and *Slate,* among other publications. He is currently at work on a prison memoir, as well as other fiction and film projects.

WAYNE KOESTENBAUM is the author of three books of poetry, including *The Milk of Inquiry* (Persea, 1999) and *Rhapsodies of a Repeat Offender* (Persea, 1994). He has also published four books of prose, including *The Queen's Throat: Opera, Homosexuality, and the Mystery of Desire* (Poseidon, 1993), which was nominated for a National Book Critics Circle Award; and *Cleavage: Essays on Sex, Stars, and Aesthetics* (Ballantine, 2000). He has received a Whiting Writers' Award, and is a professor of English at the City University of New York's Graduate School.

YUSEF KOMUNYAKAA's most recent books include *Pleasure Dome: New and Collected Poems, 1975–1999* (Wesleyan University Press, 2001), a newly published volume of poems, *Talking Dirty to the Gods* (Farrar Straus & Giroux, 2000), and *Blue Notes: Essays, Interviews, and Commentaries* (University of Michigan Press, 2000). His *Thieves of Paradise* (Wesleyan University Press, 1998) was a finalist for the National Book Critics Circle Award and *Neon Vernacular: New & Selected Poems*(1994) received the Pulitzer Prize and the Kingsley Tufts Poetry Award. He is a professor in the Council of Humanities and Creative Writing Program at Princeton University.

WENDY LESSER is the founding editor of the *Threepenny Review* and the author of five books: *The Life below the Ground, His Other Half, Pictures at an Execution, A Director Calls*, and *The Amateur.* A member of the American Academy of Arts and Sciences, she has received fellowships from the Guggenheim Foundation, the American Council of Learned Societies, the National Endowment for the Humanities, and the Open Society Institute. In 1997 her criticism won the Morton Dauwen Zabel Award given by the Academy of Arts and Letters. She lives in Berkeley, California, with her husband and son.

CATHLEEN MEDWICK is the author of *Teresa of Avila: The Progress of a Soul* (Knopf, 1999 and Doubleday Image paperback, 2001). A contributing editor to *House & Garden* magazine, she was a founding editor of *Mirabella* and a features editor and writer at *Vogue, Vanity Fair,* and *House & Garden*. Her work has also appeared in the *New York Times Magazine, Elle,* and the *Washington Post Magazine*. Her literary interviews are anthologized in Norman Mailer's *Pieces and Pontifications* and in the Louisiana University Press collections *Conversations with Truman Capote* and *Conversations with Mary McCarthy*. She lives in New York's Hudson Valley with her husband and two children.

KATHLEEN NORRIS is the award-winning author of *Dakota: A Spiritual Geography, The Cloister Walk, Amazing Grace: A Vocabulary of Faith, Meditations on Mary,* and the forthcoming memoir, *The Virgin of Bennington*. She lives in South Dakota and Hawaii.

JOSIP NOVAKOVICH was born in Croatia and now teaches at the University of Cincinnati in Ohio. Recently honored with an American Book Award, a Whiting Writers' Award, and the Friends of American Writers Award, he was also a Finalist for the PEN/Hemingway Award for First Fiction, the Midland Prize for Literature, and the Paterson Prize for Literature. His books include *Salvation and Other Disasters, Yolk, Apricots from Chernobyl,* and *Fiction Writers' Workshop*.

MOLLY PEACOCK is a writer who has relished using private life as the subject of four volumes of her poetry, including *Original Love* (W. W. Norton, 1995) as well as her memoir, *Paradise, Piece by Piece* (Riverhead, 1998). *How to Read a Poem & Start a Poetry Circle* (Riverhead, 1999) is her most recent book. Her efforts to bring that most private art, poetry, into public life have resulted in *Poetry in Motion*™ on the nation's buses and subways. And her efforts to bring that most private decision, not to have children, into public discourse have become part of our national dis-

. . . .

cussion of parenthood. She is President emerita of the Poetry Society of America and Poet-in-Residence at the Cathedral of St. John the Divine.

VICTORIA ROBERTS is a cartoonist for the *New Yorker* magazine. Her work has appeared also in the *New York Times,* the *Wall Street Journal,* and the *Boston Globe,* among other publications. Born in New York City, and raised in Mexico and Australia, her first cartoons were published in the *Sydney Morning Herald* and Mexico's *Uno Mas Uno.* She has written/illustrated seventeen books and lives in New York City.

JANNA MALAMUD SMITH, a clinical social worker, writer, and author of *Private Matters,* lives outside Boston, Massachusetts, with her husband and sons. She is currently at work on a book about mothers.

ROBIN WEST is a professor of law at Georgetown University Law Center where she teaches Jurisprudence, Feminist Legal Theory, Torts, and Law and Literature. She is the author of *Caring For Justice* (New York University Press), *Narrative Authority and Law* (Michigan Press), and *Progressive Constitutionalism* (Duke University Press). She lives in Baltimore, Maryland, with her husband and three children.

A PRIVATE LAST WORD FROM THE EDITOR:

·   ·   ·   ·   ·   ·   ·   ·   ·   ·

I am delighted to have edited this book and in the process to have discovered new friends and deepened old friendships. Each contributor privately
added a pungent, original ingredient to this now public stew. Michael
Groden deserves particular thanks for his unflagging attention to detail,
and I owe a debt of gratitude to all the folks at Graywolf Press, particularly to Editor-in-Chief Fiona McCrae for her fortitude and unflappabil-
ity, to editors Katie Dublinsky for her good sense and Anne Czarniecki for
her patience, and to publicist Jana Robbins for her zest. As always, I thank
my agent, Kathleen Anderson, for her literary grace.

This book was designed by Will Powers. It is set in Sabon and Formata type by Stanton Publication Services, Inc. and manufactured by Bang Printing on acid-free paper.

Graywolf Press is a not-for-profit, independent press. The books we publish include poetry, literary fiction, essays, and cultural criticism. We are less interested in best-sellers than in talented writers who display a freshness of voice coupled with a distinct vision. We believe these are the very qualities essential to shape a vital and diverse culture.

Thankfully, many of our readers feel the same way. They have shown this through their desire to buy books by Graywolf writers; they have told us this themselves through their e-mail notes and at author events; and they have reinforced their commitment by contributing financial support, in small amounts and in large amounts, and joining the "Friends of Graywolf."

If you enjoyed this book and wish to learn more about Graywolf Press, we invite you to ask your bookseller or librarian about further Graywolf titles; or to contact us for a free catalog; or to visit our award-winning web site that features information about our forthcoming books.

We would also like to invite you to consider joining the hundreds of individuals who are already "Friends of Graywolf" by contributing to our membership program. Individual donations of any size are significant to us: they tell us that you believe that the kind of publishing we do *matters*. Our web site gives you many more details about the benefits you will enjoy as a "Friend of Graywolf"; but if you do not have online access, we urge you to contact us for a copy of our membership brochure.

www.graywolfpress.org

Graywolf Press
2402 University Avenue, Suite 203
Saint Paul, MN 55114
Phone: (651) 641-0077
Fax: (651) 641-0036
E-mail: wolves@graywolfpress.org